JUST ENOUGH PROGRAMMING
LOGIC AND DESIGN

JUST ENOUGH PROGRAMMING LOGIC AND DESIGN

JOYCE FARRELL

COURSE TECHNOLOGY
CENGAGE Learning™

Australia • Brazil • Japan • Korea • Mexico • Singapore • Spain • United Kingdom • United States

COURSE TECHNOLOGY
CENGAGE Learning™

Just Enough **Programming Logic and Design**
Joyce Farrell

Executive Editor: Marie Lee

Acquisitions Editor: Amy Jollymore

Managing Editor: Tricia Coia

Developmental Editor: Dean Robbins

Editorial Assistant: Julia Leroux-Lindsey

Marketing Manager: Bryant Chrzan

Content Project Manager: Matt Hutchinson

Art Director: Marissa Falco

Manufacturing Coordinator: Julio Esperas

Proofreader: Harold Johnson

Indexer: Liz Cunningham

Compositor: International Typesetting and Composition

For product information and technology assistance, contact us at
Cengage Learning Customer & Sales Support, 1-800-354-9706

For permission to use material from this text or product, submit all requests online at **www.cengage.com/permissions**
Further permissions questions can be emailed to
permissionrequest@cengage.com

ISBN-13: 978-1-4390-3957-1

ISBN-10: 1-4390-3957-7

Course Technology
20 Channel Center Street
Boston, MA 02210
USA

Cengage Learning is a leading provider of customized learning solutions with office locations around the globe, including Singapore, the United Kingdom, Australia, Mexico, Brazil, and Japan. Locate your local office at:
international.cengage.com/region

Cengage Learning products are represented in Canada by Nelson Education, Ltd.

For your course and learning solutions, visit **www.cengage.com**

Purchase any of our products at your local college store or at our preferred online store **www.ichapters.com**

Printed in Canada
1 2 3 4 5 6 7 14 13 12 11 10

Brief Contents

v

Contents

vii

ix

Preface

Just Enough Programming Logic and Design is a guide to developing structured program logic for the beginning programmer. This book contains only seven chapters and two appendices—just enough to get the student comfortable with programming logic before tackling the syntax of a programming language. This book is intended to provide a complete, sound, yet compact, start in logic—just enough for a short logic course, just enough as an accompaniment to a programming language book, or just enough as a supplement to a computer literacy course.

This textbook assumes no programming language experience. The writing is nontechnical and emphasizes good programming practices. The examples are business examples; they do not assume mathematical background beyond high school business math. All the examples illustrate one or two major points; they do not contain so many features that students become lost following irrelevant and extraneous details. Advanced logical concepts such as file handling, multidimensional arrays, and overloading methods are not covered. This book provides just enough material for a solid background in logic, no matter what programming languages students eventually use to write programs.

Organization and Coverage

Just Enough Programming Logic and Design introduces students to programming concepts and enforces good style and logical thinking. General programming concepts are introduced in Chapter 1. Chapter 2 discusses the key concepts of structure, including what structure is, how to recognize it, and, most importantly, the advantages to writing structured programs. Chapters 3, 4, 5, and 6 cover selections, loops, arrays, and methods. Chapter 7 is a straightforward, plain language introduction to the concepts of object-oriented programming. Two appendices allow students to gain extra experience with using the binary numbering system and understanding `case` and `do-while` structures.

Just Enough Programming Logic and Design combines text explanation with flowcharts and pseudocode examples to provide students with alternative means of expressing structured logic. Multiple choice review questions, debugging exercises, and numerous detailed, full-program exercises at the end of each chapter illustrate the concepts explained within the chapter, and reinforce understanding and retention of the material presented.

Teaching Tools and Supplements

The following supplemental materials are available when this book is used in a classroom setting. All of the teaching tools available with this book are provided to the instructor on a single CD-ROM. *Just Enough Programming Logic and Design* is a superior textbook because it includes the following features:

- **Electronic Instructor's Manual**. The Instructor's Manual that accompanies this textbook provides additional instructional material to assist in class preparation, including items such as Sample Syllabi, Chapter Outlines, Technical Notes, Lecture Notes, Quick Quizzes, Teaching Tips, Discussion Topics, and Key Terms.

- **ExamView®**. This textbook is accompanied by ExamView, a powerful testing software package that allows instructors to create and administer printed, computer (LAN-based), and Internet exams. ExamView includes hundreds of questions that correspond to the topics covered in this text, enabling students to generate detailed study guides that include page references for further review. The computer-based and Internet testing components allow students to take exams at their computers, and save the instructor time by grading each exam automatically.

- **PowerPoint Presentations**. This book comes with Microsoft PowerPoint slides for each chapter. These are included as a teaching aid for classroom presentation, to make available to students on your network for chapter review, or to be printed for classroom distribution. Instructors can add their own slides for additional topics they introduce to the class.

- **Solutions**. Suggested solutions to Review Questions and Exercises are provided on the Instructor Resources CD-ROM and may also be found on the Course Technology Web site at *www.cengage.com/ coursetechnology*. The solutions are password protected.

- **Distance Learning**. Course Technology offers online WebCT and Blackboard (versions 5.0 and 6.0) courses for this text to provide the most complete and dynamic learning experience possible. When you add online content to one of your courses, you're adding a lot: automated tests, topic reviews, quick quizzes, and additional case projects with solutions. For more information on how to bring distance learning to your course, contact your local Course Technology sales representative.

Accompanying Software:

- **Visual Logic™, version 2.0:** Visual Logic™ is a simple but powerful tool for teaching programming logic and design without traditional high-level programming language syntax. Visual Logic uses flowcharts to explain essential programming concepts, including variables, input, assignment, output, conditions, loops, procedures, graphics, arrays, and files. It also has the ability to interpret and execute flowcharts, providing students with immediate and accurate feedback about their solutions. By executing student solutions, Visual Logic combines the power of a high-level language with the ease and simplicity of flowcharts. You may purchase Visual Logic along with your text. Please contact your Course Technology sales representative for more information.

Acknowledgments

I would like to thank all of the people who helped to make this book a reality, especially Dean Robbins, Development Editor, whose attention to detail has made this a quality textbook. Thanks also to Tricia Coia, Managing Editor, and Amy Jollymore, Acquisitions Editor, for their support of this project. I am always grateful to Green Pen QA, Technical Editors, for their expertise. I also appreciate the helpful comments from Ann Shaffer throughout this book's development. Finally, thanks to Matt Hutchinson and Anupriya Tyagi, who masterminded the process of turning the manuscript into a printed book.

I thank the reviewers who provided helpful and insightful comments during the development of this book, including Katie Danko, Grand Rapids Community College; Dawn Pantaleo, Kalamazoo Valley Community College; Marie Pullan, Farmingdale State College; and John Thacher, Gwinnett Technical College. As always, thanks to my husband, Geoff, for his constant support.

—*Joyce Farrell*

CHAPTER 1

An Overview of Computers and Logic

After completing this chapter you will be able to:

- ◎ Explain computer components and operations
- ◎ Discuss the steps involved in the programming process
- ◎ Use pseudocode statements and flowchart symbols
- ◎ Use and name variables and constants
- ◎ Explain data types and declare variables
- ◎ End a program by using sentinel values
- ◎ Discuss the evolution of programming techniques

Understanding Computer Components and Operations

Hardware and software are the two major components of any computer system.

Hardware is the equipment, or the devices, associated with a computer. For a computer to be useful, however, it needs more than equipment; a computer needs to be given instructions. Just as your stereo equipment does not do much until you provide music on a CD or tape, computer hardware needs instructions that control how and when data items are input, how they are processed, and the form in which they are output or stored.

 Software can be classified as application software or system software. Application software comprises all the programs you apply to a task—word-processing programs, spreadsheets, payroll and inventory programs, and even games. System software comprises the programs you use to manage your computer, including operating systems, such as Windows, Linux, or UNIX.

Software is computer instructions; software tells the hardware what to do. Software is **programs**; instruction sets written by programmers. You can buy prewritten programs (such as Microsoft Word, iTunes, or Halo) that are stored on a disk or that you download from the Web. Alternately, you can write your own programs. When you write software instructions, you are **programming**.

Together, computer hardware and software accomplish three major operations:

- **Input**—Hardware devices that perform input operations include keyboards and mice. Through these devices, **data**, or facts, enter the computer system.

- **Processing**—Processing data items may involve organizing them, checking them for accuracy, or performing mathematical operations on them. The hardware component that performs these sorts of tasks is the **central processing unit**, or **CPU**.

 Data items include all the text, numbers, and other information that are processed by a computer. However, many computer professionals reserve the term "information" for data items that have been processed. For example, your name, Social Security number, and hourly pay rate are data items, but your paycheck holds information.

- **Output**—After data items have been processed, the resulting information usually is sent to a printer, monitor, or some other output device so people can view, interpret, and use the results. Sometimes, you store output on hardware, such as a disk or flash media. People cannot read data directly from these storage devices, but the devices hold information for later retrieval. When you send output to a storage device, sometimes it later is used as input for another program.

You write computer instructions in a computer **programming language**, such as Visual Basic, C#, C++, or Java. Just as some people speak English and others speak Japanese, programmers also write programs in different languages. Some programmers work exclusively in one language, whereas others know several and use the one that seems most appropriate for the task at hand.

No matter which programming language a computer programmer uses, the language has rules governing its word usage and punctuation.

These rules are called the language's **syntax**. If you ask, "How the geet too store do I?" in English, most people can figure out what you probably mean, even though you have not used proper English syntax—you have mixed up the word order, misspelled a word, and used the wrong word. However, computers are not nearly as smart as most people; with a computer, you might as well have asked, "Xpu mxv ot dodnm cadf B?" Unless the syntax is perfect, the computer cannot interpret the programming language instruction at all.

Every computer operates on circuitry that consists of millions of on/off switches. Each programming language uses a piece of software to translate the specific programming language statements into the computer's on/off circuitry language, or **machine language**. Machine language is represented as a series of 0s and 1s, also called **binary** form. The language translation software that converts a programmer's statements to binary form is called a **compiler** or **interpreter**, and it tells you if you have used a programming language incorrectly. Therefore, syntax errors are relatively easy to locate and correct—the compiler or interpreter you use highlights every syntax error. If you write a computer program using a language such as C++ but spell one of its words incorrectly or reverse the proper order of two words, the compiler or interpreter lets you know that it found a mistake by displaying an error message as soon as you try to translate the program.

When a program's instructions are carried out, the program **executes**. A program that is free of syntax errors can be executed, but it might not produce correct results. For a program to work properly, you must give the instructions to the computer in a specific sequence, you must not leave any instructions out, and you must not add extraneous instructions. By doing this, you are developing the **logic** of the computer program.

Suppose you instruct someone to make a cake as follows:

Stir

Add two eggs

Add a gallon of gasoline

Bake at 350 degrees for 45 minutes

Add three cups of flour

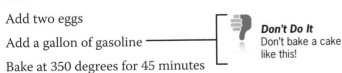

Don't Do It
Don't bake a cake like this!

The dangerous cake-baking instructions are shown with a warning icon. You will see this icon when a table or figure contains a programming practice that is being used as an example of what *not* to do.

Even though the cake-baking instructions use correct English spelling and grammar, the instructions are out of sequence, some

The instructions you write are called **program code**; when you write a program, you are **coding the program**. Program code is also called **source code**.

3

Machine language is also called **object code**.

Although there are differences in how compilers and interpreters work, their basic function is the same—to translate your programming statements into code the computer can use. Usually, you do not choose which type of translation to use—it depends on the programming language. However, there are some languages for which both compilers and interpreters are available.

4

instructions are missing, and some instructions belong to procedures other than baking a cake. If you follow these instructions, you
are not going to end up with an edible cake, and you may end up
with a disaster. Such **logical errors** are much more difficult to locate
than syntax errors. The incorrect cake recipe example is extreme, but
suppose the error was more subtle. For example, the correct recipe
might require three eggs instead of two, or might require a teaspoon
of vanilla. It is easy for you to determine whether "eggs" is spelled
incorrectly in a recipe, but perhaps impossible for you to know if
there are too few eggs until after the cake is baked and you taste
it. Similarly, it is easy for a compiler or interpreter to locate syntax
errors, but often impossible for it to locate logical errors until the
program executes.

Programmers call some code errors semantic errors. For example,
if you misspell a programming language word, you commit a syntax
error, but if you use an otherwise correct word that does not make
any sense in the current context, you commit a **semantic error**.

Just as baking directions can be given correctly in French, German,
or Spanish, the same logic of a program can be expressed in any
number of programming languages. This book is almost exclusively
concerned with the logic development process. Because this book
is not concerned with any specific language, the programming
examples could have been written in Japanese, C++, or Java. The
logic is the same in any language. For convenience, the book uses
English!

Once instructions have been input to the computer and translated
into machine language, a program can execute. You can write a
program that takes a number (an input step), doubles it (processing),
and tells you the answer (output) in a programming language such as
Java or C++, but if you were to write it using English-like statements,
it would look like this:

```
Input originalNumber.
Compute calculatedAnswer as originalNumber times 2.
Output calculatedAnswer.
```

You will learn
about the odd
elimination
of the space
between words
like "original" and "Number"
in the next few pages.

The instruction to Input originalNumber is an example of an input
operation. When the computer interprets this instruction, it knows
to look to an input device to obtain a number. Computers often have
several input devices, perhaps a keyboard, a mouse, and a CD drive.
When you learn a specific programming language, you learn how
to tell the computer which of those input devices to access for input
for the current program. Logically, however, it doesn't really matter
which hardware device is used, as long as the computer knows to look
for a number. The logic of the input operation—that the computer

must obtain a number for input, and that the computer must obtain it before multiplying it by 2—remains the same regardless of any specific input hardware device. The same is true in your daily life. If your boss says to you, "Get Joe Parker's phone number for me," it does not really matter where the number comes from. For example, you might look it up in a phone book, consult your cell phone's record of stored numbers, search for the number on the Internet, or phone a friend who knows the number.

The step that occurs when the arithmetic is performed to double `originalNumber` is an example of a processing step. Mathematical operations are not the only kind of processing, but they are very typical. After you write a program, the program can be used on computers of different brand names, sizes, and speeds. When you make a phone call, your message gets through whether you use a land line or a cell phone, and it doesn't matter whether your cell phone is made by Motorola, Nokia, or Samsung. Similarly, whether you use an IBM, Macintosh, Linux, or UNIX operating system, and whether you use a personal computer that sits on your desk or a mainframe that costs hundreds of thousands of dollars and resides in a special building in a university, multiplying by 2 is the same process. The hardware is not important; the logical process is.

A computer system needs both internal memory and external storage. Internal memory is needed to run the programs, but internal memory is **volatile**—that is, its contents are lost every time the computer loses power. External storage (such as a disk) provides a nonvolatile (or persistent) medium.

In the number-doubling program, the `Output calculatedAnswer` statement represents an output operation. Within a particular program, this statement could cause the output to appear on the monitor (which might be a flat panel screen or a cathode-ray tube), or the output could go to a printer (which could be laser or inkjet), or the output could be written to a disk or CD. The logic of the process called `Output` is the same no matter what hardware device you use.

To use a computer program, you must first load it into the computer's memory. **Memory** is the internal storage in a computer, often called **main memory** or **random access memory (RAM)**. You might type a program's instructions into memory from the keyboard, or you might load a program that has already been written and stored on a disk. Either way, a copy of the instructions must be placed in memory before the program can be run.

Computer memory consists of millions of numbered locations where data can be stored. Every named item such as `originalNumber` has a specific numeric address associated with it. Every time you refer to a named item within a program, the computer retrieves the value at the associated memory location.

Once you have a copy of a program in memory, you want to execute, or run, the program. When you run the number-doubling program, it requires a piece of data—a value for `originalNumber`. The `originalNumber`—for example, 8—is also placed in main memory at a specific location that the program will call `originalNumber`. Then, and only then, can the `calculatedAnswer`, in this case 16, be calculated and output.

Computer programmers often refer to memory addresses using hexadecimal notation, or base 16. With this system, they might use a value like 42FF01A to refer to a memory address. Despite the use of letters, such an address is still a number. Appendix A contains information on the hexadecimal numbering system.

Understanding the Programming Process

A programmer's job involves writing instructions (such as the three instructions in the doubling program in the preceding section), but a professional programmer usually does not just sit down at a computer keyboard and start typing. The programmer's job can be broken down into seven development steps:

1. Understanding the problem

2. Planning the logic

3. Coding the program

4. Using software (a compiler or interpreter) to translate the program into machine language

5. Testing the program

6. Putting the program into production

7. Maintaining the program

Figure 1-1 illustrates the program development cycle.

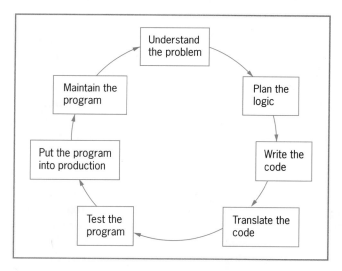

Figure 1-1 The program development cycle

Understanding the Problem

Professional computer programmers write programs to satisfy the needs of others. Examples could include a Human Resources Department that needs a printed list of all employees, a Billing Department that wants a list of clients who are 30 or more days overdue on their payments, and an Order Department that needs a Web site to provide buyers with an online shopping cart in which to gather their orders. Because programmers are providing a service to these users, programmers must first understand what it is the users want.

Suppose the director of human resources says to a programmer, "Our department needs a list of all employees who have been here more than five years, because we want to invite them to a special thank-you dinner." On the surface, this seems like a simple enough request. An experienced programmer, however, will know that he or she may not yet understand the whole problem. Does the director want a list of full-time employees only, or a list of full- and part-time employees together? Does she want people who have worked for the company on a month-to-month contractual basis over the past five years, or only regular, permanent employees? Do the listed employees need to have worked for the organization for five years as of today, as of the date of the dinner, or as of some other cutoff date? What about an employee who worked three years, took a two-year leave of absence, and has been back for three years? Does he or she qualify? The programmer cannot make any of these decisions; the user is the one who must address these questions.

More decisions still might be required. For example, what does the user want the report of five-year employees to look like? Should it contain both first and last names? Social Security numbers? Phone numbers? Addresses? Is all this data available? Several pieces of documentation are often provided to help the programmer understand the problem. This documentation might include items such as a sample of what the output will look like and lists of data that are available in company files.

Really understanding the problem may be one of the most difficult aspects of programming. On any job, the description of what the user needs may be vague—worse yet, the users may not even really know what they want, and users who think they know what they want frequently change their minds after seeing sample output. A good programmer is often part counselor, part detective!

Planning the Logic

The heart of the programming process lies in planning the program's logic. During this phase of the programming process, the programmer plans the steps of the program, deciding what steps to include and how to order them. You can plan the solution to a problem in many ways. The two most common planning tools are flowcharts and pseudocode. Both tools involve writing the steps of the program in English, much as you would plan a trip on paper before getting into the car, or plan a party theme before going shopping for food and favors.

The programmer shouldn't worry about the syntax of any particular language at this point, just about figuring out what sequence of events

You may hear programmers refer to planning a program as "developing an algorithm." An **algorithm** is the sequence of steps necessary to solve any problem.

You will learn more about flowcharts and pseudocode later in this chapter.

will lead from the available input to the desired output. Planning a program's logic includes thinking carefully about all the possible data values a program might encounter and how you want the program to handle each scenario. The process of walking through a program's logic on paper before you actually write the program is called **desk-checking**. You will learn more about planning the logic later; in fact, this book focuses on this crucial step almost exclusively.

Coding the Program

Once the programmer has developed the logic of a program, only then can he or she code the program in one of more than 400 programming languages. Programmers choose a particular language because some languages have built-in capabilities that make them more efficient than others at handling certain types of operations. Despite their differences, programming languages are quite alike—each can handle input operations, arithmetic processing, output operations, and other standard functions. The logic developed to solve a programming problem can be executed using any number of languages. It is only after a language is chosen that the programmer must worry about each command being spelled correctly and all of the punctuation getting into the right spots—in other words, using the correct syntax.

Some very experienced programmers can successfully combine logic planning and program coding in one step. This may work for planning and writing a very simple program, just as you can plan and write a postcard to a friend using one step. A good term paper or a Hollywood screenplay, however, needs planning before writing, and so do most programs.

Which step is harder, planning the logic or coding the program? Right now, it may seem to you that writing in a programming language is a very difficult task, considering all the spelling and grammar rules you must learn. However, the planning step is actually more difficult. Which is more difficult: thinking up the twists and turns to the plot of a bestselling mystery novel, or writing a translation of an already written novel from English to Spanish? And who do you think gets paid more, the writer who creates the plot or the translator? (Try asking friends to name any famous translator!)

Using Software to Translate the Program into Machine Language

Even though there are many programming languages, each computer is built knowing only one language, its machine language, which consists of many 1s and 0s. Computers understand machine language because computers themselves are made up of thousands of tiny electrical switches, each of which can be set in either the on or off state, which is represented by a 1 or 0, respectively.

Languages like Java or Visual Basic are available for programmers to use because someone has written a translator program (a compiler or interpreter) that changes the English-like **high-level programming language** in which the programmer writes into the **low-level machine language** that the computer understands. If you write a programming language statement incorrectly (for example, by mis-spelling a word, using a word that doesn't exist in the language, or using "illegal" grammar), the translator program does not know how to proceed and issues an error message identifying a syntax error—a misuse of a language's grammar rules. Although making errors is never desirable, syntax errors are not a major concern to program-mers because the compiler or interpreter catches every syntax error, and displays a message that notifies you of the problem. The com-puter will not execute a program that contains even one syntax error.

A computer program must be free of syntax errors before you can execute it. Typically, a programmer develops a program's logic, writes the code, and then attempts to compile or interpret the program using language-interpreting software. Usually, the software displays a list of syntax errors, which the programmer corrects. Then, the programmer attempts another translation. Correcting the first set of errors frequently reveals new errors that originally were not apparent to the compiler.

For example, if you could use an English compiler and submit the sentence "the dg chase the cat", the compiler at first would point out only one syntax error to you. The second word, "dg", is illegal because it is not part of the English language. Only after you corrected the word "dog" would the compiler find another syntax error on the third word, "chase", because it is the wrong verb form for the subject "dog". This doesn't mean "chase" is necessarily the wrong word. Maybe "dog" is wrong; perhaps the subject should be "dogs", in which case "chase" is right. Compilers don't always know exactly what you mean, nor do they know what the proper correction should be, but they do know when something is wrong with your syntax.

When writing a program, a programmer might need to retranslate the code several times. An executable program is created only when the code is free of syntax errors.

Testing the Program

A program that is free of syntax errors is not necessarily free of logical errors. For example, the sentence "The dog chases the cat", although syntactically perfect, is not logically correct if the dog chases a ball or the cat is the aggressor.

Once a program is free from syntax errors, the programmer can test it—that is, execute it with some sample data to see whether the results are logically correct. Recall the number-doubling program:

```
Input originalNumber.
Compute calculatedAnswer as originalNumber times 2.
Output calculatedAnswer.
```

If you provide the value 2 as input to the program and the answer 4 is displayed as output, you have executed one successful test run of the program.

However, if the answer 40 is displayed as output, maybe it's because the program contains a logical error. Maybe the second line of code was mistyped with an extra zero, so that the program reads:

> The programmer typed "20" instead of "2".

```
Input originalNumber.
Compute calculatedAnswer as originalNumber times 20.
Output calculatedAnswer.
```

The error of placing 20 instead of 2 in the multiplication statement caused a logical error. Notice that nothing is syntactically wrong with this second program—it is just as reasonable to multiply a number by 20 as by 2—but if the programmer intends only to double originalNumber, then a logical error has occurred.

Programs should be tested with many sets of data. For example, if you write the program to double a number and enter 2 and get an output value of 4, that doesn't necessarily mean you have a correct program. Perhaps you have typed this program by mistake:

> The programmer did not mean to use "plus".

```
Input originalNumber.
Compute calculatedAnswer as originalNumber plus 2.
Output calculatedAnswer.
```

An input of 2 results in an answer of 4, but that doesn't mean your program doubles numbers—it actually only adds 2 to them. If you test your program with additional data and get the wrong answer—for example, if you enter 3 and produce an answer of 5—you know there is a problem with your code.

Selecting test data is something of an art in itself, and it should be done carefully. If the Human Resources Department requests a list of the names of five-year employees, it would be a mistake to test the program you create using a small sample file of only long-term employees. If no newer employees are part of the data being used for testing, you do not really know if the program would have eliminated them from the five-year list. Many companies do not know that their software has a problem until an unusual circumstance occurs—for example, the first time an employee has more than nine dependents, the first time a customer orders more than 999 items at a time, the first time a program is executed during a leap year, or when (in an example that was well documented in the popular press) a new century begins.

Putting the Program into Production

Once the program is tested adequately, it is ready for the organization to use. Putting the program into production might mean simply running the program once, if it was written to satisfy a user's request for a special list. However, the process might take months if the program will be run on a regular basis, or if it is one of a large system of programs being developed. Perhaps data-entry people must be trained to prepare the input for the new program, users must be trained to understand the output, or existing data in the company must be changed to an entirely new format to accommodate this program. **Conversion**, the entire set of actions an organization must take to switch over to using a new program or set of programs, can sometimes take months or years to accomplish.

Maintaining the Program

After programs are put into production, making required changes is called **maintenance**. Maintenance is necessary for many reasons: for example, new tax rates are legislated, the format of an input file is altered, or the end user requires additional information not included in the original output specifications. Frequently, your first programming job will require maintaining previously written programs. When you maintain the programs others have written, you will appreciate the effort the original programmer put into writing clear code, using reasonable identifiers for values, and documenting his or her work. When you make changes to existing programs, you repeat the development cycle. That is, you must understand the changes, and plan, code, translate, and test them before putting them into production. If a substantial number of program changes are required, the original program might be retired, and the program development cycle started for a new program.

Using Pseudocode Statements and Flowchart Symbols

When programmers plan the logic for a solution to a programming problem, they often use one of two tools, pseudocode (pronounced "sue-doe-code") or flowcharts. **Pseudocode** is an English-like representation of the logical steps it takes to solve a problem A **flowchart** is a pictorial representation of the same thing. *Pseudo* is a prefix that means "false," and to *code* a program means to put it in a programming language; therefore, *pseudocode* simply means "false code," or sentences that appear to have been written in a computer programming language but do not necessarily follow all the syntax rules of any specific language.

You have already seen examples of statements that represent pseudocode earlier in this chapter, and there is nothing mysterious about them. The following five statements constitute a pseudocode representation of a number-doubling problem:

```
start
   input originalNumber
   compute calculatedAnswer as originalNumber times 2
   output calculatedAnswer
stop
```

Using pseudocode involves writing down all the steps you will use in a program. Usually, programmers preface their pseudocode statements with a beginning statement like `start` and end them with a terminating statement like `stop`. The statements between `start` and `stop` look like English and are indented slightly so that `start` and `stop` stand out. Most programmers do not bother with punctuation such as periods at the end of pseudocode statements, although it would not be wrong to use them if you prefer that style. Similarly, there is no need to capitalize the first word in a sentence, although you might choose to do so. This book follows the conventions of using lowercase letters for verbs that begin pseudocode statements and omitting periods at the end of statements.

Pseudocode is fairly flexible because it is a planning tool, and not the final product. Therefore, you might prefer, for example, to use the terms `begin` and `end` instead of `start` and `stop`. Instead of writing `input originalNumber`, many pseudocode developers would write `get originalNumber` or `read originalNumber`. Instead of writing `output calculatedAnswer`, many pseudocode developers would write `display calculatedAnswer` or `write calculatedAnswer`. The point is, the pseudocode statements mean to retrieve an original number from an input device and store it in memory where it can be used in a calculation, and then to get the calculated answer from memory and send it to an output device so a person can see it. When you eventually convert your pseudocode to a specific programming language, you do not have such flexibility because specific syntax will be required. For example, if you use the C# programming language, you will code `Console.Write(calculatedAnswer);`. The capitalization, exact use of words, and punctuation are important in the C# statement; they are not important in the pseudocode statement.

Some professional programmers prefer writing pseudocode to drawing flowcharts, because using pseudocode is more similar to writing the final statements in the programming language. Others prefer drawing flowcharts to represent the logical flow, because flowcharts allow programmers to visualize more easily how the program statements will connect. Especially for beginning programmers, flowcharts are an excellent tool to help visualize how the statements in a program are interrelated.

When you create a flowchart, you draw geometric shapes around the individual statements and connect them with arrows. You use a parallelogram to represent an **input symbol**, which indicates an input operation. You write an input statement, in English, inside the parallelogram, as shown in Figure 1-2.

```
input
originalNumber
```

Figure 1-2   Input symbol

Because the parallelogram is used for both input and output, it is often called the **input/output symbol** or the **I/O symbol**.

Arithmetic operation statements are examples of processing. In a flowchart, you use a rectangle as the **processing symbol** that contains a processing statement, as shown in Figure 1-3.

```
compute calculatedAnswer
as originalNumber times 2
```

Figure 1-3   Processing symbol

To represent an output statement, you use the same symbol as for input statements—the **output symbol** is a parallelogram, as shown in Figure 1-4.

```
output
calculatedAnswer
```

Figure 1-4   Output symbol

Some software programs that use flowcharts (such as Visual Logic) represent output with a left-slanting parallelogram. As long as the flowchart creator and the flowchart reader are communicating, the actual shape used is irrelevant. This book will follow the most standard convention of always using the right-slanting parallelogram for both input and output.

To show the correct sequence of these statements, you use arrows, or **flowlines**, to connect the steps. Whenever possible, most of a flowchart should read from top to bottom or from left to right on a page. That's the way we read English, so when flowcharts follow this convention, they are easier for us to understand.

To be complete, a flowchart should include two more elements: **terminal symbols**, or start/stop symbols, at each end. Often, you place a word like start or begin in the first terminal symbol and a word like end or stop in the other. The standard terminal symbol is shaped like a racetrack; many programmers refer to this shape as a lozenge, because it resembles the shape of a medicated candy lozenge you might use to soothe a sore throat. Figure 1-5 shows a complete flowchart for the program that doubles a number, and the pseudocode for the same problem.

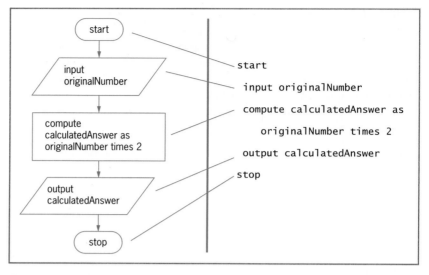

Figure 1-5   Flowchart and pseudocode of program that doubles a number

When you instruct a friend how to get to your house you might write a series of instructions, or you might draw a map. Pseudocode is similar to written, step-by-step instructions, and a flowchart, like a map, is a visual representation of the same thing.

Programmers seldom create both pseudocode and a flowchart for the same problem. You usually use one or the other. In a large program, you might even prefer to pseudocode some parts and draw a flowchart for others.

The Advantages of Repetition

After the programmer has developed the flowchart or pseudocode to double a number, he or she only needs to: (1) buy a computer, (2) buy a language compiler, (3) learn the programming language, (4) code the program, (5) attempt to compile it, (6) fix the syntax errors, (7) compile it again, (8) test it with several sets of data, and (9) put it into production.

"Whoa!" you are probably saying to yourself. "This is simply not worth it! All that work to create a flowchart or pseudocode, and *then* all those other steps? For five dollars, I can buy a pocket calculator that will double any number for me instantly!" You are absolutely right. If this were a real computer program, and all it did was double the value of a number, it simply would not be worth all the effort. Writing a computer program would be worth the effort only if you had many—let's say 10,000—numbers to double in a limited amount of time; let's say the next two minutes. Then it would be worth your while to create a computer program.

Unfortunately, the number-doubling program represented in Figure 1-5 does not double 10,000 numbers; it doubles only one. You could execute the program 10,000 times, of course, but that would require you to sit at the computer telling it to run the program over and over again. You would be better off with a program that could process 10,000 numbers, one after the other.

One solution is to write the program as shown in Figure 1-6 and execute the same steps 10,000 times. Of course, writing this program would be very time consuming; you might as well buy the calculator.

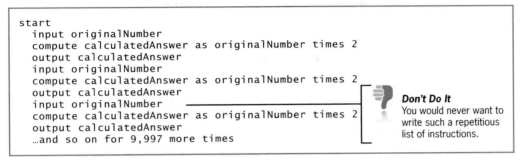

```
start
   input originalNumber
   compute calculatedAnswer as originalNumber times 2
   output calculatedAnswer
   input originalNumber
   compute calculatedAnswer as originalNumber times 2
   output calculatedAnswer
   input originalNumber
   compute calculatedAnswer as originalNumber times 2
   output calculatedAnswer
   ...and so on for 9,997 more times
```

Don't Do It
You would never want to write such a repetitious list of instructions.

Figure 1-6 Inefficient pseudocode for program that doubles 10,000 numbers

A better solution is to have the computer execute the same set of three instructions over and over again, as shown in Figure 1-7. With this approach, the computer gets a number, doubles it, displays the answer, and then starts over again with the first instruction. The same spot in memory, called originalNumber, is reused for the second number and for any subsequent numbers. The spot in memory named calculatedAnswer is reused each time to store the different results of the repeated multiplication operations. The logic illustrated in the flowchart shown in Figure 1-7 contains a major problem—the sequence of instructions never ends. You will learn to handle this problem later in the chapter.

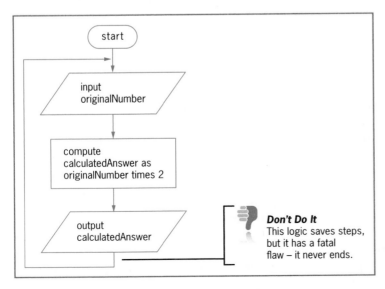

Don't Do It
This logic saves steps, but it has a fatal flaw – it never ends.

Figure 1-7 Flowchart of infinite number-doubling program

Every variable has a data type and a name. You will learn more about both of these features later in this chapter.

Fifty or 60 years ago, programmers had to deal with memory addresses and had to remember where variables were stored on their computer. Today, we are very fortunate that high-level computer languages allow us to pick a reasonable "English" name for a memory address and let the computer keep track of where it is located.

Using and Naming Variables and Constants

Programmers commonly refer to the locations in memory called `originalNumber` and `calculatedAnswer` as variables. **Variables** are named memory locations, whose contents can vary over time. At any moment in time, a variable holds just one value. Sometimes, `originalNumber` holds 2 and `calculatedAnswer` holds 4; at other times, `originalNumber` holds 6 and `calculatedAnswer` holds 12. It is the ability of memory variables to change in value that makes computers and programming worthwhile. Because one memory location can be used repeatedly with different values, you can write program instructions once and then use them for thousands of separate calculations. *One* set of payroll instructions at your company produces each individual's paycheck, and *one* set of instructions at your electric company produces each household's bill.

The number-doubling program example requires two variables, `originalNumber` and `calculatedAnswer`. These can just as well be named `userEntry` and `programSolution`, or `inputValue` and `twiceTheValue`. As a programmer, you choose reasonable names for your variables. The language interpreter then associates the names you choose with specific memory addresses.

A variable name is also called an **identifier**. Every computer programming language has its own set of rules for creating identifiers. Most languages allow both letters and digits within identifiers. Some languages allow hyphens in identifiers—for example, `hourly-wage`. Others allow underscores, as in `hourly_wage`. Still others allow neither. Some languages allow dollar signs or other special characters in variable names (for example, `hourly$`); others allow foreign alphabet characters, such as π or Ω.

Different languages put different limits on the length of identifiers, although in general, newer languages allow longer names. For example, in some very old versions of BASIC, a variable name could consist of only one or two letters and one or two digits. You could have some cryptic variable names like `hw` or `a3`. Fortunately, most modern languages allow variable names to be much longer; in the newest versions of C++, C#, and Java, the length of identifiers is virtually unlimited. These languages are case sensitive, so `HOURLYWAGE`, `hourlywage`, and `hourlyWage` are considered three separate variable names; the last example, in which the new word begins with an uppercase letter, is easiest to read. This format is called **camel casing**, because such variable names, like `hourlyWage`, have a "hump" in the middle. The variable names in this text are shown using camel casing.

When the first letter of a variable name is upper-case, as in `HourlyWage`, the format is known as **Pascal casing**.

Even though every language has its own rules for naming variables, when designing the logic of a computer program, you should not concern yourself with the specific syntax of any particular computer language. The logic, after all, works with any language. The variable names used throughout this book follow only two rules:

1. *Variable names must be one word.* The name can contain letters, digits, hyphens, underscores, or any other characters you choose, with the exception of *spaces*. Therefore, r is a legal variable name, as is `rate`, as is `interestRate`. The variable name `interest rate` is not allowed because of the space. No programming language allows spaces within a variable name. If you see a name such as `interest rate` in a flowchart or pseudocode, you should assume that the programmer is discussing two variables, `interest` and `rate`, each of which individually would be a fine variable name.

2. *Variable names should have some appropriate meaning.* This is not a rule of any programming language. When computing an interest rate in a program, the computer does not care if you call the variable g, u84, or `fred`. As long as the correct numeric result is placed in the variable, its actual name doesn't really matter. However, it's much easier to follow the logic of a program with a statement in it like `compute finalBalance as equal to initialInvestment times interestRate` than one with a statement in it like `compute someBanana as equal to j89 times myFriendLinda`. You might think you will remember how you intended to use a cryptic variable name within a program, but several months or years later when a program requires changes, you, and other programmers working with you, will appreciate clear, descriptive variable names.

Notice that the flowchart in Figure 1-7 follows these two rules for variables: both variable names, `originalNumber` and `calculatedAnswer`, are one word without embedded spaces, and they have appropriate meanings. Some programmers have fun with their variable names by naming them after friends or creating puns with them, but such behavior is unprofessional and marks those programmers as amateurs.

Assigning Values to Variables

When you create a flowchart or pseudocode for a program that doubles numbers, you can include the following statement to perform arithmetic:

```
compute calculatedAnswer as originalNumber times 2
```

As a convention, this book begins variable names with a lowercase letter. You might find programming texts in languages such as Visual Basic and C++ in which the author has chosen to begin variable names with an uppercase letter. As long as you adopt a convention and use it consistently, your programs will be easier to read and understand.

When you write a program using an editor that is packaged with a compiler, the compiler may display variable names in a different color from the rest of the program. This visual aid helps your variable names stand out from words that are part of the programming language.

Another general rule in all programming languages is that variable names may not begin with a digit, although usually they may contain digits. Thus, in most languages budget2013 is a legal variable name, but 2013Budget is not.

When you create an assignment statement, it may help to imagine the word "let" or "assign" in front of the statement. Thus, you can read the statement calculatedAnswer = originalNumber * 2 as "Let calculatedAnswer equal originalNumber times 2" or "Assign calculatedAnswer the value of originalNumber times 2."

This statement incorporates two actions. First, the computer calculates the arithmetic value of originalNumber times 2. Second, the computed value is stored in the calculatedAnswer memory location. Most programming languages allow a shorthand expression for **assignment statements** similar to the following:

calculatedAnswer = originalNumber * 2

The equal sign is the **assignment operator**. It always requires the name of a memory location on its left side—the name of the location where the result will be stored. According to the rules of algebra, a statement like calculatedAnswer = originalNumber * 2 should be exactly equivalent to the statement in which the two sides are reversed: originalNumber * 2 = calculatedAnswer. That's because in algebra, the equal sign always represents equivalency; in other words, it means "is equal to." In most programming languages, however, the equal sign represents assignment, and calculatedAnswer = originalNumber * 2 means "multiply originalNumber by 2 and store the result in the variable called calculatedAnswer". Whatever operation is performed to the right of the equal sign results in a value that is placed in the memory location to the left of the equal sign. The assignment operator means that calculatedAnswer *becomes equal to* the value calculated on the right side.

Besides variables, most programming languages allow you to create named constants. A **named constant** is similar to a variable, except it can be assigned a value only once. You use a named constant when you want to assign a useful name to a value that will never be changed during a program's execution. Using named constants makes your programs easier to understand by eliminating magic numbers. A **magic number** is an unnamed constant, like 0.06, whose meaning is not immediately apparent.

For example, if a program uses a sales tax rate of 6%, you might want to declare a named constant as follows:

num SALES_TAX = 0.06

You then might use SALES_TAX in a program statement similar to the following:

finalPrice = price + price * SALES_TAX

The way in which named constants are declared differs among programming languages. This book will follow the convention of using all uppercase letters in constant identifiers, and using underscores to separate words for readability. Using these conventions makes named constants easier to recognize.

Performing Arithmetic Operations

Most programming languages use the following standard arithmetic operators:

+ (plus sign)—addition

− (minus sign)—subtraction

* (asterisk)—multiplication

/ (slash)—division

Many languages also support operators that calculate the remainder after division and that raise a number to a higher power.

For example, the following statement adds two test scores and assigns the sum to a variable named `totalScore`:

```
totalScore = test1 + test2
```

In programming languages, you can combine arithmetic statements. When you do, every operator follows **rules of precedence** that dictate the order in which operations in the same statement are carried out. For example, multiplication and division always take precedence over addition and subtraction. So in an expression such as a + b * c, b and c are multiplied, producing a temporary result before a is added to it. The assignment operator has a very low precedence, meaning in a statement such as d = e + f + g, the operations on the right of the assignment operator are always performed before the final assignment to the variable on the left is made.

In arithmetic statements, the rules of precedence can be overridden using parentheses. For example, consider the following two arithmetic expressions:

```
firstAnswer = 2 + 3 * 4
secondAnswer = (2 + 3) * 4
```

After these statements execute, the value of `firstAnswer` is 14, because, according to the rules of precedence, multiplication is carried out before addition, so 3 is multiplied by 4, giving 12, then 2 and 12 are added, and 14 is assigned to `firstAnswer`. The value of `secondAnswer`, however, is 20, because the parentheses force the contained addition operation to be performed first. The 2 and 3 are added, producing 5, and then 5 is multiplied by 4, producing 20.

Forgetting about the rules of arithmetic precedence, or forgetting to add parentheses when you need them, can be a source of difficult-to-find logical errors in programs. You are free to add parentheses even when you don't need them to force a different order of operations; sometimes you use them just to make your intensions clearer.

Understanding Data Types and Declaring Variables

Computers deal with two basic types of data—text and numeric. When you use a specific numeric value, such as 43, within a program, you write it using the digits and no quotation marks. A specific

You cannot assign values to constants. For example, 43 = 82 is an illegal assignment. You assign values to variables or constants.

In most languages, there are separate data types for numeric variables that hold integers (whole number values), such as 21, and floating-point number values (those with decimal places), such as 13.45. Many languages even have more specific data types for larger and smaller numeric values.

In many languages, there are separate data types for variables that hold a single character value such as *A*, and strings of characters, such as *Andrea*.

For the programs you develop in this book, assume that each variable is one of the two broad types, numeric (or *num*, for short) or *string*.

numeric value is often called a **numeric constant** (or a **literal numeric constant** or an **unnamed numeric constant**) because it does not change—a 43 always has the value 43. When you use a specific text value, or string of characters, such as "Amanda", you enclose the unnamed, literal **string constant** within quotation marks.

Similarly, most computer languages allow at least two distinct types of variables. A variable's **data type** describes the kind of values the variable can hold, how much memory the value occupies, and the types of operations that can be performed with the data stored there.

- A **numeric variable** is one that can have mathematical operations performed on it; it can hold digits, and usually can hold a decimal point and a sign indicating positive or negative if you want. In the statement calculatedAnswer = originalNumber * 2, both calculatedAnswer and originalNumber are numeric variables; that is, their intended contents are numeric values, such as 6 and 3, 150 and 75, or −18 and −9.

- A **string variable** is a separate type of variable that can hold letters of the alphabet and other special characters such as punctuation marks. If a working program contains the statement lastName = "Lincoln", then lastName is a text or string variable.

Programmers must distinguish between numeric and string variables, because computers handle the two types of data differently. Therefore, means are provided within the syntax rules of computer programming languages to tell the computer which type of data to expect. When you tell the computer what type of variable to expect, you **declare the variable**. Before you can use any variable in a program, you must declare it. Declaring a variable is the act of providing it with a data type and an identifier. For example, if a program needs to use an employee's last name and salary, you might make the following declarations:

```
string lastName
num salary
```

Variables must always be declared before the first time they are used in a program. In many languages, it would be possible to mix declarations and other program statements. However, it is easier to locate variables if they are all declared in one location, so this book follows the convention of declaring all variables at the start of the program.

After a variable is declared, you can assign a value to it, send it to output, or perform any operations that are allowed for its data type. For example, after lastName and salary are declared, you might assign values to them as follows:

```
lastName = "Brown"
salary = 15.25
```

When you declare variables, you have the option of assigning initial values to them. For example, the following variables are **initialized** when they are declared:

```
string heading = "Employee Report"
num countOfEmployees = 0
```

In some languages, uninitalized variables are assigned a default value. It is more common, however, for uninitialized variables to have an unknown or garbage value until a valid assignment is made. For example, in most languages, if you write the following statements, depending on the programming language you use, either your program will display unpredictable results, or your language translator will issue an error message:

Don't Do It
Don't display or try to perform arithmetic with an unassigned variable.

```
num salary
output salary
```

Data can be assigned to a variable only if it is the correct type. You can assign either a constant or another variable's value to a variable.

Ending a Program by Using Sentinel Values

Recall that the logic in the flowchart for doubling numbers, shown in Figure 1-7, has a major flaw—the program never ends. This programming situation is an **infinite loop**—a repeating flow of logic with no end. If, for example, the input numbers are being entered at the keyboard, the program will keep accepting numbers and outputting their doubled values forever. Of course, the user could refuse to type in any more numbers. But the computer is very patient, and if you refuse to give it any more numbers, it will sit and wait forever. When you finally type in a number, the program will double it, display the result, and wait for another. The program cannot progress any further while it is waiting for input; meanwhile, the program is occupying computer memory and tying up operating system resources. Refusing to enter any more numbers is not a practical solution. Another way to end the program is simply to turn off the computer. But again, that's neither the best nor an elegant way to bring the program to an end.

A superior way to end the program is to use a sentinel value. A **sentinel value** is a predetermined value that means "Stop the program!" For example, the programmer and the user could agree that the user will never need to know the double of 0 (zero), so the user could enter a 0 when he or she wants to stop. The program could then test any incoming value contained in `originalNumber` and, if it is a 0, stop the program. Testing a value is also called **making a decision**.

By convention, this book encloses string data like "Employee Report" within quotation marks to distinguish the string of characters from a variable name. Also by convention, numeric data values are not enclosed within quotation marks; there is no chance of confusing numbers with variable names because variable names cannot start with digits.

21

The preselected ending value is called a sentinel value because it protects a logical entry or exit point, like a sentinel who guards a fortress.

A yes-or-no decision is called a **binary decision**, because there are two possible outcomes.

A preselected value that stops the execution of a program is often called a **dummy value** because it does not represent real data, but just a signal to stop.

You represent a decision in a flowchart by drawing a **decision symbol**, which is shaped like a diamond. The diamond usually contains a question, the answer to which is one of two mutually exclusive options—often yes or no. All good computer questions have only two mutually exclusive answers, such as yes and no or true and false. For example, "What day of the year is your birthday?" is not a good computer question because there are 366 possible answers. But "Is your birthday June 24?" is a good computer question because, for everyone in the world, the answer is either yes or no.

The question to stop the doubling program should be "Is the value of originalNumber just entered equal to 0?" or originalNumber = 0? for short. The complete flowchart will now look like the one shown in Figure 1-8. It includes the variable declarations and a check for value that indicates the end of the data.

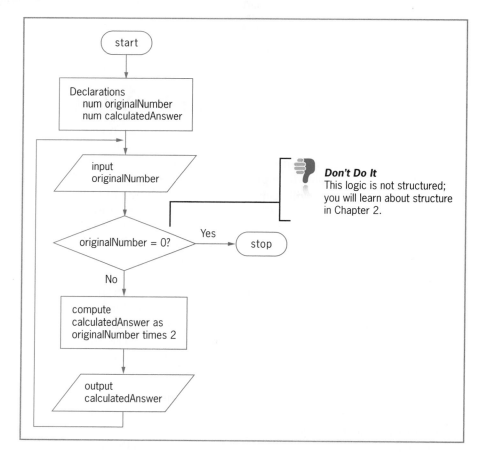

Figure 1-8   Flowchart of number-doubling program with sentinel value of 0

One drawback to using 0 to stop a program, of course, is that it won't work if the user does need to find the double of 0. In that case, some other data-entry value that the user never will need, such as 999 or −1, could be selected to signal that the program should end.

Not all programs rely on user data entry from a keyboard; many read data from an input device, such as a disk. When organizations store data on a disk or other storage device, they do not commonly use a dummy value to signal the end of the file. For one thing, an input record might have hundreds of fields, and if you store a dummy record in every file, you are wasting a large quantity of storage on "nondata." Additionally, it is often difficult to choose sentinel values for fields in a company's data files. Any balanceDue, even a zero or a negative number, can be a legitimate value, and any customerName, even "ZZ", could be someone's name. Fortunately, programming languages can recognize the end of data in a file automatically, through a code that is stored at the end of the data. Many programming languages use the term **eof** (for "end of file") to talk about this marker that automatically acts as a sentinel. This book uses eof to indicate the end of data, regardless of whether the code is a special disk marker or a dummy value such as 0 that comes from the keyboard. Therefore, the flowchart can look like the example shown in Figure 1-9.

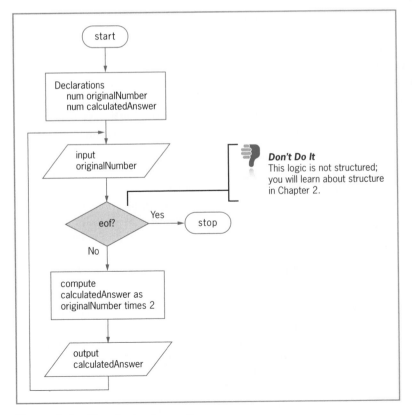

Figure 1-9 Flowchart using eof

Understanding the Evolution of Programming Techniques

People have been writing modern computer programs since the 1940s. The oldest programming languages required programmers to work with memory addresses and to memorize awkward codes associated with machine languages. Newer programming languages look much more like natural language and are easier for programmers to use. Part of the reason it is easier to use newer programming languages is that they allow programmers to name variables instead of using awkward memory addresses. Another reason is that newer programming languages provide programmers with the means to create self-contained modules or program segments that can be pieced together in a variety of ways. The oldest computer programs were written in one piece, from start to finish. Modern programs are rarely written that way—they are created by teams of programmers, each developing his or her own reusable and connectable program procedures. Writing several small modules is easier than writing one large program, and most large tasks are easier when you break the work into units and get other workers to help with some of the units.

 Modularity—the ability to build programs from smaller segments—is an important feature of modern programs, You will learn more about this topic in Chapter 6.

Currently, there are two major techniques used to develop programs and their procedures. One technique, **procedural programming**, focuses on the procedures that programmers create. That is, procedural programmers focus on the actions that are carried out—for example, getting input data for an employee and writing the calculations needed to produce a paycheck from the data. Procedural programmers would approach the job of producing a paycheck by breaking down the paycheck-producing process into manageable subtasks.

The other popular programming technique, **object-oriented programming**, focuses on objects, or "things," and describes their features, or attributes, and their behaviors. For example, object-oriented programmers might design a payroll application by thinking about employees and paychecks, and describing their attributes (such as last name or check amount) and behaviors (such as the calculations that result in the check amount).

With either approach, procedural or object-oriented, you can produce a correct paycheck, and both techniques employ reusable program modules. The major difference lies in the focus the programmer takes during the earliest planning stages of a project. To start, this book focuses on procedural programming techniques. In Chapter 7, you will learn the basics of the object-oriented approach. The skills you gain will serve you well whether you eventually write programs in a procedural or object-oriented fashion, or in both.

Review Questions

1. The two major components of any computer system are its _____.

   a. input and output   c. hardware and software

   b. data and programs   d. memory and disk drives

2. The major computer operations include _____.

   a. hardware and software

   b. input, processing, and output

   c. sequence and looping

   d. spreadsheets, word processing, and data communications

3. Another term meaning "computer instructions" is _____.

   a. hardware   c. queries

   b. software   d. data

4. Visual Basic, C++, and Java are all examples of computer _____.

   a. operating systems   c. machine languages

   b. hardware   d. programming languages

5. A programming language's rules are its _____.

   a. syntax   c. format

   b. logic   d. options

6. The most important task of a compiler or interpreter is to _____.

   a. create the rules for a programming language

   b. translate English statements into a language such as Java

   c. translate programming language statements into machine language

   d. execute machine language programs to perform useful tasks

7. Which of the following pairs of steps in the programming process is in the correct order?

   a. code the program, plan the logic

   b. test the program, translate it into machine language

   c. put the program into production, understand the problem

   d. code the program, translate it into machine language

8. The two most commonly used tools for planning a program's logic are _____.

   a. flowcharts and pseudocode

   b. ASCII and EBCDIC

   c. Java and Visual Basic

   d. word processors and spreadsheets

9. The most important task a programmer must do before planning the logic to a program is _____.

   a. decide which programming language to use

   b. code the problem

   c. train the users of the program

   d. understand the problem

10. Writing a program in a language such as C++ or Java is known as _____ the program.

   a. translating   c. interpreting

   b. coding   d. compiling

11. A compiler would find all of the following programming errors *except* _____.

   a. the misspelled word "prrint" in a language that includes the word "print"

   b. the use of an "X" for multiplication in a language that requires an asterisk

   c. newBalanceDue calculated by adding customerPayment to oldBalanceDue instead of subtracting it

   d. an arithmetic statement written as regularSales + discountedSales = totalSales

12. In a flowchart, a terminal symbol looks most like a _____.

    a. lozenge   c. rectangle

    b. circle   d. parallelogram

13. The parallelogram is the flowchart symbol representing _____.

    a. input   c. both a and b

    b. output   d. none of the above

14. Which of the following is not a legal variable name in any programming language?

    a. `semester grade`   c. `GradeInCIS100`

    b. `fall2011_grade`   d. `MY_GRADE`

15. In flowcharts, the decision symbol is a _____.

    a. parallelogram   c. lozenge

    b. rectangle   d. diamond

Find the Bugs

Your student disk contains files named DEBUG01-01.txt, DEBUG01-02.txt, and DEBUG01-03.txt. Each file starts with some comments that describe the problem. Comments are lines that begin with two slashes (//). Following the comments, each file contains pseudocode segments with one or more bugs that you must find and correct.

Exercises

1. Match the definition with the appropriate term.

    i.   Computer system equipment   a. compiler

    ii. Another word for programs   b. syntax

    iii. Language rules   c. logic

    iv. Order of instructions   d. hardware

    v.   Language translator   e. software

2. In your own words, describe the steps to writing a computer program.

Since the early days of computer programming, program errors have been called "bugs." The term is often said to have originated from an actual moth that was discovered trapped in the circuitry of a computer at Harvard University in 1945. Actually, the term "bug" was in use prior to 1945 to mean trouble with any electrical apparatus; even during Thomas Edison's life, it meant an "industrial defect." However, the process of finding and correcting program errors has come to be known as debugging.

3. Consider a student file that contains the following data:

Last Name	First Name	Major	Grade Point Average
Andrews	David	Psychology	3.4
Brown	Chris	Computer Science	4.0
Brogan	Lindsey	Biology	3.8
Carson	Kelly	Computer Science	2.8
Eisfelder	Katie	Mathematics	3.5
Faris	Natalie	Biology	2.8
Fredricks	Zachary	Psychology	2.0
Gonzales	Eduardo	Biology	3.1

Would this set of data be suitable and sufficient to use to test each of the following programs? Explain why or why not.

a. a program that displays a list of Psychology majors

b. a program that displays a list of Art majors

c. a program that displays a list of students on academic probation—those with a grade point average under 2.0

d. a program that displays a list of students on the dean's list

e. a program that displays a list of students from Wisconsin

f. a program that displays a list of female students

4. Suggest a good set of test data to use for a program that gives an employee a $50 bonus check if the employee has produced more than 1,000 items in a week. For example, one record might include the following:

Last name	First Name	Items produced this week
Foster	Samantha	1,315

5. Suggest a good set of test data for a program that computes gross paychecks (that is, before any taxes or other deductions) based on hours worked and rate of pay. The program computes gross as hours times rate, unless hours are over 40. If so, the program computes gross as regular rate of pay for 40 hours, plus one and a half times the rate of pay for the hours over 40.

6. Suggest a good set of test data for a program that is intended to output a student's grade point average based on letter grades (A, B, C, D, or F) in five courses.

7. Suggest a good set of test data for a program for an automobile insurance company that wants to increase its premiums by $50 per month for every ticket a driver receives in a three-year period.

8. Which of the following names seem like good variable names to you? If a name doesn't seem like a good variable name, explain why not.

   a. c

   b. cost

   c. costAmount

   d. cost amount

   e. cstofdngbsns

   f. cost2011

   g. costOfDoingBusinessThisFiscalYear

9. If myAge and yourRate are numeric variables, and departmentName is a string variable, which of the following statements are valid assignments? If a statement is not valid, explain why not.

   a. myAge = 23

   b. myAge = yourRate

   c. myAge = departmentName

   d. myAge = "departmentName"

   e. 42 = myAge

   f. yourRate = 3.5

   g. yourRate = myAge

   h. yourRate = departmentName

   i. 6.91 = yourRate

   j. departmentName = Personnel

   k. departmentName = "Personnel"

   l. departmentName = 413

   m. departmentName = "413"

   n. departmentName = myAge

   o. departmentName = yourRate

   p. 413 = departmentName

   q. "413" = departmentName

10. Draw a flowchart or write pseudocode that represents the directions from your house to your best friend's house.

11. Develop the logic that represents your favorite recipe.

12. Develop the logic of a program that allows the user to enter two values and displays their sum and difference.

13. Develop the logic of a program that allows a new employee to enter his or her birth year and the current year. Display

the years in which the employee becomes eligible for medical insurance (after one year with the company), is vested in the retirement plan (after five years with the company), and is eligible for a pension (at age 65).

14. Body mass index (BMI) is a statistical measurement that compares a person's weight and height. To calculate BMI, you multiply your weight in pounds by 703 and divide the result by the square of your height in inches. Develop the logic for a BMI calculator.

15. Develop the logic of a program that allows the user to enter his or her hourly pay rate, the number of hours worked this pay period, and the percentage of gross salary that is withheld. The program multiplies the hourly pay rate by the number of hours worked, giving the gross pay; then, it multiplies the gross pay by the withholding percentage, giving the withholding amount. Finally, it subtracts the withholding amount from the gross pay, giving the net pay after taxes. The program displays the net pay.

16. Mad Libs is a children's game in which players provide a few words that are then incorporated into a silly story. The game helps children understand different parts of speech because they are asked to provide specific types of words. For example, you might ask a child for a noun, another noun, an adjective, and a past-tense verb. The child might reply with such answers as "table," "book," "silly," and "studied." The newly created Mad Lib might be:

Mary had a little table

Its book was silly as snow

And everywhere that Mary studied

The table was sure to go.

Create the logic for a Mad Lib program that displays a message asking the user to provide five words, and then accept those words and create and display a short story or nursery rhyme that uses them.

CHAPTER 2

Understanding Structure

After completing this chapter you will be able to:

- ◎ Describe the features of unstructured spaghetti code
- ◎ Identify the three basic structures—sequence, selection, and loop
- ◎ Use a priming input
- ◎ Discuss the need for structure
- ◎ Recognize structure and structure unstructured logic

Understanding Unstructured Spaghetti Code

Professional computer programs usually get far more complicated than the number-doubling program developed in Chapter 1, and the logic of which is shown in Figure 2-1.

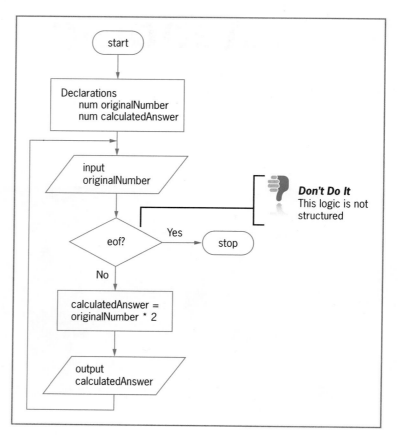

Figure 2-1   Number-doubling program

Imagine the number of instructions in the computer program that NASA uses to calculate the launch angle of a space shuttle, or in the program the IRS uses to audit your income tax return. Even the program that produces your paycheck contains many, many instructions. Designing the logic for such a program can be a time-consuming task. When you add several thousand instructions to a program, including several hundred decisions, it is easy to create a complicated mess. The popular name for logically snarled program statements is **spaghetti code**. The reason for the name is that the code is as confusing to read as following one noodle through a plate of spaghetti. Programs that use spaghetti code logic are **unstructured programs**;

that is, they do not follow the rules of structured logic that you will learn in this chapter.

For example, suppose you start a job as a dog washer, and you receive the instructions shown in Figure 2-2 on how to wash a dog. This kind of flowchart is an example of unstructured spaghetti code. A computer program that is structured similarly might "work"—that is, it might produce correct results—but would be difficult to read and maintain, and its logic would be difficult to follow.

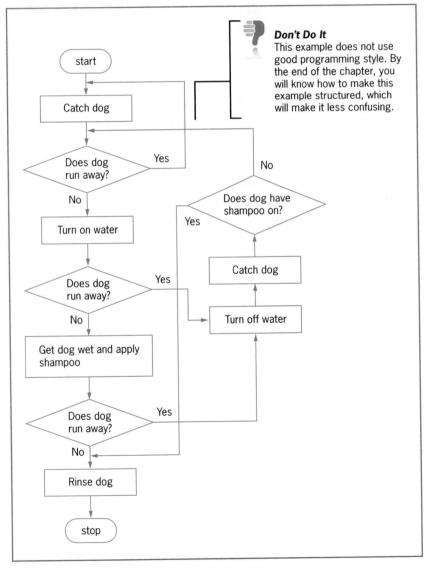

Don't Do It
This example does not use good programming style. By the end of the chapter, you will know how to make this example structured, which will make it less confusing.

Figure 2-2   Spaghetti code logic for washing a dog

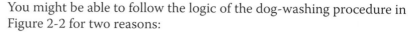

You might be able to follow the logic of the dog-washing procedure in Figure 2-2 for two reasons:

- You probably already know how to wash a dog.

- The flowchart contains a very limited number of steps.

However, imagine that the described process was far more complicated or that you were not familiar with the process. (For example, imagine you must wash 100 dogs concurrently while applying flea and tick medication, giving them haircuts, and researching their genealogy.) Depicting more complicated logic in an unstructured way would be cumbersome. By the end of this chapter, you will understand how to make the unstructured process in Figure 2-2 clearer and less error-prone.

Understanding the Three Basic Structures: Sequence, Selection, and Loop

In the mid-1960s, mathematicians proved that any program, no matter how complicated, can be constructed using one or more of only three structures. A **structure** is a basic unit of programming logic; each structure is a sequence, selection, or loop. With these three structures alone, you can diagram any task, from doubling a number, to washing a dog, to performing brain surgery. You can diagram each structure with a specific configuration of flowchart symbols.

The first of these structures is a sequence, as shown in Figure 2-3. With a **sequence structure**, you perform an action or task, and then you perform the next action, in order. A sequence can contain any number of tasks, but there is no chance to branch off and skip any of the tasks. Once you start a series of actions in a sequence, you must continue step-by-step until the sequence ends.

Many times, directions are given as a sequence. For example, to tell a friend how to get to your house from school, you might provide the following sequence in which one step follows the other and no steps can be skipped:

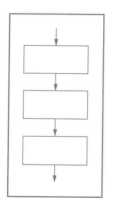

Figure 2-3   Sequence structure

```
go north on First Avenue for 3 miles
turn left on Washington Boulevard
go west on Washington for 2 miles and stop at 634 Washington
```

The second structure is called a **selection structure** or **decision structure**, as shown in Figure 2-4. With this structure, you ask a question, and, depending on the answer, you take one of two courses of action. Then, no matter which path you follow, you continue with the next task.

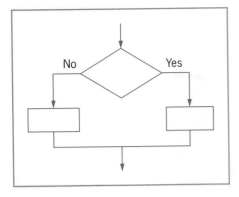

Figure 2-4 Selection structure

Some people call the selection structure an **if-then-else** because it fits the following statement:

```
if someCondition is true then
   do oneProcess
else
   do theOtherProcess
```

For example, you might provide part of the directions to your house as follows:

```
if traffic is backed up on Washington Boulevard then
   continue for 1 block on First Avenue
   turn left on Adams Lane
else
   turn left on Washington Boulevard
```

Similarly, a payroll program might include a statement such as:

```
if hoursWorked is more than 40 then
   calculate regularPay and overtimePay
else
   calculate regularPay
```

The previous examples can also be called **dual-alternative ifs** (or **dual-alternative selections**), because they contain two alternatives—the action taken when the tested condition is true and the action taken when it is false. Note that it is perfectly correct for one branch of the selection to be a "do nothing" branch. For example:

```
if it is raining then
   take anUmbrella
```

or

```
if employee belongs to dentalPlan then
   deduct $40 from employeeGrossPay
```

The previous examples are **single-alternative if**s (or **single-alternative selection**s), and a diagram of their structure is shown

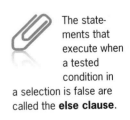 The statements that execute when a tested condition in a selection is false are called the **else clause**.

in Figure 2-5. In these cases, you don't take any special action if it is not raining or if the employee does not belong to the dental plan. The case where nothing is done is often called the **null case**.

The third structure, shown in Figure 2-6, is a loop. In a **loop structure**, you continue to repeat actions while a condition remains true. The action or actions that occur within the loop are known as the **loop body**. In the most common type of loop, a condition is evaluated; if the answer is true, you execute the loop body and evaluate the condition again. If the condition is still true, you execute the loop body again and then reevaluate the original condition. This continues until the condition becomes false; then you exit the structure. You may hear programmers refer to looping as **repetition** or **iteration**.

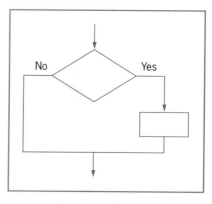

Figure 2-5   Single-alternative selection structure

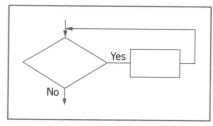

Figure 2-6   Loop structure

Some programmers call this structure a **while...do**, or more simply, a **while loop**, because it fits the following statement:

while testCondition continues to be true
    do someProcess

When you provide directions to your house, part of the directions might be:

while the address of the house you are passing remains below 634
    travel forward to the next house

You encounter other examples of looping every day, as in:

while you continue to beHungry
    take another biteOfFood

or

while unreadPages remain in the readingAssignment
    read another unreadPage

All logic problems can be solved using only these three structures—sequence, selection, and loop. The three structures can be combined in an infinite number of ways. For example, you can have a sequence of tasks followed by a selection, or a loop followed by a sequence. Attaching structures end-to-end is called **stacking structures**. For example, Figure 2-7 shows a structured flowchart achieved by stacking structures, and shows pseudocode that might follow that flowchart logic.

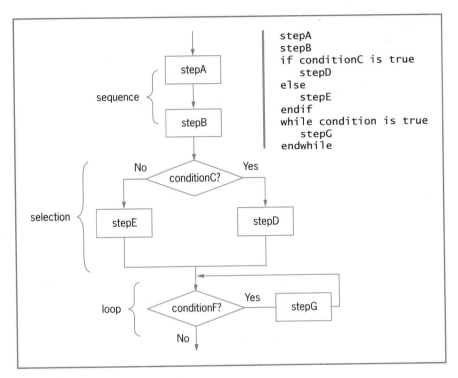

```
stepA
stepB
if conditionC is true
    stepD
else
    stepE
endif
while condition is true
    stepG
endwhile
```

Figure 2-7 Structured flowchart and pseudocode

The pseudocode in Figure 2-7 shows two **end-structure statements**—endif and endwhile. You can use an endif statement to clearly show where the actions that depend on a decision end. The instruction that follows if occurs when its tested condition is true, the instruction that follows else occurs when the tested condition is false, and any instructions that follow endif execute in either case—instructions after the endif are not dependent on the if statement at all. In other words, statements beyond the endif statement are "outside" the decision structure. Similarly, you use an endwhile statement to show where a loop structure ends. In Figure 2-7, while conditionF continues to be true, stepG continues to execute. If any statements followed the endwhile statement, they would be outside of, and not a part of, the loop.

Whether you are drawing a flowchart or writing pseudocode, you can use either of the following pairs to represent decision outcomes: Yes and No or True and False. This book follows the convention of using Yes and No in flowchart diagrams and true and false in pseudocode.

When you write the pseudocode for the logic shown in Figure 2-7, the convention is to align an `if` with its `else`, if it has one, and also with its `endif`. Then, you indent any dependent statements a few spaces. Similarly, you align a `while` and an `endwhile` pair, and indent any dependent statements.

Besides stacking structures, you can replace any individual tasks or steps in a structured flowchart diagram or pseudocode segment with additional structures. In other words, any sequence, selection, or loop can contain other sequences, selections, or loops. Placing a structure within another structure is called **nesting structures**. For example, you can have a sequence of three tasks on one side of a selection, as shown in Figure 2-8.

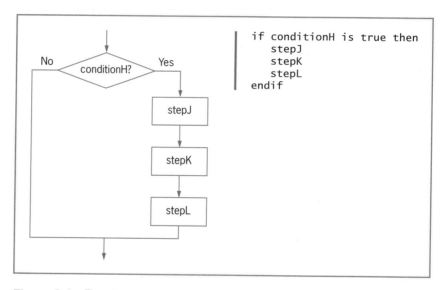

Figure 2-8 Flowchart and pseudocode showing a sequence nested within a selection

In the pseudocode for the logic shown in Figure 2-8, the indentation shows that all three statements (`stepJ`, `stepK`, and `stepL`) must execute if `conditionH` is true. The three statements constitute a **block**, or a group of statements that executes as a single unit.

In place of one of the steps in the sequence in Figure 2-8, you can insert a selection. In Figure 2-9, the process named `stepK` has been replaced with a loop structure that begins with a test of the condition named `conditionM`.

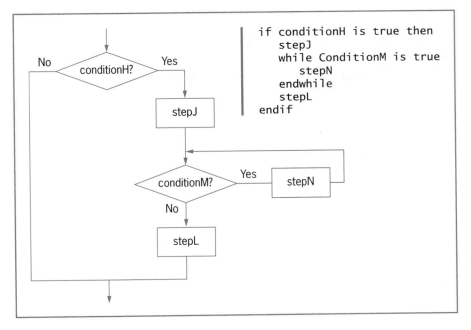

Figure 2-9 Selection in a sequence within a selection

In the pseudocode shown in Figure 2-9, notice that `if` and `endif` are vertically aligned. This shows that they are all "on the same level." Similarly, `stepJ`, `while`, `endwhile`, and `stepL` are aligned, and they are evenly indented. If you look at the same problem flowcharted in Figure 2-9, you see that you could draw a vertical line through the symbols containing `stepJ`, `while`, `endwhile`, and `stepL`. The flowchart and the pseudocode represent exactly the same logic.

There is no end to the number of levels you might need when you nest and stack structures. For example, Figure 2-10 shows logic that has been made more complicated by replacing `stepN` with a selection. The structure that performs `stepP` or `stepQ` based on the outcome of **conditionO** is nested within the loop that is controlled by **conditionO**. In the pseudocode in Figure 2-10, notice how the `if`, `else`, and `endif` that describe the condition selection are aligned with each other and within the `while` structure that is controlled by `conditionM`. As before, the indentation used in the pseudocode reflects the logic you can see laid out graphically in the flowchart.

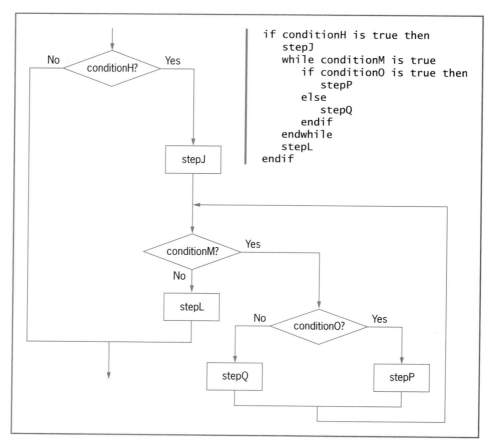

```
if conditionH is true then
    stepJ
    while conditionM is true
        if conditionO is true then
            stepP
        else
            stepQ
        endif
    endwhile
    stepL
endif
```

Figure 2-10   Flowchart and pseudocode for loop within selection within sequence within selection

Many of the examples you have just studied in this chapter are generic so that you can focus on the relationships of the shapes without worrying what they do. Keep in mind that generic instructions like stepA and generic conditions like conditionC can stand for anything. For example, Figure 2-11 shows the process of buying and planting flowers outdoors in the spring after the danger of frost is over. The flowchart and the pseudocode structures are identical to the ones in Figure 2-10. In the exercises at the end of this chapter, you will be asked to come up with more scenarios that fit the same pattern.

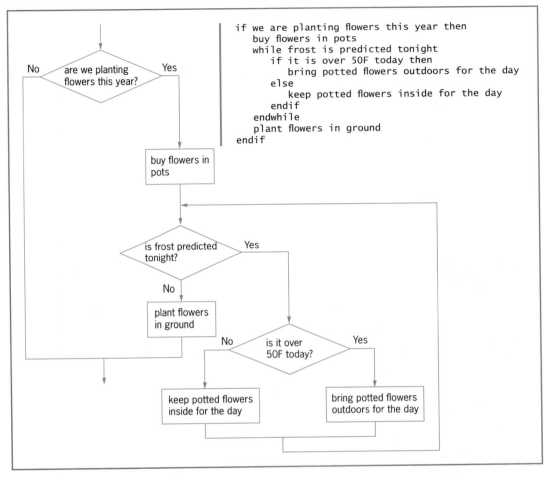

```
if we are planting flowers this year then
    buy flowers in pots
    while frost is predicted tonight
        if it is over 50F today then
            bring potted flowers outdoors for the day
        else
            keep potted flowers inside for the day
        endif
    endwhile
    plant flowers in ground
endif
```

Figure 2-11   The process of buying and planting flowers in the spring

The possible combinations of logical structure are endless, but each of a structured program's segments is a sequence, a selection, or a loop. The three structures are shown together in Figure 2-12. Notice that each structure has one entry and one exit point. One structure can attach to another only at one of these points.

 Try to imagine physically picking up any of the three structures in Figure 2-12 using the ends of the flowlines that enter from the top and emerge from the bottom. These are the spots at which you could connect a structure to any of the others. Similarly, any complete structure, from its entry point to its exit point, can be inserted within the process symbol of any other structure.

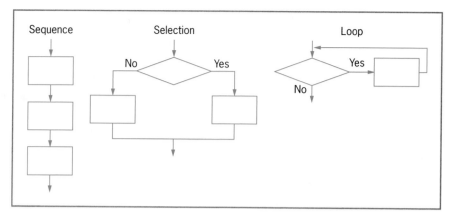

Figure 2-12 The three structures

A structured program is never required to contain examples of all three structures; a structured program might contain only one or two of them. For example, many simple programs contain only a sequence of several tasks that execute from start to finish without any needed selections or loops. As another example, a program might display a series of numbers, looping to do so, but never making any decisions about the numbers.

In summary, a structured program has the following characteristics:

- A structured program includes only combinations of the three basic structures—sequence, selection, and loop. Any structured program might contain one, two, or all three types of structures.

- Structures can be stacked or connected to one another only at their entry or exit points.

- Any structure can be nested within another structure.

Using the Priming Input

For a program to be structured and work the way you want it to, sometimes you need to add extra steps. The priming read is one kind of added step. A **priming input** or **priming read** is the statement that reads the first input value in a program. For example, if a program will read 100 values, you read the first value in a statement that is separate from the other 99. You must do this to keep the program structured.

Recall the number-doubling program in Figure 2-1 and repeated in Figure 2-13. The program gets a number and checks for the end-of-file condition. If it is not the end of file, then the number is doubled, the answer is displayed, and the next number is input.

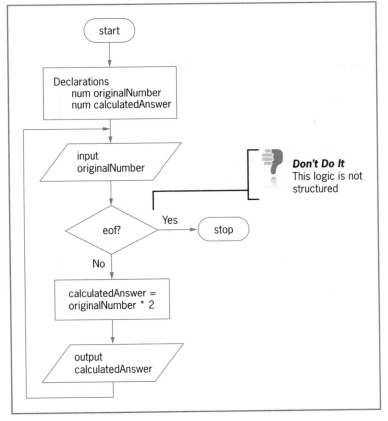

Figure 2-13   Unstructured flowchart of a number-doubling program

Is the program represented by Figure 2-13 structured? At first, it might be hard to tell. Remember the three allowed structures that were illustrated in Figure 2-12. The flowchart in Figure 2-13 does not look exactly like any of the three shapes shown in Figure 2-12. However, because you may stack and nest structures while retaining overall structure, it might be difficult to determine whether a flowchart as a whole is structured. It's easiest to analyze the flowchart in Figure 2-13 one step at a time. The beginning of the flowchart looks like Figure 2-14.

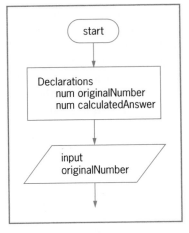

Figure 2-14   Beginning of a number-doubling flowchart

Is this portion of the flowchart structured? Yes, it's a sequence of two events.

Adding the next piece of the flowchart looks like Figure 2-15. The sequence is finished; either a selection or a loop is starting. You might not know which one, but you do know the sequence is not continuing, because sequences can't contain questions. With a sequence, each task or step must follow without any opportunity to branch off. Therefore, which type of structure starts with the question in Figure 2-15? Is it a selection or a loop?

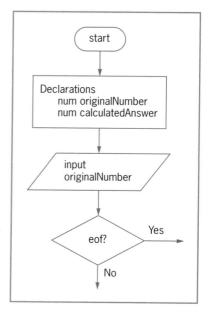

Figure 2-15 Number-doubling flowchart continued

Selection and loop structures differ as follows:

- In a selection structure, the logic goes in one of two directions after the question, and then the flow comes back together; the question is not asked a second time.

- In a loop, if the answer to the question results in the loop being entered and the loop statements executing, then the logic returns to the question that started the loop; when the body of a loop executes, the question that controls the loop is always asked again.

In the number-doubling problem in the original Figure 2-13, if it is not **eof** (that is, if the end-of-file condition is not met), then some math is done, an answer is output, a new number is obtained, and the logic returns to the **eof** question. In other words, while the answer to the **eof** question continues to be *No*, a body of statements continues to execute. Therefore, the **eof** question starts a structure that is more like a loop than it is like a selection.

The number-doubling problem *does* contain a loop, but it's not a structured loop. In a structured loop, the rules are:

1. You ask a question.

2. If the answer indicates you should execute the loop body, then you do so.

3. If you execute the loop body, then you must go right back to repeat the question.

The flowchart in Figure 2-13 asks a question; if the answer is *No* (that is, while it is true that the `eof` condition has not been met), then the program performs two tasks in the loop body: it does the arithmetic and it displays the results. Doing two things is acceptable because two tasks with no possible branching constitute a sequence, and it is fine to nest a structure within another structure. However, when the sequence ends, the logic doesn't flow right back to the question. Instead, it goes *above* the question to get another number. For the loop in Figure 2-13 to be a structured loop, the logic must return to the `eof` question when the embedded sequence ends.

The flowchart in Figure 2-16 shows the flow of logic returning to the `eof` question immediately after the sequence. Figure 2-16 shows a structured flowchart, but the flowchart has one major flaw—it doesn't do the job of continuously doubling different numbers.

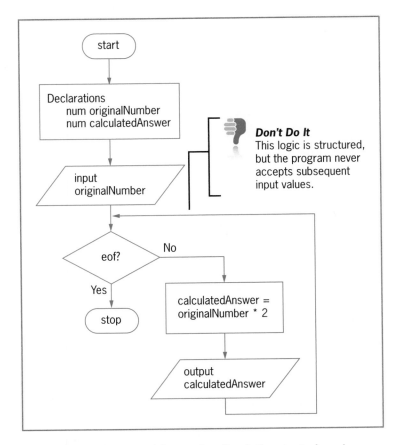

Figure 2-16 Structured, but nonfunctional, flowchart of number-doubling problem

Follow the flowchart in Figure 2-16 through a typical program run, assuming the eof value is 0. Suppose when the program starts, the user enters a 9 for the value of originalNumber. That's not eof, so the number is multiplied by 2, and 18 is displayed as the value of calculatedAnswer. Then the question eof? is asked again. It can't be eof because a new value representing the sentinel (ending) value can't be entered. The logic never returns to the input originalNumber task, so the value of originalNumber never changes. Therefore, 9 doubles again and the answer 18 is displayed again. It's still not eof, so the same steps are repeated. This goes on *forever*, with the answer 18 displaying repeatedly because the user can never enter a second or subsequent values. The program logic shown in Figure 2-16 is structured, but it doesn't work as intended; the program in Figure 2-17 works, but it isn't structured!

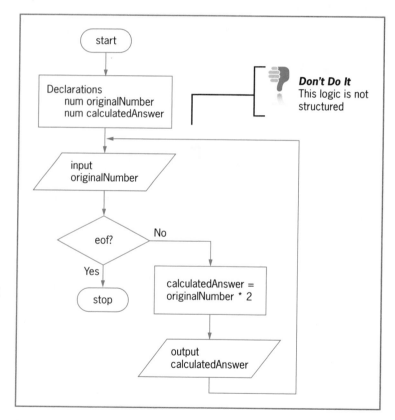

The loop in Figure 2-17 is not structured because in a structured loop, after the tasks execute within the loop, the flow of logic must return directly to the loop-controlling question. In Figure 2-17, the logic does not return to the loop-controlling question; instead, it goes "too high" outside the loop to repeat the input originalNumber task.

Figure 2-17   Functional but unstructured flowchart

How can the number-doubling problem be both structured and work as intended? Often, for a program to be structured, you must add something extra. In this case, it's an extra input originalNumber step. Consider the solution in Figure 2-18; it's structured *and* it does what it's supposed to do. The program logic illustrated in Figure 2-18 contains a sequence and a loop. The loop contains another sequence.

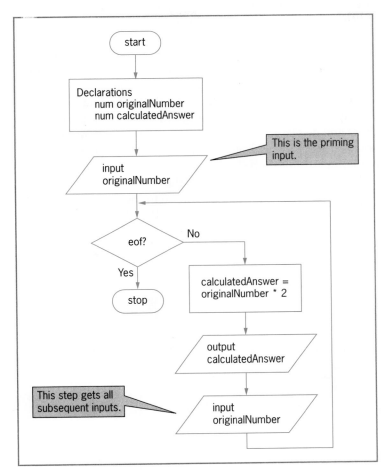

Figure 2-18 Functional, structured flowchart and pseudocode for the number-doubling problem

The additional `input originalNumber` step shown in Figure 2-18 is typical in structured programs. The first of the two input steps is the priming input, or priming read. The term *priming* comes from the fact that the read is first, or *primary* (what gets the process going, as in "priming the pump"). The purpose of the priming input step is to control the upcoming loop that begins with the eof question. The last element within the structured loop gets the next, and all subsequent, input values. This is also typical in structured loops—the last step executed within the loop alters the condition tested in the question that begins the loop, which in this case is the eof question.

 Years ago, programmers could avoid using structure by inserting a "go to" statement into their pseudocode. A "go to" statement would say something like "after displaying the answer, go to the first input step." Because "go to" statements cause spaghetti code, they are not allowed in structured programming. Some programmers call structured programming "goto-less" programming.

Figure 2-19 shows another way you might attempt to draw the logic for the number-doubling program. At first glance, the figure might seem to show an acceptable solution to the problem—it is structured, contains a single loop with a sequence of three steps within it, and appears to eliminate the need for the priming input statement. When the program starts, the eof question is asked. The answer is *No*, so the program gets an input number, doubles it, and displays it. Then, if it is still not eof, the program gets another number, doubles it, and displays it. The program continues until eof is encountered when getting input. The last time the input originalNumber statement executes, it encounters eof, but the program does not stop—instead, it calculates and displays a result one last time. This last output is extraneous—the eof value should not be doubled and output. As a general rule, an eof question should always come immediately after an input statement because it is at input that the end-of-file condition will be detected. Therefore, the best solution to the number-doubling problem remains the one shown in Figure 2-18—the solution containing the priming input statement.

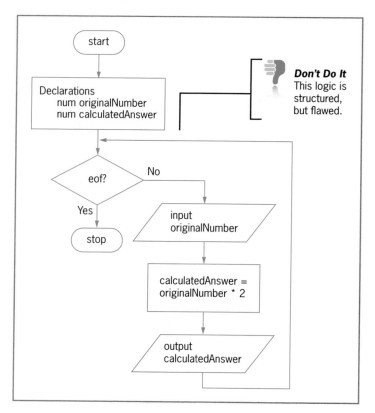

Figure 2-19   Structured but incorrect solution to the number-doubling problem

Understanding the Reasons for Structure

At this point, you may very well be saying, "I liked the original number-doubling program back in Figure 2-13 just fine. I could follow it. Also, the second program had an extra step in it, so it was more work. Who cares if a program is structured?"

Until you have some programming experience, it is difficult to appreciate the reasons for using only the three structures—sequence, selection, and loop. However, staying with these three structures is better for the following reasons:

- *Clarity*—The number-doubling program is a small program. As programs get bigger, they get more confusing if they're not structured.

- *Professionalism*—All other programmers (and programming teachers you might encounter) expect your programs to be structured. It's the way things are done professionally.

- *Efficiency*—Most newer computer languages are structured languages with syntax that lets you deal efficiently with sequence, selection, and looping. Older languages, such as assembly languages, COBOL, and RPG, were developed before the principles of structured programming were discovered. However, even programs that use those older languages can be written in a structured form, and structured programming is expected on the job today. Newer languages such as C#, C++, and Java enforce structure by their syntax.

- *Maintenance*—You, as well as other programmers, will find it easier to modify and maintain structured programs as changes are required in the future.

- *Modularity*—Structured programs can be easily broken down into routines or **modules** that can be assigned to any number of programmers. The routines then are pieced back together like modular furniture at each routine's single entry or exit point. Additionally, often a module can be used in multiple programs, saving development time in the new project. You will learn more about this concept in Chapter 6.

Recognizing Structure and Structuring Unstructured Logic

When you are just learning about structured program design, it is difficult to detect whether a flowchart of a program's logic is structured. For example, is the flowchart segment in Figure 2-20 structured?

Yes, it is. It has a sequence and a selection structure.

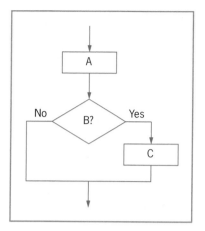

Figure 2-20   Example 1

Is the flowchart segment in Figure 2-21 structured?

Yes, it is. It has a loop, and within the loop is a selection.

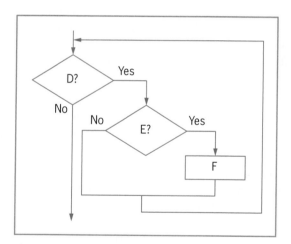

Figure 2-21   Example 2

Is the flowchart segment in Figure 2-22 structured?

No, it isn't; it is not constructed from the three basic structures. One way to straighten out a flowchart segment that isn't structured is to use what you can call the "spaghetti bowl" method; that is, picture the flowchart as a bowl of spaghetti that you must untangle. Imagine you can grab one piece of pasta at the top of the bowl and start pulling. As you "pull" each symbol out of the tangled mess, you can untangle the separate paths until the entire segment is structured.

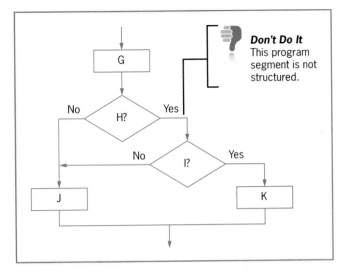

Figure 2-22 Example 3

For example, with the diagram in Figure 2-22, if you start pulling at the top, you encounter a procedure box, labeled G. (See Figure 2-23.) A single process like G is part of an acceptable structure—it constitutes at least the beginning of a sequence structure.

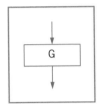

Figure 2-23
Untangling Example 3, first step

Imagine you continue pulling symbols from the tangled segment. The next item in the flowchart is a question that tests a condition labeled H, as you can see in Figure 2-24. At this point, you know the sequence that started with G has ended. Sequences never have decisions in them, so the sequence is finished; either a selection or a loop is beginning with question H. A loop must return to the question at some later point.

You can see from the original logic in Figure 2-22 that whether the answer to H is yes or no, the logic never returns to H. Therefore, H begins a selection structure, not a loop structure.

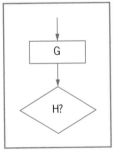

Figure 2-24
Untangling Example 3, second step

To continue detangling the logic, you (imaginarily) pull up on the flowline that emerges from the left side (the "No" side) of Question H. You encounter J, as shown in Figure 2-25. When you continue beyond J, you reach the end of the flowchart.

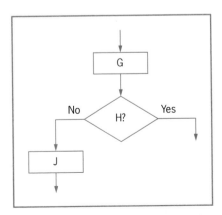

Figure 2-25 Untangling Example 3, third step

Now you can turn your attention to the "Yes" side (the right side) of the condition tested in H. When you pull up on the right side, you encounter Question I. (See Figure 2-26.)

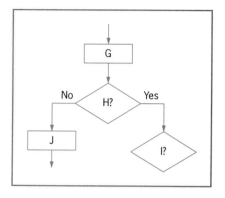

In the original version of the logic in Figure 2-22, follow the line on the left side of Question I. The line extending from the selection is attached to a task outside the selection. The line emerging from the left side of selection I is attached to Step J. You might

Figure 2-26 Untangling Example 3, fourth step

say the I selection is becoming entangled with the H selection, so you must untangle the structures by repeating the step that is causing the tangle. (In this example, you repeat Step J to untangle it from the other usage of J.) Continue pulling on the flowline that emerges from process J until you reach the end of the program segment, as shown in Figure 2-27.

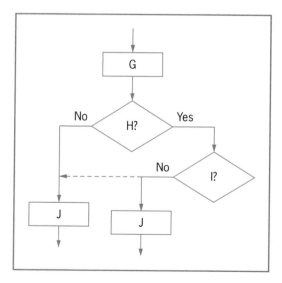

Figure 2-27 Untangling Example 3, fifth step

Now pull on the right side of Question I. Process K pops up, as shown in Figure 2-28; then you reach the end of the flowchart segment.

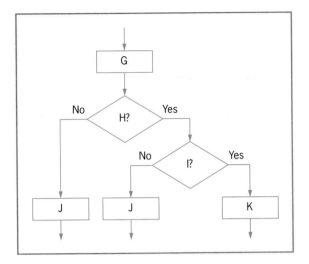

Figure 2-28   Untangling Example 3, sixth step

At this point, the untangled flowchart has three loose ends. The loose ends of Question I can be brought together to form a selection structure; then the loose ends of Question H can be brought together to form another selection structure. The result is the flowchart shown in Figure 2-29. The entire flowchart segment is structured—it has a sequence followed by a selection inside a selection.

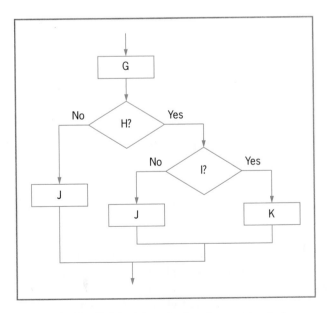

Figure 2-29   Finished flowchart and pseudocode for untangling Example 3

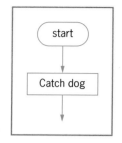

Figure 2-30   Washing the dog, part 1

Structuring the Dog-Washing Process

Recall the dog-washing process illustrated in Figure 2-2 at the beginning of this chapter. When you look at it now, you should recognize it as an unstructured process. Can this process be reconfigured to perform precisely the same tasks in a structured way? Of course!

Figure 2-30 shows the beginning of the process. The first step, *Catch the dog*, is a simple sequence.

Figure 2-31 contains the next part of the process. When a question is encountered, the sequence is over, and either a loop or a selection starts. In this case, after the dog runs away, you must catch the dog, and determine whether he runs away again, so a loop begins. To create a structured loop like the ones you have seen earlier in this chapter, you can repeat the *Catch the dog* process and return immediately to the *Does dog run away?* question.

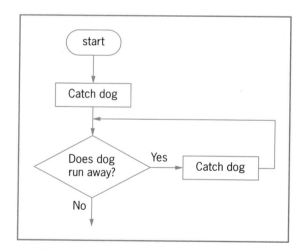

Figure 2-31   Washing the dog, part 2

In the original flowchart in Figure 2-2, when the dog does not run away, you turn on the water. This step is a simple sequence, so it can correctly be added to the bottom of the loop. When the water is turned on, the original process checks to see whether the dog runs away after this new development. This starts a loop. In the original flowchart, the lines cross, creating a tangle, so you repeat as many steps as necessary to detangle the lines. After you turn off the water and catch the dog, you encounter the question *Does dog have shampoo on?* Because the logic has not yet reached the shampooing step, there is no need to ask this question; the answer at this point always will be *No*. When one of the logical paths emerging from a question can never be traveled, you can eliminate the question. Figure 2-32 shows that if the dog runs away after you turn on the water, but before you've gotten the dog wet and shampooed him, you must turn the water off, catch the dog, and return to the step that asks whether the dog runs away.

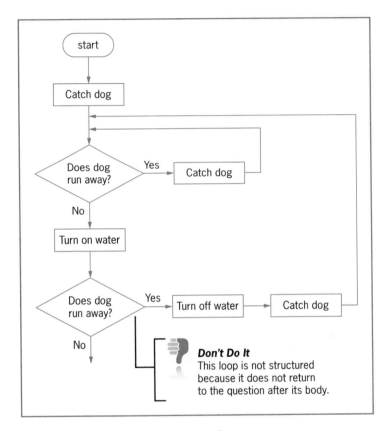

Figure 2-32 Washing the dog, part 3

The logic in Figure 2-32 is not structured because the second loop that begins with the question *Does dog run away?* does not immediately return to the question after its body executes. So, to make the loop structured, you can repeat the actions that occur before returning to the loop-controlling question. (See Figure 2-33.)

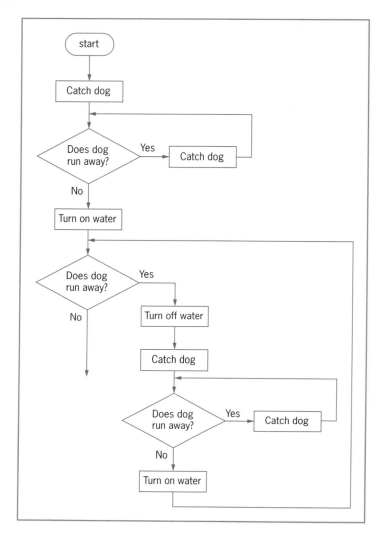

Figure 2-33 Washing the dog, part 4

The flowchart segment in Figure 2-33 is structured; it contains a sequence, a loop, a sequence, and a final, larger loop. This last loop contains its own sequence, loop, and sequence.

After the dog is caught, and the water is on, you wet and shampoo the dog, as shown in Figure 2-34. Then, according to the original flowchart in Figure 2-2, you once again check to see whether the dog has run away. If he has, you turn off the water and catch the dog. From this location in the logic, the answer to the *Does dog have shampoo on?* question will always be *Yes*; so, as before, there is no need to ask this question. So, if the dog runs away, the last loop executes. You turn off the water, continue to catch the dog as he repeatedly escapes, and turn the water on. When the dog is caught, you rinse the dog and end the program. Figure 2-34 shows both the complete flowchart and pseudocode.

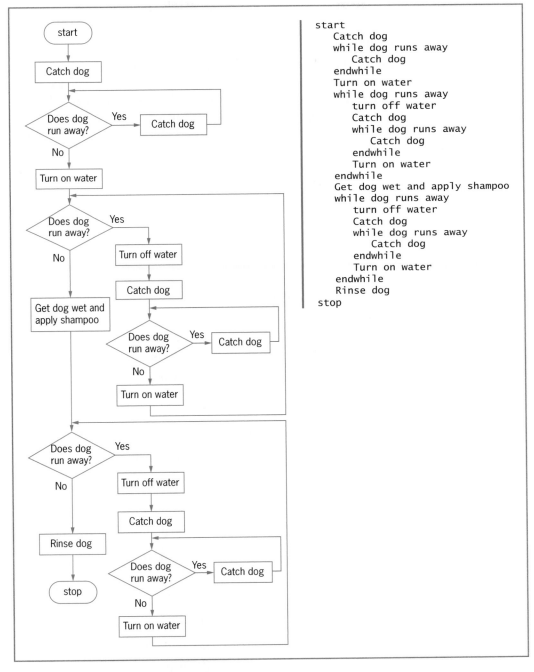

```
start
    Catch dog
    while dog runs away
        Catch dog
    endwhile
    Turn on water
    while dog runs away
        turn off water
        Catch dog
        while dog runs away
            Catch dog
        endwhile
        Turn on water
    endwhile
    Get dog wet and apply shampoo
    while dog runs away
        turn off water
        Catch dog
        while dog runs away
            Catch dog
        endwhile
        Turn on water
    endwhile
    Rinse dog
stop
```

Figure 2-34 Structured dog-washing flowchart and pseudocode

For convenience, many programming languages allow two supplemental structures—the do loop and the case structure. You can learn about these two structures in Appendix B. Even though these extra structures can be used in most programming languages, all logical problems can be solved without them. All processes can be described using sequence, selection, and loop.

The flowchart in Figure 2-34 is complete, and is structured. It contains alternating sequence and loop structures. You might notice that the two loops are identical, so if you wanted to, you could modularize the *Does dog run away?* loop so that the repeated instruction sets are written once and contained in their own process using a single name. You will learn to do this in Chapter 6.

No matter how complicated any set of steps is, it can always be reduced to combinations of the three basic structures sequence, selection, and loop. These structures can be nested and stacked in an infinite number of ways to describe the logic of any process and to create the logic for every computer program that ever has been or ever will be written.

Review Questions

1. Snarled program logic is called _____ code.

   a. snake

   b. spaghetti

   c. string

   d. gnarly

2. A sequence structure can contain _____.

   a. any number of tasks

   b. exactly three tasks

   c. no more than three tasks

   d. only one of task

3. Which of the following is not another term for a selection structure?

   a. decision structure

   b. if-then-else structure

   c. dual-alternative if structure

   d. loop structure

4. The structure in which you ask a question, and, depending on the answer, take some action and then ask the question again, can be called all of the following except _____.

   a. iteration

   b. loop

   c. repetition

   d. if-then-else

5. Placing a structure within another structure is called _____ the structures.

   a. stacking   c. building

   b. untangling   d. nesting

6. Attaching structures end-to-end is called _____.

   a. stacking   c. building

   b. untangling   d. nesting

7. The action or actions that occur within the loop are known as the _____.

   a. loop mass   c. loop body

   b. reiterations   d. nested statements

8. The statement `if age >= 65 then seniorDiscount = "yes"` is an example of a _____.

   a. sequence   c. dual-alternative selection

   b. loop   d. single-alternative selection

9. The statement `if age < 13 then movieTicket = 4.00 else movieTicket = 8.50` is an example of a _____.

   a. sequence   c. dual-alternative selection

   b. loop   d. single-alternative selection

10. Which of the following attributes do all three basic structures share?

   a. Their flowcharts all contain exactly three processing symbols.

   b. They all contain a decision.

   c. They all have one entry and one exit point.

   d. They all begin with a process.

11. When you read input data in a loop within a program, the input statement that precedes the loop _____.

   a. is the only part of a program allowed to be unstructured

   b. cannot result in `eof`

   c. is called a priming input

   d. executes hundreds or even thousands of times in most business programs

12. A group of statements that execute as a unit is a _____.

    a. block   c. chunk

    b. family   d. cohort

13. Which of the following is acceptable in a structured program?

    a. placing a sequence within the true half of a dual-alternative decision

    b. placing a decision within a loop

    c. placing a loop within one of the steps in a sequence

    d. All of these are acceptable.

14. Which of the following is not a reason for enforcing structure rules in computer programs?

    a. Structured programs are clearer to understand than unstructured ones.

    b. Other professional programmers will expect programs to be structured.

    c. Structured programs usually are shorter than unstructured ones.

    d. Structured programs can be broken down into modules easily.

15. Which of the following is true of structured logic?

    a. You can use structured logic with newer programming languages, such as Java and C#, but not with older ones.

    b. Any task can be described using some combination of the three structures.

    c. Structured programs require that you break the code into modules.

    d. All of these are true.

Find the Bugs

Your student disk contains files named DEBUG02-01.txt, DEBUG02-02.txt, and DEBUG02-03.txt. Each file contains pseudocode segments with one or more bugs that you must find and correct.

Exercises

1. In Figure 2-11 the process of buying and planting flowers in the spring was shown using the same structures as
    the generic example in Figure 2-10. Describe some other
    process with which you are familiar using exactly the
    same logic.

2. Each of the flowchart segments in Figure 2-35 is unstructured. Redraw each flowchart segment so that it does the
    same thing but is structured.

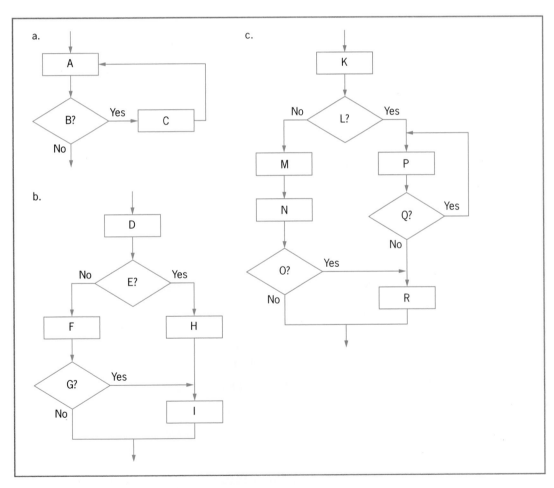

Figure 2-35 Flowcharts for Exercise 2 (*continues*)

(continued)

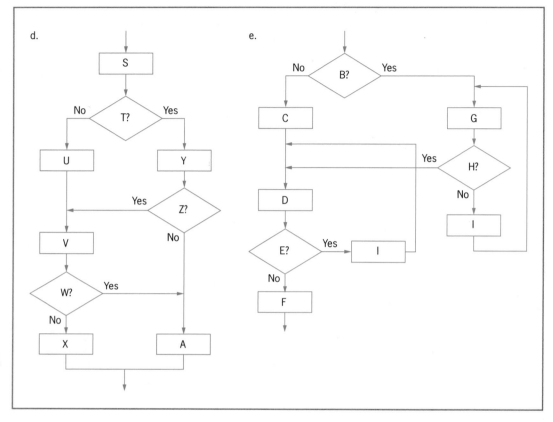

Figure 2-35 Flowcharts for Exercise 2

3. Write pseudocode for each example (a through e) in Exercise 2 making sure your pseudocode is structured but accomplishes the same tasks as the flowchart segment.

4. Assume you have created a mechanical arm that can hold a pen. The arm can perform the following tasks:

• Lower the pen to a piece of paper.

• Raise the pen from the paper.

• Move the pen one inch along a straight line. (If the pen is lowered, this action draws a one-inch line from left to right; if the pen is raised, this action just repositions the pen one inch to the right.)

• Turn 90 degrees to the right.

• Draw a circle that is one inch in diameter.

Draw a structured flowchart or write structured pseudocode describing the logic that would cause the arm to draw the following:

a.   a one-inch square

b.   a 21-inch by one-inch rectangle

c.   a string of three beads

d.   a short word (for example, "cat")

Have a fellow student act as the mechanical arm and carry out your instructions. Do not tell your mechanical arm partner what he or she will be drawing (or writing) before the partner attempts to carry out your instructions.

5.   Assume you have created a mechanical robot that can perform the following tasks:

• Stand up.

• Sit down.

• Turn left 90 degrees.

• Turn right 90 degrees.

• Take a step.

Additionally, the robot can determine the answer to one test condition:

• Am I touching something?

Place two chairs 20 feet apart, directly facing each other. Draw a structured flowchart or write pseudocode describing the logic that would allow the robot to start from a sitting position in one chair, cross the room, and end up sitting in the other chair.

Have a fellow student act as the robot and carry out your instructions.

6.   Looking up a word in a dictionary can be a complicated process. For example, assume you want to look up "logic." You might proceed by opening the dictionary to a random page and seeing "juice." You know that word comes alphabetically before "logic," so you flip forward and see "lamb." That is still not far enough, so you flip forward and see "monkey." That means you have gone too far, so now you flip back, and so on. Draw a structured flowchart or write pseudocode that describes the process of looking up a word in a dictionary.

Pick a word at random and have a fellow student attempt to carry out your instructions.

7. Draw a structured flowchart or write structured pseudocode describing your preparation to go to work or school in the morning. Include at least two decisions and two loops.

8. Draw a structured flowchart or write structured pseudocode describing your preparation to go to bed at night. Include at least two decisions and two loops.

9. Draw a structured flowchart or write structured pseudocode describing how your paycheck is calculated. Include at least two decisions.

10. Draw a structured flowchart or write structured pseudocode describing the steps a retail store employee should follow to process a customer purchase. Include at least two decisions.

11. Choose a very simple children's game and describe its logic, using a structured flowchart or pseudocode. For example, you might try to explain Rock, Paper, Scissors; Musical Chairs; Duck, Duck, Goose; the card game War; or the elimination game Eenie, Meenie, Minie, Moe.

12. Choose a television game show such as *Deal or No Deal* or *Jeopardy!* and describe its rules using a structured flowchart or pseudocode.

13. Choose a professional sport such as baseball or football and describe the actions in one play period using a structured flowchart or pseudocode.

CHAPTER 3

Making Decisions

After completing this chapter you will be able to:

- ◎ Evaluate Boolean expressions to make comparisons
- ◎ Use relational comparison operators
- ◎ Explain AND logic
- ◎ Explain OR logic
- ◎ Make selections within ranges
- ◎ Explain precedence when combining AND and OR selections

This book follows the convention that the two logical paths emerging from a decision are drawn to the right and left in a flowchart. Some programmers draw one flowline emerging from the side of the diamond shape that represents a selection, and then draw the other emerging from the bottom. The exact format of the diagram is not as important as the idea that one logical path flows into a selection, and two possible outcomes emerge.

You can call a single-alternative decision (or selection) a *single-sided decision*. Similarly, a dual-alternative decision is a *double-sided decision* (or selection).

Evaluating Boolean Expressions to Make Comparisons

The reason people frequently think computers are smart lies in the computer program's ability to make decisions. A medical diagnosis program that can decide if your symptoms fit various disease profiles seems quite intelligent, as does a program that can offer different potential vacation routes based on your destination.

The selection structure (sometimes called a decision structure) involved in such programs is not new to you—it's one of the basic structures you learned about in Chapter 2. Take a moment to review Figures 3-1 and 3-2.

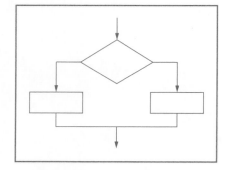

Figure 3-1   The dual-alternative selection structure

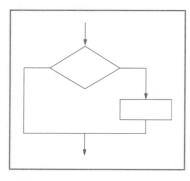

Figure 3-2   The single-alternative selection structure

In Chapter 2 you learned that you can refer to the structure in Figure 3-1 as a dual-alternative selection because an action is associated with each of two possible outcomes: depending on the answer to the question represented by the diamond, the logical flow proceeds either to the left branch of the structure or to the right. The choices are mutually exclusive; that is, the logic can flow only to one of the two alternatives, never to both. This selection structure is also called an if-then-else structure or a **binary selection**.

The flowchart segment in Figure 3-2 represents a single-alternative selection where action is required for only one outcome of the question. You can call this form of the selection structure an **if-then**, because no alternative or "else" action is necessary.

Figure 3-3 shows the flowchart and pseudocode for a program that contains a typical if-then-else decision in a business program. Many organizations pay employees time and a half (one and one-half times their usual hourly rate) for hours worked in excess of 40 per week.

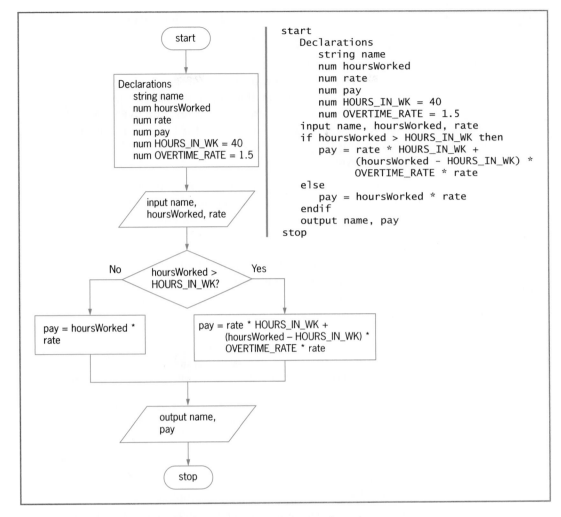

```
start
    Declarations
        string name
        num hoursWorked
        num rate
        num pay
        num HOURS_IN_WK = 40
        num OVERTIME_RATE = 1.5
    input name, hoursWorked, rate
    if hoursWorked > HOURS_IN_WK then
        pay = rate * HOURS_IN_WK +
                (hoursWorked - HOURS_IN_WK) *
                OVERTIME_RATE * rate
    else
        pay = hoursWorked * rate
    endif
    output name, pay
stop
```

Figure 3-3 Flowchart and pseudocode for overtime payroll program

Throughout this book, you will see many examples presented in both flowchart and pseudocode form. When you first analyze a solution, you might find it easier if you concentrate on just one of the two design tools. When you understand how the program works using one tool (for example, the flowchart), you can proceed to confirm that the solution is identical using the other tool (for example, the pseudocode).

In Chapter 1 you learned that named constants conventionally are created using all uppercase letters.

In the program in Figure 3-3, several variables and constants are declared. The variables include those that will be retrieved from input (name, which is a string, and hoursWorked and rate, which are numbers) and one that will be calculated from the input values (grossPay, which is a number). The program in Figure 3-3 also uses two named constants: HOURS_IN_WK, which represents the number of hours in a standard workweek, and OVERTIME_RATE, which represents a multiplication factor for the premium rate at which an employee is paid after working the standard number of hours in a week.

After the input data is retrieved in the program in Figure 3-3, a decision is made about the value of hoursWorked. The longer calculation, which adds a time-and-a-half factor to an employee's gross pay, is found in the if clause of the decision—the part of the decision that holds the action or actions that execute when the tested condition in the decision is true. The shorter calculation, which produces grossPay by multiplying hoursWorked by rate, constitutes the else clause of the decision—the part that executes only when the tested condition in the decision is false.

> The statement input name, hoursWorked, rate is intended to represent any type of input whether interactive or from a file. With interactive input, you would want to add a prompt before each data item was retrieved. A **prompt** is a displayed statement that advises a user what to do. For example, you might use a statement such as output "Please enter employee's name". On the other hand, if the input comes from a storage device, such as a disk, no prompt is needed.

Suppose that an employee's paycheck should be reduced if the employee participates in the company dental plan and that no action is taken if the employee is not a dental plan participant. Figure 3-4 shows how this decision might be added to the payroll program. The additions from Figure 3-3 are shaded.

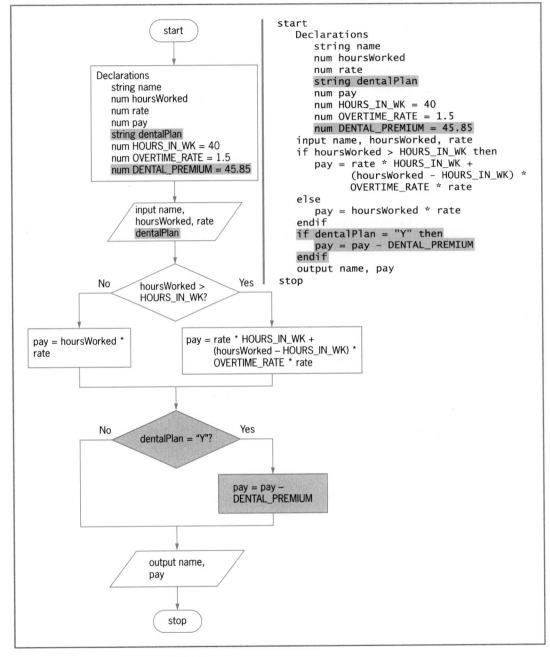

```
start
    Declarations
        string name
        num hoursWorked
        num rate
        string dentalPlan
        num pay
        num HOURS_IN_WK = 40
        num OVERTIME_RATE = 1.5
        num DENTAL_PREMIUM = 45.85
    input name, hoursWorked, rate
    if hoursWorked > HOURS_IN_WK then
        pay = rate * HOURS_IN_WK +
              (hoursWorked - HOURS_IN_WK) *
              OVERTIME_RATE * rate
    else
        pay = hoursWorked * rate
    endif
    if dentalPlan = "Y" then
        pay = pay - DENTAL_PREMIUM
    endif
    output name, pay
stop
```

Figure 3-4   Flowchart and pseudocode for payroll program with dental insurance determination

Mathematician George Boole (1815–1864) approached logic more simply than his predecessors did, by expressing logical selections with common algebraic symbols. Boolean (true/false) expressions are named for him.

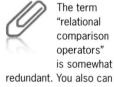

The term "relational comparison operators" is somewhat redundant. You also can call these operators **relational operators** or **comparison operators**.

The expressions hoursWorked > HOURS_IN_WK and dentalPlan = "Y" in Figures 3-3 and 3-4 are Boolean expressions. A **Boolean expression** is one that represents only one of two states, usually expressed as true or false. Every decision you make in a computer program involves evaluating a Boolean expression. True/false evaluation is "natural" from a computer's standpoint, because computer circuitry consists of two-state on-off switches, often represented by 1 or 0. Every computer decision yields a true-or-false, yes-or-no, 1-or-0 result.

Using the Relational Comparison Operators

Table 3-1 describes the six relational comparison operators supported by all modern programming languages. Each of these operators is binary—that is, each requires two operands. An **operand** is a value on either side of an operator. When you construct an expression using two operands and one of the operators described in Table 3-1, the expression evaluates to true or false based on the operands' values. Usually, both operands in a comparison must be the same data type; that is, you can compare numeric values to other numeric values, and text strings to other strings.

Operator	Name	Discussion
=	Equivalency operator	Evaluates as true when its operands are equivalent Many languages use a double equal sign (==) to avoid confusion with the assignment operator.
>	Greater than operator	Evaluates as true when the left operand is greater than the right operand.
<	Less than operator	Evaluates as true when the left operand is less than the right operand.
>=	Greater than or equal to operator	Evaluates as true when the left operand is greater than or equivalent to the right operand. When an operator is formed using two keystrokes, you never insert a space between them.
<=	Less than or equal to operator	Evaluates as true when the left operand is less than or equivalent to the right operand. When an operator is formed using two keystrokes, you never insert a space between them.
<>	Not equal to operator	Evaluates as true when its operands are not equivalent. Some languages use an exclamation point followed by an equal sign to indicate not equal to (!=). When an operator is formed using two keystrokes, you never insert a space between them.

Table 3-1   Relational comparison operators

In any Boolean expression, the two values compared can be either variables or constants. For example, the expression `currentTotal = 100?` compares a variable, `currentTotal`, to a numeric constant, 100. Depending on the `currentTotal` value, the expression is true or false. In the expression `currentTotal = previousTotal?`, both values are variables, and the result is also true or false depending on the values stored in each of the two variables. Although it's legal to do so, you would never use expressions in which you compare two constants— for example 20 = 20? or 30 = 40?. Such expressions are considered **trivial expressions** because each will always evaluate to the same result: true for 20 = 20? and false for 30 = 40?.

Any decision can be made using combinations of just three types of comparisons: equal, greater than, and less than. You never need the three additional comparisons (greater than or equal, less than or equal, or not equal), but using them often makes decisions more convenient. For example, assume you need to issue a 10 percent discount to any customer whose age is 65 or greater, and charge full price to other customers. You can use the greater-than-or-equal-to symbol to write the logic as follows:

```
if customerAge >= 65 then
    discount = 0.10
else
    discount = 0
endif
```

As an alternative, if you want to avoid using the >= operator, you can express the same logic by writing:

```
if customerAge < 65 then
    discount = 0
else
    discount = 0.10
endif
```

In any decision for which a >= b is true, then a < b is false. Conversely, if a >= b is false, then a < b is true. By rephrasing the question and swapping the actions taken based on the outcome, you can make the same decision in multiple ways. The clearest route is often to ask a question so the positive or true outcome results in the action that was your motivation for making the test. When your company policy is to "provide a discount for those who are 65 and older," the phrase "greater than or equal to" comes to mind, so it is the most natural to use. On the other hand, if your policy is to "provide no discount for those under 65," then it is more natural to use the "less than" syntax. Either way, the same people receive a discount.

Comparing two amounts in order to decide if they are *not* equal to each other is the most confusing of all the comparisons. Using "not equal to" in decisions involves thinking in double negatives, which makes you prone to include logical errors in your programs. For example, consider the flowchart segment in Figure 3-5.

Some programming languages allow you to compare a character to a number. If you do, then a single character's numeric code value is used in the comparison. For example, many computers use the American Standard Code for Information Interchange (ASCII) system or the Unicode system. Appendix A contains more information on coding systems.

Usually, string variables are not considered to be equal unless they are identical, including the spacing and whether they appear in uppercase or lowercase. For example, "black pen" is *not* equal to "black-pen", "BLACK PEN", or "Black Pen".

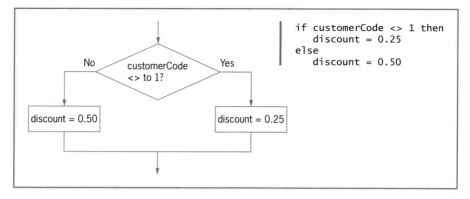

```
if customerCode <> 1 then
    discount = 0.25
else
    discount = 0.50
```

Figure 3-5   Using a negative comparison

Although negative comparisons can be awkward to use, your meaning is sometimes clearest if you use one. Frequently, this occurs when you use an if without an else, taking action only when some comparison is false. An example would be: if customerZipCode <> LOCAL_ZIP_CODE then add deliveryCharge to total.

In Figure 3-5, if the value of customerCode *is* equal to 1, the logical flow follows the false branch of the selection. If customerCode not equal to 1 is true, the discount is 0.25; if customerCode not equal to 1 is not true, it means the customerCode *is* 1, and the discount is 0.50. Even using the phrase "customerCode not equal to 1 is not true" is awkward.

Figure 3-6 shows the same decision, this time asked in the positive. Making the decision if customerCode *is* 1 then discount = 0.50 is clearer than trying to determine what customerCode is *not*.

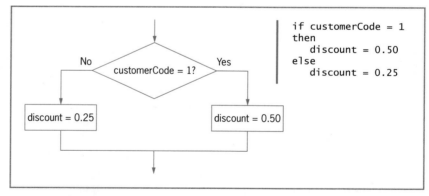

```
if customerCode = 1
then
    discount = 0.50
else
    discount = 0.25
```

Figure 3-6   Using the positive equivalent of the negative comparison in Figure 3-5

Understanding AND Logic

Often, you need more than one selection structure to determine whether an action should take place. When you need to ask multiple questions before an outcome is determined, you must create a **compound condition**. One type of compound condition is needed when the results of at least two decisions must be true for some action to take place.

For example, suppose you have salespeople for whom you calculate bonus payments based on sales performance. A salesperson receives a $50 bonus only if the salesperson sells more than three items that total at least $1,000. This type of situation is known as an **AND decision** because the salesperson's data must pass two tests—a minimum number of items sold *and* a minimum value—before the salesperson receives the bonus. An AND decision can be constructed using a **nested decision**, or a **nested if**—that is, a decision "inside of" another decision. The flowchart and pseudocode for the program are shown in Figure 3-7.

 Later in this chapter you will learn an alternate way to create AND logic by using a logical operator.

 You first learned about nesting structures in Chapter 2. You can always stack and nest any of the basic structures.

 A series of nested if statements is also called a **cascading if statement**.

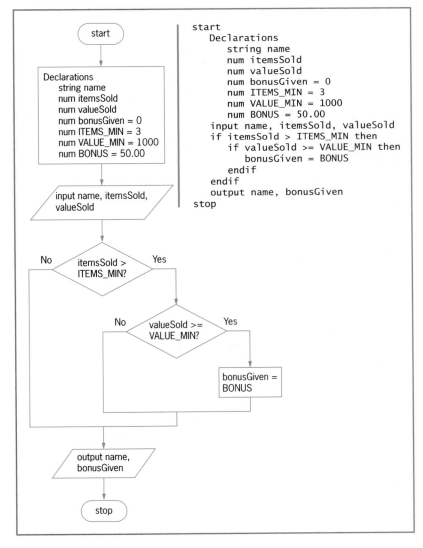

```
start
    Declarations
        string name
        num itemsSold
        num valueSold
        num bonusGiven = 0
        num ITEMS_MIN = 3
        num VALUE_MIN = 1000
        num BONUS = 50.00
    input name, itemsSold, valueSold
    if itemsSold > ITEMS_MIN then
        if valueSold >= VALUE_MIN then
            bonusGiven = BONUS
        endif
    endif
    output name, bonusGiven
stop
```

Figure 3-7 Flowchart and pseudocode for salesperson bonus-determining program in which salesperson must meet two criteria to get a bonus

In Figure 3-7, variables are declared to hold a salesperson's name, the number of items the salesperson has sold, the value of the items sold, and the bonus the salesperson will receive. Constants are declared to hold the minimums needed to receive a bonus and for the value of the potential bonus. In the nested if structure in Figure 3-7, the expression itemsSold > ITEMS_MIN is evaluated first. If this expression is true, then, and only then, is the second Boolean expression (valueSold >= VALUE_MIN) evaluated. If that expression is also true, then the salesperson is assigned the $50 bonus. If neither of the tested conditions is true, the salesperson's bonus value is never altered, and it retains its initial value of 0.

Nesting and Decisions for Efficiency

When you nest decisions because the resulting action requires that two conditions be true, you must decide which of the two decisions to make first. Logically, either selection in an AND decision can come first. However, when there are two selections, you often can improve your program's performance by correctly choosing which selection to make first.

For example, Figure 3-8 shows two ways to design the nested decision structure that assigns a $50 bonus to salespeople who sell more than three items valued at $1,000 or more. If you want to assign this bonus, you can take one of two approaches:

- You can ask about the items sold first, eliminate those salespeople who do not qualify, and ask about the value of the items sold only for those salespeople who "pass" the number of items test.

- You can ask about the value of the items first, eliminate those who do not qualify, and ask about the number of items only for those salespeople who "pass" the value test.

Either way, only salespeople who pass both tests receive the $50 bonus. Does it make a difference which question is asked first? As far as the result goes, no. Either way, the same salespeople receive the bonus—those who qualify on the basis of both criteria. As far as program efficiency goes, however, it *might* make a difference which question is asked first.

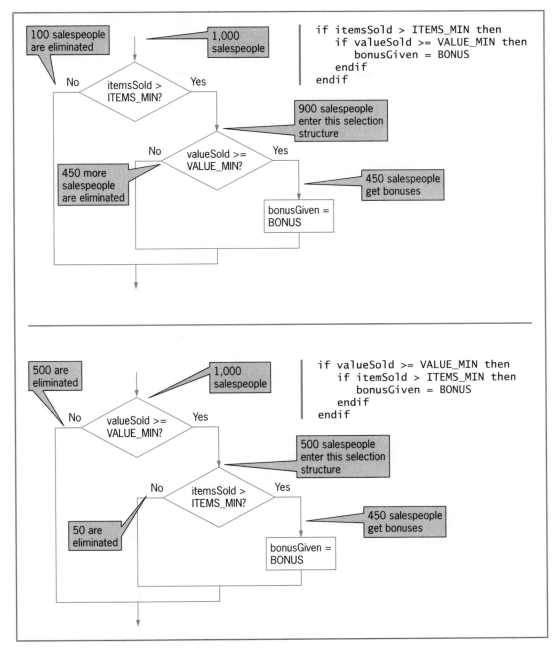

Figure 3-8 Two ways to select bonus recipients using identical criteria

Assume you know two facts about salesperson performance in your company:

- Out of 1,000 salespeople, about 90 percent, or 900, sell more than three items in a pay period.

- Only about half the 1,000 salespeople, or 500, sell items valued at $1,000 or more.

If you use the logic shown first in Figure 3-8, and you need to determine bonuses for 1,000 salespeople, the first question, itemsSold > ITEMS_MIN?, will execute 1,000 times. For approximately 90 percent of the salespeople, or 900 of them, the answer is true, so 100 salespeople are eliminated from the bonus assignment, and 900 proceed to the next question about the value of the items sold. Only about half the salespeople sell at least $1,000 worth of merchandise, so 450 of the 900 receive the bonus.

Using the alternate logic in Figure 3-8, the first question valueSold >= VALUE_MIN? will also be asked 1,000 times—once for each salesperson. Because only about half the company's salespeople sell at this higher dollar level, only 500 will "pass" this test and proceed to the question for number of items sold. Then about 90 percent of the 500, or 450 salespeople, will pass this second test and receive the bonus.

Whether you use the first or second decision order in Figure 3-8, the same 450 employees who surpass both sales criteria receive the bonus. The difference is that when you ask about the items sold first, the program must ask 1,900 questions to assign the correct bonuses—the first question tests the data for all 1,000 salespeople, and 900 continue to the second question. If you use the alternate logic, asking about valueSold first, the program asks only 1,500 questions—all 1,000 records are tested with the first question, but only 500 proceed to the second question. By asking about the dollar value of the goods first, you "save" 400 decisions.

The 400-question difference between the first and second set of decisions doesn't take much time on most computers. But it does take *some* time, and if a corporation has hundreds of thousands of salespeople instead of only 1,000, or if many such decisions have to be made within a program, performance time can be significantly improved by asking questions in the proper order.

In many programs where you must make AND decisions, you have no idea which of two events is more likely to occur; in that case, you can legitimately ask either question first. In addition, even though you know the probability of each of two conditions, the two events might not be mutually exclusive; that is, one might depend on the other. For example, salespeople who sell more items are also likely to have surpassed a requisite dollar value. Depending on the relationship between these questions, the order in which you ask them might matter less or not matter at all. However, if you do know the probabilities of the conditions, or can make a reasonable guess, the general rule is: *In an AND decision, first ask the question that is less likely to be true.* This eliminates as many instances of the second decision as possible, which speeds up processing time.

Combining Decisions Using the AND Operator

Most programming languages allow you to ask two or more questions in a single comparison by testing a **compound condition**. When you test a compound condition in a single expression to determine if each part of the expression is true, you use a **logical AND operator**, or more simply, an **AND operator**.

For example, Figure 3-9 shows the original bonus-determining logic from Figure 3-7 along with an example that uses a compound decision that contains an AND operator. The figure shows that if you want to provide a bonus for salespeople who sell more than ITEMS_MIN items and at least VALUE_MIN in value, you can use nested ifs, or you can include both decisions in a single statement by using the expression itemsSold > ITEMS_MIN AND valueSold >= VALUE_MIN?. When you use one or more AND operators to combine two or more Boolean expressions, each Boolean expression must be true for the entire expression to be evaluated as true. For example, if you ask, "Are you at least 18, and are you a registered voter, and did you vote in the last election?" the answer to all three parts of the question must be "yes" before the response can be a single, summarizing "yes." If any part of the expression is false, then the entire expression is false.

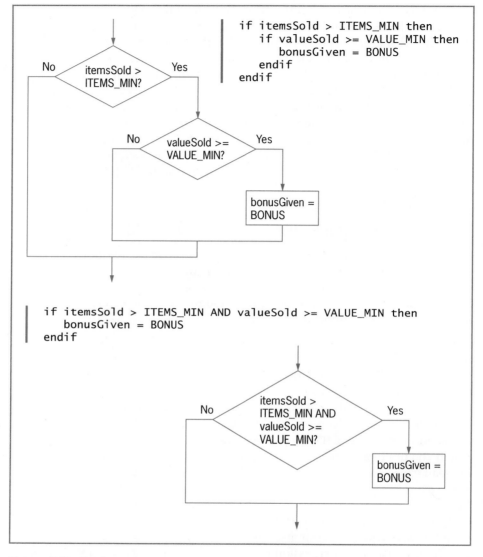

Figure 3-9   Testing a compound condition using nested decisions and using an AND operator

One tool that can help you understand the AND operator is a truth table. **Truth tables** are diagrams used in mathematics and logic to help describe the truth of an entire expression based on the truth of its parts. Table 3-2 shows a truth table that lists all the possibilities with an AND decision. As the table shows, for

x	y	x AND y
True	True	True
True	False	False
False	True	False
False	False	False

Table 3-2   Truth table for the AND operator

any two expressions x and y, the expression x AND y is true only if both x and y are individually true. If either x or y alone is false, or if both are false, then the expression x AND y is false.

If the programming language you use allows an AND operator, you must realize that the question you place first is the one that will be asked first, and cases that are eliminated based on the first question will not proceed to the second question. In other words, each part of an expression that uses an AND operator is evaluated only as far as necessary to determine whether the entire expression is true or false. This feature is called **short-circuit evaluation**. The computer can ask only one question at a time; even when you design your logic using the AND operator like the second example in Figure 3-9, the computer will execute the logic shown in the nested example.

You never are required to use the AND operator because using nested if statements can always achieve the same result. However, using the AND operator often makes your code more concise, less error-prone, and easier to understand. Using an AND operator in a decision that involves multiple conditions does not eliminate your responsibility for determining which condition to test first. Even when you use an AND operator, the computer makes decisions one at a time, and makes them in the order you ask them. If the first question in an AND expression evaluates to false, then the entire expression is false, and the second question is not even tested.

Logically, the AND operation corresponds to multiplication. If you assume 1 is true and 0 is false, then true AND true is true because 1 * 1 is 1. All the other combinations are false because 1 * 0, 0 * 1, and 0 * 0 all evaluate to 0.

The conditional AND operator in Java, C++, and C# consists of two ampersands, with no spaces between them (&&). In Visual Basic, you use the word And.

Avoiding Common Errors in an AND Selection

When you must satisfy two or more criteria to initiate an event in a program, you must make sure that the second decision is made entirely within the first decision. For example, if a program's objective is to assign a $50 bonus to salespeople who sell more than ITEMS_MIN items with a value of at least VALUE_MIN, then the program segment shown in Figure 3-10 contains three different types of logic errors.

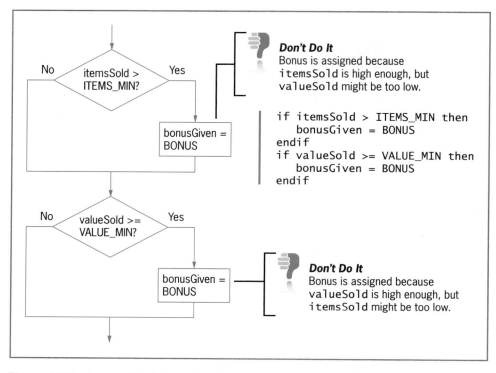

Figure 3-10 Incorrect logic to assign bonuses to salespeople who meet two criteria

The logic in Figure 3-10 shows that a salesperson who sells more than the minimum required items receives a $50 bonus. This salesperson should not necessarily receive the bonus—the dollar value might not be high enough, and it has not yet been tested. In addition, a salesperson who has not sold the minimum number of items is not eliminated from the second question. Instead, all salespeople endure the dollar value question, and some are assigned the bonus even though they might not have passed the criterion for number of items sold. Additionally, any salesperson who passes both tests has a bonus assigned twice. This does not result in an error, because the second $50 assignment replaces the first one, but processing time is wasted. For many reasons, the logic shown in Figure 3-10 is *not* correct for this problem.

Beginning programmers often make another type of error when they must make two comparisons on the same variable while using a logical **AND** operator. For example, suppose you want to assign a $75 bonus to those who have sold between 5 and 10 items inclusive. When you make this type of decision, you are basing it on a **range of values**—every value between low and high limits. For example, you want to select salespeople whose itemsSold value is greater than or equal to 5 *and* whose itemsSold value is less than or equal to 10; therefore, you need to make two comparisons on the same variable. Without the logical AND operator, the comparison is:

```
Declarations
    num itemsSold
    num bonusGiven
    num MIN_FOR_BONUS = 5
    num MAX_FOR_BONUS = 10
    num BONUS = 75
if itemsSold >= MIN_FOR_BONUS then
    if itemsSold <= MAX_FOR_BONUS then
        bonusGiven = BONUS
    endif
endif
```

The correct way to make this comparison with the AND operator is as follows:

```
if itemsSold >= MIN_FOR_BONUS AND itemsSold <= MAX_FOR_BONUS then
    bonusGiven = BONUS
endif
```

You substitute the AND operator for the phrase then if. However, some programmers might try to make the comparison as follows:

```
if itemsSold >= MIN_FOR_BONUS AND <= MAX_FOR_BONUS then
    bonusGiven = BONUS
endif
```

Don't Do It
This second relational comparison operator (<=) is missing an operand.

In most programming languages, the phrase `itemsSold >= MIN_FOR_BONUS AND <= MAX_FOR_BONUS` is incorrect. The logical AND operator is usually a binary operator that requires a complete Boolean expression on each side. When `<=` immediately follows AND, the second comparison is not a complete Boolean expression; you must indicate *what* is being compared to MAX_FOR_BONUS each time you make a comparison.

For clarity, many programmers prefer to surround each Boolean expression in a compound Boolean expression with its own set of parentheses. When you use this format, it is easier to remember to include each operand. Use this format if it is clearer to you. For example:

```
if (itemsSold >= MIN_FOR_BONUS) AND (itemsSold <= MAX_FOR_BONUS)
   bonusGiven = BONUS
endif
```

Understanding OR Logic

Sometimes you want to take action when one *or* the other of two conditions is true. This type of compound condition is called an **OR decision** because either one condition must be met *or* some other condition must be met in order for an event to take place. If someone asks, "Do you have a pen or pencil I can borrow?" only one of the two conditions has to be true for the answer to the whole question to be "yes"; only if the answers to both halves of the question are false is the value of the entire expression false.

For example, suppose you want to assign a $300 bonus to salespeople when they have achieved one of two goals—selling at least five items, or selling at least $2,000 worth of merchandise. Figure 3-11 shows a program that accomplishes this objective.

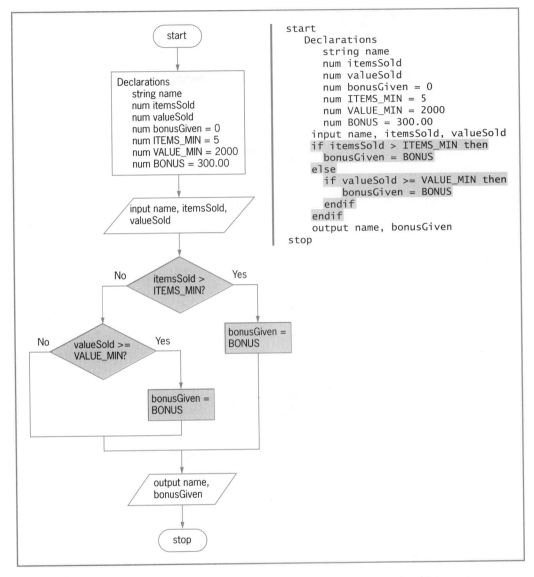

Figure 3-11 Flowchart and pseudocode for bonus-determining program in which a salesperson must meet one or both of two criteria to get a bonus

After a salesperson's data is input in the program in Figure 3-11, you ask the question `itemsSold >= ITEMS_MIN?`, and if the result is true, you assign the $300 bonus. Because selling ITEMS_MIN items is enough to qualify for the bonus, there is no need for further questioning. If the salesperson has not sold enough items, only then do you need to ask `if valueSold >= VALUE_MIN?`. If the employee did not sell ITEMS_MIN items, but did sell a high dollar value nonetheless, the salesperson receives the bonus.

Writing OR Decisions for Efficiency

As with an AND selection, when you use an OR selection, you can choose to ask either question first. For example, you can assign a bonus to salespeople who meet one or the other of two criteria using the logic in either part of Figure 3-12.

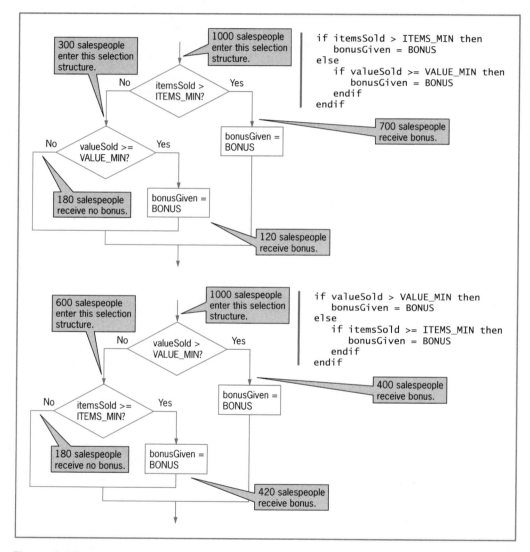

Figure 3-12 Two ways to select bonus recipients using identical criteria

You might have guessed that one of these selections is superior to the other when you have some background information about the relative likelihood of each condition you are testing. For example, assume you know the following sales statistics:

- Out of 1,000 employees in your company, about 70 percent, or 700, sell at least ITEMS_MIN items during a given period of time.

- Only 40 percent of salespeople, or 400, sell VALUE_MIN worth of goods or more.

When you use the logic shown in the first half of Figure 3-12 to assign bonuses, you first ask about the number of items sold. For 700 salespeople the answer is true and you assign the bonus. Only about 300 records continue to the next question regarding the dollar amount sold, where about 40 percent of the 300, or 120, fulfill the bonus requirement. In the end, you have made 1,300 decisions to correctly assign bonuses to 820 employees (700 plus 120).

If you use the OR logic in the second half of Figure 3-12, you ask about the dollar value sold first—1,000 times, once each for 1,000 salespeople. The result is true for 40 percent, or 400 employees, who receive a bonus. For 600 salespeople, you ask whether itemsSold is at least the minimum required. For 70 percent of the 600, the result is true, so bonuses are assigned to 420 additional people. In the end, the same 820 salespeople (400 plus 420) receive a bonus, but after executing 1,600 decisions—300 more decisions than when using the first decision logic.

The general rule is: *In an OR decision, first ask the question that is more likely to be true.* In the preceding example, a salesperson qualifies for a bonus as soon as the person's data passes one test. Asking the question that is more likely true first eliminates as many repetitions as possible of the second decision, and the time it takes to process all the salespeople is decreased. As with the AND situation, you might not always know which question is more likely to be true, but when you can make a reasonable guess, it is more efficient to eliminate as many extra decisions as possible.

Combining Decisions in an OR Selection

If you need to take action when either one or the other of two conditions is met, you can use two separate, nested selection structures, as in the previous examples. However, most programming languages allow you to ask two or more questions in a single comparison by using a **logical OR operator** (or simply the **OR operator**). When you use the logical OR operator, only one of the listed conditions must be met for the resulting action to take place. Table 3-3 shows the truth table for the OR operator. As you can

C#, C++, C, and Java use the symbol || to represent the logical OR. In Visual Basic, the operator is Or.

As with the AND operator, most programming languages require a complete Boolean expression on each side of the OR.

x	y	x OR y
True	True	True
True	False	True
False	True	True
False	False	False

Table 3-3   Truth table for the OR operator

Logically, the OR operation corresponds to arithmetic addition. If you assume 1 is true and 0 is false, then `false OR false` is false because 0 + 0 is 0. All the other combinations (1 + 1, 1 + 0, and 0 + 1) are true because their results are not 0.

see in the table, the entire expression x OR y is false only when x and y each is false individually.

If the programming language you use supports the OR operator, you still must realize that the question you place first is the question that will be asked first, and cases that pass the test of the first question will not proceed to the second question. As with the AND operator, this feature is called short-circuiting. The computer can ask only one question at a time; even when you write code as shown at the top of Figure 3-13, the computer will execute the logic shown at the bottom.

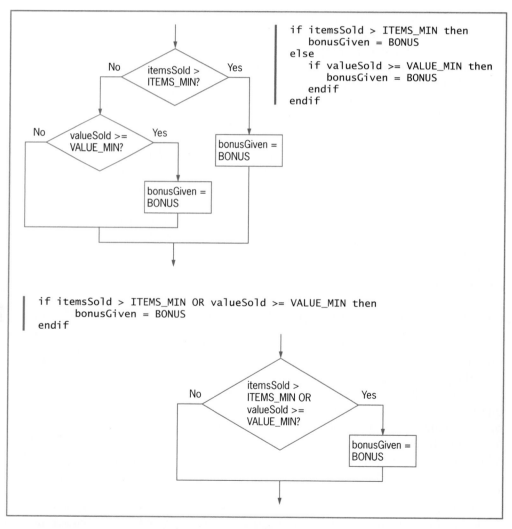

Figure 3-13 Using an OR operator and the logic behind it

Avoiding Common Errors in an OR Selection

You might have noticed that the assignment statement bonusGiven = BONUS appears twice in the decision-making processes in Figures 3-11, 3-12, and 3-13. When you create a flowchart, the temptation is to draw the logic to look like Figure 3-14. Logically, you can argue that the flowchart in Figure 3-14 is correct because the correct salespeople receive bonuses. However, this flowchart is not allowed because it is not structured. The second question is not a self-contained structure with one entry and exit point; instead, the flowline "breaks out" of the inner selection structure to join the true side of the outer selection structure.

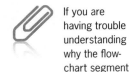

If you are having trouble understanding why the flowchart segment in Figure 3-14 is unstructured, go back and review Chapter 2.

87

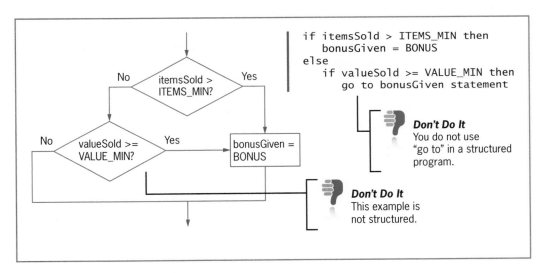

Figure 3-14 Unstructured flowchart for determining bonuses

An additional source of error that is specific to the OR selection stems from a problem with language and the way people use it more casually than computers do. When a sales manager wants to assign bonuses to salespeople who have sold three or more items or who have achieved $2,000 in sales, she is likely to say, "Give a bonus to anyone who has sold at least three items and to anyone who has achieved $2,000 in sales." Her request contains the word "and" between two types of people—those who sold three items and those who sold $2,000 worth—placing the emphasis on the people. However, each decision you make is about a bonus for a single salesperson who has surpassed one goal *or* the other *or* both. The logical situation requires an OR decision. It would be clearer if the manager said, "Give a bonus to anyone who has sold at least three items or has achieved $2,000 in sales." In other words, because you are making each decision about a single salesperson, it is more correct to put the "or" conjunction between the achieved sales goals than between types of people, but bosses and other human beings often do not speak like computers. As a programmer, you have the job of clarifying what really is being requested. Often, a request for A *and* B means a request for A *or* B.

The way we casually use English can cause another type of error when you are required to find whether a value falls between two other values. For example, a movie theater manager might say, "Provide a discount to patrons who are under 13 years old and those who are over 64 years old; otherwise, charge the full price." Because the manager has used the word "and" in the request, you might be tempted to create the decision shown in Figure 3-15; however, this logic will not provide a discounted price for any movie patron. You must remember that every time the decision is made in Figure 3-15, it is made for a single movie patron. If `patronAge` contains a value lower than 13, then it cannot possibly contain a value over 64. Similarly, if it contains a value over 64, there is no way it can contain a lesser value. Therefore, no value could be stored in `patronAge` for which both parts of the AND question could be true—and the price will never be set to the discounted price for any patron. Figure 3-16 shows the correct logic.

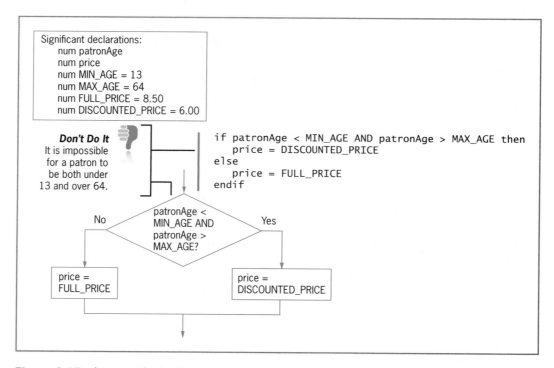

Figure 3-15 Incorrect logic that attempts to provide a discount for young and old movie patrons

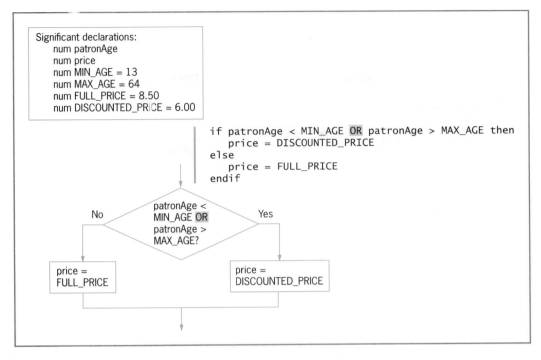

Significant declarations:
    num patronAge
    num price
    num MIN_AGE = 13
    num MAX_AGE = 64
    num FULL_PRICE = 8.50
    num DISCOUNTED_PRICE = 6.00

```
if patronAge < MIN_AGE OR patronAge > MAX_AGE then
    price = DISCOUNTED_PRICE
else
    price = FULL_PRICE
endif
```

patronAge <
MIN_AGE OR
patronAge >
MAX_AGE?

No   Yes

price =
FULL_PRICE

price =
DISCOUNTED_PRICE

Figure 3-16   Correct logic that provides a discount for young and old movie patrons

A similar error can occur in your logic if the theater manager says something like, "Don't give a discount—that is, charge full price—if a patron is over 12 or under 65." Because the word "or" appears in the request, you might plan your logic to resemble Figure 3-17. As in Figure 3-15, no patron ever receives a discount, because every patron is either over 12 or under 65. Remember, in an OR decision, only one of the conditions needs to be true for the entire expression to be evaluated as true. So, for example, because a patron who is 10 is under 65, the full price is charged, and because a patron who is 70 is over 12, the full price also is charged. Figure 3-18 shows the correct logic for this decision. In the figure the shaded AND operator produces the correct result.

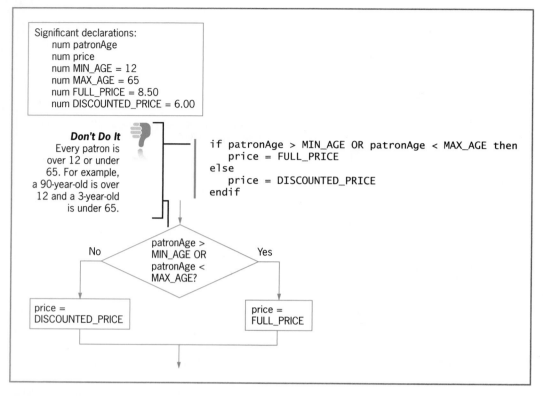

Significant declarations:
  num patronAge
  num price
  num MIN_AGE = 12
  num MAX_AGE = 65
  num FULL_PRICE = 8.50
  num DISCOUNTED_PRICE = 6.00

Don't Do It
Every patron is over 12 or under 65. For example, a 90-year-old is over 12 and a 3-year-old is under 65.

```
if patronAge > MIN_AGE OR patronAge < MAX_AGE then
    price = FULL_PRICE
else
    price = DISCOUNTED_PRICE
endif
```

No — patronAge > MIN_AGE OR patronAge < MAX_AGE? — Yes

price = DISCOUNTED_PRICE

price = FULL_PRICE

Figure 3-17 Incorrect logic that attempts to charge full price for patrons over 12 and under 65

In C++, Java, and C#, the exclamation point is the symbol used for the NOT operator. In Visual Basic, the operator is Not.

Understanding Negative Logic

Besides AND and OR, most languages support a NOT operator. You use the logical NOT operator to reverse the meaning of a Boolean expression. For example, the statement if NOT age < 21 output "OK" displays "OK" when age is greater than or equal to 21. The NOT operator is unary instead of binary—that is, you do not use it between two expressions, but in front of a single expression.

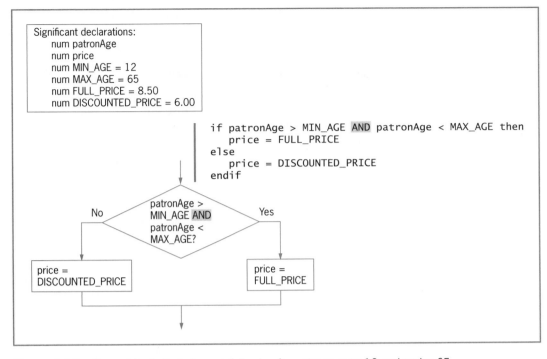

Significant declarations:
```
    num patronAge
    num price
    num MIN_AGE = 12
    num MAX_AGE = 65
    num FULL_PRICE = 8.50
    num DISCOUNTED_PRICE = 6.00
```

```
if patronAge > MIN_AGE AND patronAge < MAX_AGE then
    price = FULL_PRICE
else
    price = DISCOUNTED_PRICE
endif
```

No — patronAge > MIN_AGE AND patronAge < MAX_AGE? — Yes

price = DISCOUNTED_PRICE

price = FULL_PRICE

Figure 3-18   Correct logic that charges full price for patrons over 12 and under 65

Making Selections Within Ranges

You often need to make selections based on a variable falling within a range of values. For example, suppose your company provides various customer discounts based on the number of items ordered as shown in Figure 3-19.

When you write the program that determines a discount rate based on the number of items, you could make hundreds of decisions, such as itemQuantity = 1?, itemQuantity = 2?, and so on. However, it is more convenient to find the correct discount rate by using a range check.

When you use a **range check**, you compare a variable to a series of values that mark the limiting ends of ranges. To perform a range check, make comparisons using either the lowest or highest value in each range of values. For example, to find each discount rate as listed in Figure 3-19, you can use the values 0, 11, 25, and 51, which represent the low ends of each item number range.

Figure 3-20 shows the flowchart and pseudocode that represent the logic for a program that determines the correct discount for each

Items ordered	Discount Rate(%)
0 to 10	0
11 to 24	10
25 to 50	15
51 or more	20

Figure 3-19
Discount rates based on items ordered

In the pseudo-code in Figure 3-20, notice how each if, else, and endif group aligns vertically.

order quantity. In the decision-making process, itemsOrdered is compared to the high end of the lowest range group (RANGE1). If itemsOrdered is less than or equal to that value, then you know the correct discount, DISCOUNT1; if not, you continue checking. If itemsOrdered is less than or equal to the high end of the next range (RANGE2), then the customer's discount is DISCOUNT2; if not you continue checking, and the customer's discount eventually is set to DISCOUNT3 or DISCOUNT4.

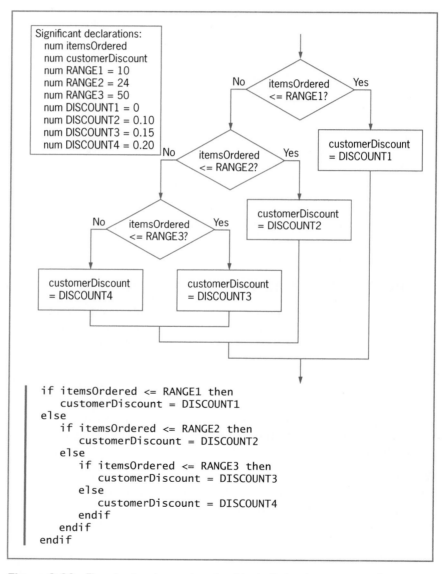

```
if itemsOrdered <= RANGE1 then
   customerDiscount = DISCOUNT1
else
   if itemsOrdered <= RANGE2 then
      customerDiscount = DISCOUNT2
   else
      if itemsOrdered <= RANGE3 then
         customerDiscount = DISCOUNT3
      else
         customerDiscount = DISCOUNT4
      endif
   endif
endif
```

Figure 3-20 Flowchart and pseudocode of logic that selects correct discount based on items

For example, consider an order for 30 items. The expression `itemsOrdered <= RANGE1` evaluates as `false`, so the `else` clause of the decision executes. There, `itemsOrdered <= RANGE2` also evaluates to `false`, so its `else` clause executes. The expression `itemsOrdered <= RANGE3` is `true`, so `customerDiscount` becomes `DISCOUNT3`, 0.15. Walk through the logic with other values for `itemsOrdered` and verify for yourself that the correct discount is applied each time.

Avoiding Common Errors When Using Range Checks

When new programmers perform range checks, they are prone to using logic that includes too many decisions, entailing more work than is necessary.

Figure 3-21 shows a program segment that contains a range check in which the programmer has asked one question too many—the shaded question in the figure. If you know that `itemsOrdered` is not less than or equal to RANGE1, not less than or equal to RANGE2, and not less than or equal to RANGE3, then `itemsOrdered` must be greater than RANGE3. Asking whether `itemsOrdered` is greater than RANGE3 is a waste of time; no customer order can ever travel the logical path on the far left of the flowchart. You might say that the path that can never be traveled is a **dead** or **unreachable path**, and that the statements written there constitute dead or unreachable code. Although a program that contains such logic will execute and assign the correct discount to customers who order more than 50 items, providing such a path is inefficient.

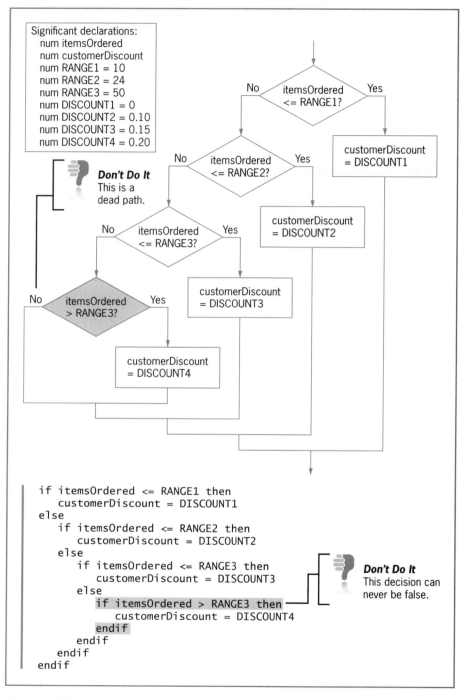

Figure 3-21   Inefficient range selection including unreachable path

In Figure 3-21, it is easier to see the useless path in the flowchart than in the pseudocode representation of the same logic. However, any- time you use an if without an else you are doing nothing when the question's answer is false.

Another error that programmers make when writing the logic to perform a range check also involves asking unnecessary questions. You should never ask a question if there is only one possible answer or outcome. Figure 3-22 shows an inefficient range selection that asks two unneeded questions. In the figure, if itemsOrdered is less than or equal to RANGE1, customerDiscount is set to DISCOUNT1. If itemsOrdered is not less than or equal to RANGE1, then it must be greater than RANGE1, so the next decision (shaded in the figure) does not have to check for greater than RANGE1. The computer logic will never execute the shaded decision unless itemsOrdered is already greater than RANGE1—that is, unless it follows the false branch of the first selection. If you use the logic in Figure 3-22, you are wasting computer time asking a question that has previously been answered. The same logic applies to the second shaded decision in Figure 3-21.

When you ask questions of human beings, you some- times ask a question to which you already know the answer. For example, a good trial lawyer seldom asks a question in court if the answer will be a surprise. With computer logic, however, such questions are an inefficient waste of time.

Beginning programmers sometimes jus- tify their use of unnecessary questions as "just making really sure." Such caution is unnecessary when writ- ing computer logic.

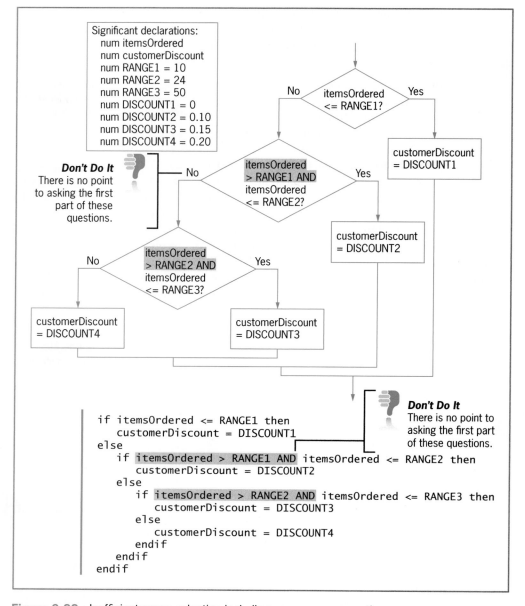

Figure 3-22   Inefficient range selection including unnecessary questions

Understanding Precedence When Combining AND and OR Operators

Most programming languages allow you to combine as many AND and OR operators in an expression as you need. For example, assume you need to achieve a score of at least 75 on each of three tests to pass a course. You can declare a constant MIN_SCORE equal to 75 and test the multiple conditions with a statement like the following:

```
if score1 >= MIN_SCORE AND score2 >= MIN_SCORE ↵
↳ AND score3 >= MIN_SCORE then
   classGrade = "Pass"
else
   classGrade = "Fail"
endif
```

On the other hand, if you are enrolled in a course in which you need to pass only one of three tests to pass the course, then the logic is as follows:

```
if score1 >= MIN_SCORE OR score2 >= MIN_SCORE ↵
↳ OR score3 >= MIN_SCORE then
   classGrade = "Pass"
else
   classGrade = "Fail"
endif
```

The logic becomes more complicated when you combine AND and OR operators within the same statement. When you combine AND and OR operators, the AND operators take **precedence**, meaning their Boolean values are evaluated first.

For example, consider a program that determines whether a movie theater patron can purchase a discounted ticket. Assume discounts are allowed for children (age 12 and under) and senior citizens (age 65 and older) who attend "G"-rated movies. The following code looks reasonable, but produces incorrect results because the expression that contains the AND operator (see shading) evaluates before the one that contains the OR operator.

```
if age <= 12 OR age >= 65 AND rating = "G" then
   output "Discount applies"
endif
```

Don't Do It
The AND evaluates first, which is not the intention.

For example, assume a movie patron is 10 years old and the movie rating is "R". The patron should not receive a discount (or be allowed to see the movie!). However, within the if statement, the part of the expression that contains the AND, age >= 65 AND rating = "G" is evaluated first. For a 10-year-old and an "R"-rated movie, the question

In Chapter 1 you learned that in every programming language, multiplication has precedence over addition in an arithmetic statement. That is, the value of 2 + 3 * 4 is 14 because the multiplication occurs before the addition. Similarly, in every programming language, AND has precedence over OR. That's because computer circuitry treats the AND operator as multiplication and the OR operator as addition.

is false (on both counts), so the entire if statement becomes the equivalent of the following:

```
if age <= 12 OR aFalseExpression then
    output "Discount applies"
endif
```

Because the patron is 10, age <= 12 is true, so the original if statement becomes the equivalent of:

```
if aTrueExpression OR aFalseExpression then
    output "Discount applies"
endif
```

The combination true OR false evaluates as true. Therefore, the string "Discount applies" is output when it should not be.

Many programming languages allow you to use parentheses to correct the logic and force the OR expression to be evaluated first, as shown in the following pseudocode.

```
if (age <= 12 OR age >= 65) AND rating = "G" then
    output "Discount applies"
endif
```

With the added parentheses, if the patron's age is 12 or under, or the age is 65 or over, the expression is evaluated as:

```
if aTrueExpression AND rating = "G" then
    output "Discount applies"
endif
```

When the age value qualifies a patron for a discount, then the rating value must also be acceptable before the discount applies. This was the original intention.

You can use the following techniques to avoid the confusion of mixing AND and OR operators:

- You can use parentheses to override the default order of operations. If a movie patron must be attending a "G" rated movie and either be under 13 or over 64 to receive a discount, then you can code the decision as follows:

```
if (age <= 12 OR age >= 65) AND rating = "G" then
    output "Discount applies"
endif
```

When several decisions are based on the value of the same variable, in many programming languages you can use a shortcut called the case structure. Appendix B describes this structure.

- You can use nesting if statements instead of using AND and OR operators. With the flowchart and pseudocode shown in Figure 3-23, it is clear which movie patrons receive the discount. In the flowchart, you can see that the OR is nested entirely within the Yes branch of the rating = "G"? selection. Similarly, in the pseudocode in Figure 3-23, you can see by the alignment that if the rating is not "G", the logic proceeds directly to the last `endif` statement, bypassing any checking of `age` at all.

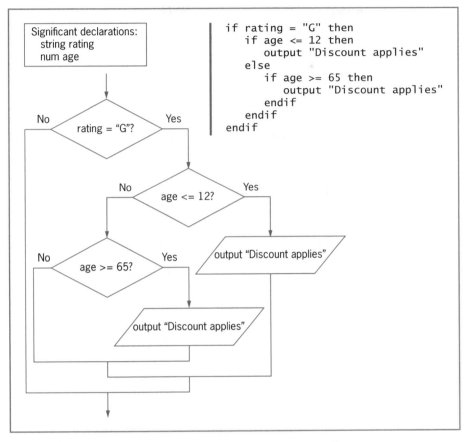

```
if rating = "G" then
    if age <= 12 then
        output "Discount applies"
    else
        if age >= 65 then
            output "Discount applies"
        endif
    endif
endif
```

Figure 3-23 Nested decisions that determine movie patron discount

Review Questions

1. The selection statement `if quantity > 100 then discountRate = RATE` is an example of a _____.

    a. dual-alternative selection

    b. single-alternative selection

    c. structured loop

    d. all of these

2. The selection statement `if dayOfWeek = "Sunday" then price = LOWER_PRICE else price = HIGHER_PRICE` is an example of a _____.

   a. dual-alternative selection

   b. single-alternative selection

   c. unary selection

   d. all of the above

3. All selection statements must have _____.

   a. an `if` clause

   b. an `else` clause

   c. both of these

   d. none of these

4. An expression like `amount < 10` is a _____ expression.

   a. Gregorian

   b. Edwardian

   c. Machiavellian

   d. Boolean

5. Usually, you compare only variables that have the same _____.

   a. type

   b. size

   c. name

   d. value

6. Symbols such as > and < are known as _____ operators.

   a. arithmetic

   b. sequential

   c. relational comparison

   d. scripting accuracy

7. If you could use only three relational comparison operators, you could get by with _____.

   a. greater than, less than, and greater than or equal to

   b. equal to, less than, and greater than

   c. less than, less than or equal to, and not equal to

   d. equal to, not equal to, and less than

8. If `a > b` is false, then which of the following is always true?

   a. `a <= b`

   b. `a < b`

   c. `a = b`

   d. `a >= b`

9. Usually, the most difficult comparison operator to work with is _____.

   a. equal to   c. less than

   b. greater than   d. not equal to

10. The Acme Computer Company operates in all 50 states of the United States. The Midwest Sales region consists of five states—Illinois, Indiana, Iowa, Missouri, and Wisconsin. Suppose you have input records containing Acme customer data, including state of residence. To most efficiently select and display all customers who live in the Midwest Sales region, you would use _____.

   a. five completely separate unnested if statements

   b. nested if statements using AND logic

   c. nested if statements using OR logic

   d. Not enough information is given.

11. The Midwest Sales region of Acme Computer Company consists of five states—Illinois, Indiana, Iowa, Missouri, and Wisconsin. About 50 percent of the regional customers reside in Illinois, 20 percent in Indiana, and 10 percent in each of the other three states. Suppose you have input records containing Acme customer data, including state of residence. To most efficiently select and display all customers who live in the Midwest Sales region, you would ask first about residency in _____.

   a. Illinois

   b. Indiana

   c. Either Iowa, Missouri, or Wisconsin—it does not matter which one of these three is first.

   d. Any of the five states—it does not matter which one is first.

12. The Boffo Balloon Company makes helium balloons. Large balloons cost $13.00 a dozen, medium-sized balloons cost $11.00 a dozen, and small balloons cost $8.60 a dozen. About 60 percent of the company's sales are the smallest balloons, 30 percent are the medium, and large balloons constitute only 10 percent of sales. Customer order records include customer information, quantity ordered, and size. When you write a

program to determine price based on size, for the most efficient decision, you should ask first whether the size is _____.

a. large   c. small

b. medium   d. It does not matter.

13. The Boffo Balloon Company makes helium balloons in three sizes, 12 colors, and with a choice of 40 imprinted sayings. As a promotion, the company is offering a 25 percent discount on orders of large, red "Happy Valentine's Day" balloons. To most efficiently select the orders to which a discount applies, you would use _____.

a. nested if statements using OR logic

b. nested if statements using AND logic

c. three completely separate unnested if statements

d. Not enough information is given.

14. When you use a range check, you compare a variable to the _____ value in the range.

a. lowest   c. highest

b. middle   d. lowest or highest

15. Assume a is 10 and b is 20. Which of the following evaluates to true?

a. a > 3 AND a > b OR b > 100

b. a > b OR b < 4 OR b = 10

c. a <= 10 OR b > a AND a not = b

d. Two of these are true.

Find the Bugs

Your student disk contains files named DEBUG03-01.txt and DEBUG03-02.txt. Each file contains pseudocode segments with one or more bugs that you must find and correct.

Exercises

1. Assume the following variables contain the values shown:

   ```
   num numberRed = 100        string wordRed = "Wagon"
   num numberBlue = 200       string wordBlue = "Sky"
   num numberGreen = 300      string wordGreen = "Grass"
   ```

   For each of the following Boolean expressions, decide whether the statement is true, false, or illegal.

   a. numberRed = numberBlue?

   b. numberBlue > numberGreen?

   c. numberGreen < numberRed?

   d. numberBlue = wordBlue?

   e. numberGreen = "Green"?

   f. wordRed = "Red"?

   g. wordBlue = "Blue"?

   h. numberRed <= numberGreen?

   i. numberBlue >= 200?

   j. numberGreen >= numberRed + numberBlue?

   k. numberRed > numberBlue AND numberBlue < numberGreen

   l. numberRed = 100 OR numberRed > numberBlue

   m. numberGreen < 10 OR numberBlue > 10

   n. numberBlue = 30 AND numberGreen = 300 OR numberRed = 200

2. Chocolate Delights Candy Company manufactures several types of candy. Design a flowchart or pseudocode for the following:

   a. A program that accepts a candy name (for example, "chocolate-covered blueberries"), price per pound, and number of pounds sold in the average month, and displays the item's data only if it is a best-selling item. Best-selling items are those that sell more than 2,000 pounds per month.

   b. A program that accepts candy data continuously until eof and displays a list of only high-priced, best-selling items. Best-selling items are those that sell more than 2,000 pounds per month. High-priced items are those that sell for $10 per pound or more.

3. Pastoral College is a small college in the Midwest. Design a flowchart or pseudocode for the following:

    a. A program that accepts a student's data: an ID number, first and last name, major field of study, and grade point average. Display a student's data if the student's grade point average is below 2.0.

    b. A program that continuously accepts students' data until eof and displays a list of all students whose grade point averages are below 2.0.

    c. A program for the Literary Honor Society that continuously reads student data and displays every student who is an English major with a grade point average of 3.5 or higher.

4. The Summerville Telephone Company charges 10 cents per minute for all calls outside the customer's area code that last over 20 minutes. All other calls are 13 cents per minute. Design a flowchart or pseudocode for the following:

    a. A program that accepts data about one phone call: customer area code (three digits), customer phone number (seven digits), called area code (three digits), called number (seven digits), and call time in minutes (four digits). Display the calling number, called number, and price for the call only if the call is one in which the area code where the call originated is different from the called area code.

    b. A program that accepts data about a phone call and displays all the details only about a call that costs over $10.

    c. A program that continuously accepts data about phone calls until eof is reached and displays details only about calls placed from the 212 area code to the 704 area code that last over 20 minutes.

    d. A program that prompts the user for a three-digit area code. Then the program continuously accepts phone call data until eof is reached, and displays data for any phone call to or from the specified area code.

5. The Drive-Rite Insurance Company provides automobile insurance policies for drivers. Design a flowchart or pseudocode for the following:

    a. A program that accepts insurance policyholder data including a policy number, customer last name, customer first name, age, premium due month, day and year, and the number of accidents in which the driver has been involved in the last three years. If a policy number entered is not between 1000 and 9999 inclusive, then set the policy number to 0. If the month is not between 1 and 12 inclusive, or the day is not correct for the month (that is, between 1 and 31 for January, 1 and 29 for February, and so on), then set the month, day, and year all to 0. Display the policyholder data after any revisions have been made.

b. A program that accepts a policyholder's data and displays the data for any policyholder over 35 years old.

c. A program that accepts a policyholder's data and displays the data for any policyholder who is at least 21 years old.

d. A program that accepts a policyholder's data and displays the data for any policyholder no more than 30 years old.

e. A program that accepts a policyholder's data and displays the data for any policyholder whose premium is due no later than March 15 any year.

f. A program that accepts a policyholder's data and displays the data for any policyholder whose premium is due up to and including January 1, 2011.

g. A program that accepts a policyholder's data and displays the data for any policyholder whose premium is due by April 27, 2010.

h. A program that accepts a policyholder's data and displays the data for any policyholder who has a policy number between 1000 and 4000 inclusive, whose policy comes due in April or May of any year, and has had fewer than three accidents.

6. The Barking Lot is a dog daycare center. Design a flowchart or pseudocode for the following:

a. A program that accepts data for an ID number of a dog's owner, and the name, breed, age, and weight of the dog. Display a bill containing all the input data as well as the weekly daycare fee, which is $55 for dogs under 15 pounds, $75 for dogs at least 15 pounds but no more than 30 pounds, $105 for dogs over 30 pounds but no more than 80 pounds, and $125 for dogs over 80 pounds.

b. A program that continuously accepts dogs' data until eof is reached and displays billing data for each dog.

c. A program that continuously accepts dogs' data until eof is reached and displays billing data for dog owners who owe more than $100.

7. Rick Hammer is a carpenter who wants an application to compute the price of any desk a customer orders, based on the following: desk length and width in inches, type of wood, and number of drawers. The price is computed as follows:

   • The minimum charge for all desks is $200.

   • If the surface (length * width) is over 750 square inches add $50.

   • If the wood is "mahogany" add $150; for "oak" add $125. No charge is added for "pine."

   • For every drawer in the desk, there is an additional $30 charge.

   Design a flowchart or pseudocode for the following:

   a. A program that accepts data for an order number, customer name, length, and width of the desk ordered, type of wood, and number of drawers. Display all the entered data and the final price for the desk.

   b. A program that continuously accepts desk order data and displays all the relevant information for oak desks that are over 36 inches long and have at least one drawer.

8. Black Dot Printing is attempting to organize carpools to save energy. Each input record contains an employee's name and town of residence. Ten percent of the company's employees live in Wonder Lake; 30 percent live in Woodstock. Because these towns are both north of the company, Black Dot wants to encourage employees who live in either town to drive to work together. Design a flowchart or pseudocode for the following:

   a. A program that accepts an employee's data and displays it with a message that indicates whether the employee is a candidate for the carpool.

   b. A program that continuously accepts employee data until eof is reached and displays a list of all employees who are carpool candidates.

9. Diana Lee, a supervisor in a manufacturing company, wants to know which employees have increased their production this year over last year so that she can issue them certificates of commendation and bonuses. Design a flowchart or pseudocode for the following:

    a. A program that continuously accepts each worker's first and last names, this year's number of units produced, and last year's number of units produced. Display each employee with a message indicating whether the employee's production has increased over last year's production.

    b. A program that accepts each worker's data and displays the name and a bonus amount. The bonuses will be distributed as follows:

    If this year's production is greater than last year's production and this year's production is:

- 1,000 units or fewer, the bonus is $25
- 1,001 to 3,000 units, the bonus is $50
- 3,001 to 6,000 units, the bonus is $100
- 6,001 units and up, the bonus is $200

    c. Modify Exercise 9b to reflect the following new facts, and have the program execute as efficiently as possible:

- Thirty percent of employees have greater production this year than last year.
- Sixty percent of employees produce over 6,000 units per year; 20 percent produce 3,001 to 6,000 units; 15 percent produce 1,001 to 3,000 units; and only 5 percent produce fewer than 1,001 units.

10. In many programming languages you can generate a random number between 1 and a limiting value named LIMIT by using a statement similar to `randomNumber = random(LIMIT)`. Create the logic for a guessing game in which the application generates a random number and the player tries to guess it. Display a message indicating whether the player's guess was correct, too high, or too low. (After you finish Chapter 4, you will be able to modify the application so that the user can continue to guess until the correct answer is entered.)

11. In many programming languages you can generate a random number between 1 and a limiting value named LIMIT by using a statement similar to `randomNumber = random(LIMIT)`. Create a lottery game application. Generate three random numbers, each between 0 and 9. Allow the user to guess three numbers. Compare each of the user's guesses to the three random numbers and display a message that includes the user's guess, the randomly determined three-digit number, and the amount of money the user has won as shown in the accompanying table.

Matching Numbers	Award ($)
Any one matching	10
Two matching	100
Three matching, not in order	1000
Three matching in exact order	1,000,000
No matches	0

Make certain that your application accommodates repeating digits. For example, if a user guesses 1, 2, and 3, and the randomly generated digits are 1, 1, and 1, do not give the user credit for three correct guesses—just one.

CHAPTER 4

Looping

After completing this chapter you will be able to:

◎ Explain the advantages of looping

◎ Control loops with counters and sentinel values

◎ Nest loops

◎ Avoid common loop mistakes

◎ Use a `for` loop

◎ Perform common loop applications

Understanding the Advantages of Looping

While making decisions is what makes computers seem intelligent, it's looping that makes computer programming both efficient and worthwhile. When you use a loop within a computer program, you can write one set of instructions that operates on multiple, separate sets of data. Consider the following set of tasks required for each employee in a typical payroll program:

- Determine regular pay.

- Determine overtime pay, if any.

- Determine federal withholding tax based on gross wages and number of dependents.

- Determine state withholding tax based on gross wages, number of dependents, and state of residence.

- Determine insurance deduction based on insurance code.

- Determine Social Security deduction based on gross pay.

- Subtract federal tax, state tax, Social Security, and insurance from gross pay.

In reality, this list is too short—companies deduct stock option plans, charitable contributions, union dues, and other items from checks in addition to the items mentioned in this list. Also, they might pay bonuses and commissions and provide sick days and vacation days that must be taken into account and handled appropriately. As you can see, payroll programs are complicated.

The advantage of having a computer perform payroll calculations is that all of the deduction instructions need to be written only once and can be repeated over and over again for each paycheck, using a **loop**, the structure that repeats actions while some condition continues.

The decision that controls every loop is always based on a Boolean comparison. In Chapter 3 you learned about six comparison operators that you can use in a selection. You can use any of the same six to control a loop. The operators are equal to, greater than, less than, greater than or equal to, less than or equal to, and not equal to.

Controlling Loops with Counters and Sentinel Values

Recall the loop structure that you learned about in Chapter 2. There you learned about `while` loops that look like Figure 4-1. As long as a Boolean expression remains true, a `while` loop's body executes. When you write a loop, you must control the

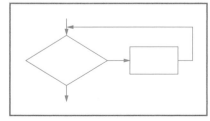

Figure 4-1   The `while` loop

110

number of repetitions it performs; if you do not, you run the risk of creating an infinite loop. Commonly, you control a loop's repetitions by using either a counter or a sentinel value.

You first learned about infinite loops in Chapter 2.

Using a Definite while Loop with a Counter

You can use a while loop to execute a body of statements continuously as long as some condition continues to be true. To make a while loop end correctly, you have to make sure your program performs three separate actions:

- Initialize a variable, the **loop control variable** (before the loop's while expression; that is, before the loop begins executing).

- Test the loop control variable in the while expression; if the result is true, the loop body begins executing.

- Alter the value of the loop control variable, so that the while expression eventually evaluates as false (this action occurs within the loop body).

For example, the code in Figure 4-2 shows a loop that displays "Hello" four times. The variable count is the loop control variable. The loop executes as follows:

- The loop control variable is initialized to 0.

- The while expression compares count to 4.

- The value is less than 4, so the loop body executes. The loop body shown in Figure 4-2 consists of two statements. The first statement prints "Hello" and the second statement adds 1 to count.

- The next time count is evaluated, its value is 1, which is still less than 4, so the loop body executes again. "Hello" displays a second time and count becomes 2, "Hello" displays a third time and count becomes 3, then "Hello" displays a fourth time and count becomes 4.

- Now when the expression count < 4 is evaluated, it is false, so the loop ends.

Just as with a selection, the Boolean comparison that controls a while loop must compare same-type values: numeric values are compared to other numeric values, and string values to other string values.

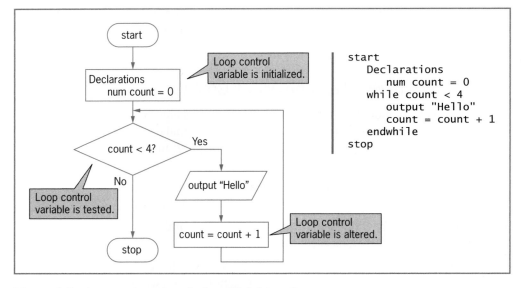

Figure 4-2 A `while` loop that displays "Hello" four times

To an algebra student, a statement such as

`count = count + 1` looks wrong—a value can never be one more than itself. In programming languages, however, the expression isn't a mathematical equation; rather, it is a statement that takes the value of `count`, adds 1 to it, and assigns the new value back into `count`.

Within a correctly functioning loop's body, you can change the value of the loop control variable in a number of ways. When a loop control variable is numeric, its value is often altered by **incrementing** it, or adding to it as in Figure 4-2. Other loops are controlled by reducing, or **decrementing**, a variable and testing whether the value remains greater than some benchmark value. For example, the loop in Figure 4-2 could be rewritten so that `count` is initialized to 4, and reduced by 1 on each pass through the loop. The revised loop should then continue while `count` remains greater than 0.

A loop such as the one in Figure 4-2, for which the number of iterations is predetermined, is called a **definite loop** or **counted loop**. The looping logic shown in Figure 4-2 uses the `count` variable as a counter. A **counter** is any numeric variable you use to count the

Because you so frequently need to increment a variable, many programming languages contain a shortcut operator for incrementing. You will learn about these shortcut operators when you study a programming language that uses them.

number of times an event has occurred. In everyday life, people usually count things starting with 1. Many programmers prefer starting their counted loops with a variable containing a 0 value for two
reasons. First, in many computer applications, numbering starts
with 0 because of the 0-and-1 nature of computer circuitry. Second,
when you learn about arrays in Chapter 5, you will discover that
array manipulation naturally lends itself to 0-based loops. However,
although it is common, you are not required to start counting
using 0. You could achieve exactly the same results in a program
such as the one in Figure 4-2 by initializing count to 1 and continuing the loop while it remains less than 5. You could even initialize
count to some arbitrary value such as 23 and continue while it
remains less than 27 (which is 4 greater than 23). This last choice is
not recommended, because it is confusing; however, the program
would work just as well.

Often, the value of a loop control variable is not altered by arithmetic,
but instead is altered by user input. For example, perhaps you want
to continue performing some task while the user indicates a desire to
continue. In that case, you do not know when you write the program
whether the loop will be executed two times, 200 times, or not at all.
This type of loop is an **indefinite loop**.

Using an Indefinite while Loop with a Sentinel Value

Consider an interactive program that displays a bank balance and
asks if the user wants to see what the balance will be after one
year of interest has accumulated. Each time the user indicates she
wants to continue, an increased balance appears. When the user
finally indicates she is done, the program ends. The loop is indefinite because each time the program executes, the loop might be
performed a different number of times. The program appears in
Figure 4-3.

You might
prefer to
revise a
longer pro-
gram like the
one in Figure 4-3 to break
it down into shorter mod-
ules. In Chapter 6 you will
learn to modularize your
programs.

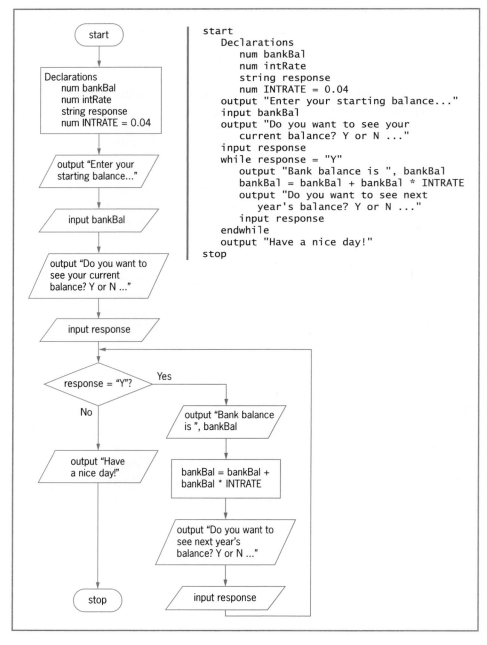

```
start
    Declarations
        num bankBal
        num intRate
        string response
        num INTRATE = 0.04
    output "Enter your starting balance..."
    input bankBal
    output "Do you want to see your
        current balance? Y or N ..."
    input response
    while response = "Y"
        output "Bank balance is ", bankBal
        bankBal = bankBal + bankBal * INTRATE
        output "Do you want to see next
            year's balance? Y or N ..."
        input response
    endwhile
    output "Have a nice day!"
stop
```

Figure 4-3 Looping bank balance program

The program shown in Figure 4-3 contains three variables that are involved in the looping process: a bank balance, an interest rate, and a response. The variable named **response** is the loop control variable. It is initialized when the program asks the user, "Do you want to see your current balance?" and reads the response. The loop control variable is tested with `response = "Y"`?. If the user has entered any response other than *Y*, then the test expression is false, and the loop body never executes; instead, the next statement to execute is to display "Have a nice day!". However, if the user enters *Y*, then the test expression is true and all four statements within the loop body execute. Within the loop body, the current balance is displayed, and the program increases the balance by the interest rate percentage; this value will not be displayed unless the user requests another loop repetition. Within the loop, the program prompts the user and reads in a new value for `response`. This is the statement that potentially alters the loop control variable. The loop body ends when program control returns to the top of the loop, where the Boolean expression in the `while` statement is tested again. If the user typed *Y* at the last prompt, then the loop is entered and the increased `bankBal` value that was calculated during the last loop cycle is finally displayed.

Figure 4-4 shows how the bank balance program might look when it is executed at the command prompt and in a GUI environment. The **command prompt** is the location on your computer screen at which you type entries to communicate with the computer's operating system using text. Many programs are not run at the command prompt in a text environment, but are run using a **graphical user interface**, or **GUI** (pronounced "gooey"), which allows users to interact with a program in a graphical environment. The screen at the right in Figure 4-4 shows a program that performs exactly the same tasks as the one that appears on the left, but this program uses a GUI. The user is presented with a prompt and an empty text box. When the user types a number in the text box, and continues to press the "Y" button, new bank balances appear. When the user eventually selects the "N" button, the program ends with the "Have a nice day!" message.

The first `input response` statement in the application in Figure 4-3 is a priming input statement. You learned about the priming input statement in Chapter 2.

115

The program shown in Figure 4-3 continues to display bank balances while `response` is *Y*. It could also be written to display while `response` is not *N*. In Chapter 2, you learned that a value such as "Y" or "N" that a user must supply to stop a loop is called a sentinel value.

In most programming languages, comparisons are case sensitive. If a program tests `response = "Y"`, a user response of *y* will result in a `false` evaluation.

Figure 4-4 Typical executions of the looping bank balance program in command-line and GUI environments

The body of a loop might contain any number of statements, including method calls, decisions, and other loops. Once your logic enters the body of a structured loop, the entire loop body must execute. Your program can leave a structured loop only at the comparison that tests the loop control variable.

The flowchart and pseudocode segments in Figure 4-3 contain three steps that must occur in every loop, and these crucial steps are shaded in Figure 4-5:

1. You must provide a starting value that will control the loop.

2. You must test the loop control variable to determine whether the loop body executes.

3. Within the loop, you must alter the loop control variable.

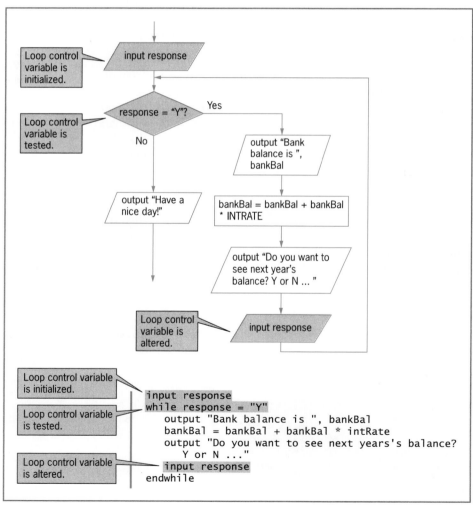

Figure 4-5 Crucial steps that must occur in every loop

Nested Loops

Program logic gets more complicated when you must use loops within loops, creating **nested loops**. When one loop is nested within another, the containing loop is the **outer loop**, and the loop that is contained is the **inner loop**. You need to create nested loops when the values of two (or more) variables repeat to produce every combination of values.

For example, suppose you want to write a program that produces a quiz answer sheet like the one shown in Figure 4-6. The quiz has five parts with three questions in each part, and you want a fill-in-the-blank line for each question. You could write a program that uses 21 separate output statements to produce the sheet, but it is more efficient to use nested loops.

Part 1
1.——
2.——
3.——

Part 2
1.——
2.——
3.——

Part 3
1.——
2.——
3.——

Part 4
1.——
2.——
3.——

Part 5
1.——
2.——
3.——

Figure 4-6   A quiz answer sheet

Figure 4-7 shows the logic of the program that produces the answer sheet. Two variables, named `partCounter` and `questionCounter`, are declared to keep track of the answer sheet parts and questions, respectively. Four named constants are also declared to hold the number of parts and questions in each, and to hold the text that will be printed—the word "Part" with each part number, and a period, space, and underscores to form a fill-in line for each question. When the program starts, `partCounter` is initialized to 1. The `partCounter` variable is the loop control variable for the outer loop in this program. The outer loop continues while `partCounter` is less than or equal to PARTS. The last statement in the outer loop adds 1 to `partCounter`. In other words, the outer loop will execute when `partCounter` is 1, 2, 3, 4, and 5.

In the program in Figure 4-7, it is important that `questionCounter` is reset to 1 within the outer loop, just before entering the inner loop. If this step was omitted, Part 1 would contain questions 1, 2, and 3, but Part 2 would contain questions 4, 5, and 6, and so on.

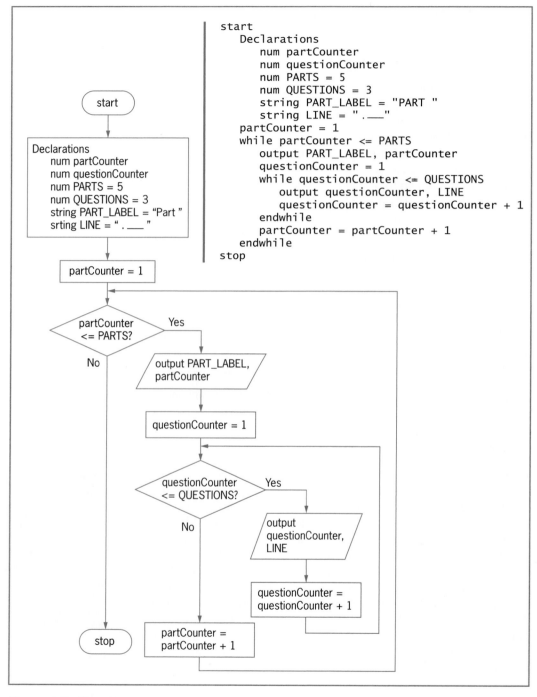

```
start
    Declarations
        num partCounter
        num questionCounter
        num PARTS = 5
        num QUESTIONS = 3
        string PART_LABEL = "PART "
        string LINE = ".___"
    partCounter = 1
    while partCounter <= PARTS
        output PART_LABEL, partCounter
        questionCounter = 1
        while questionCounter <= QUESTIONS
            output questionCounter, LINE
            questionCounter = questionCounter + 1
        endwhile
        partCounter = partCounter + 1
    endwhile
stop
```

Figure 4-7   Flowchart and pseudocode for `AnswerSheet` program

In the outer loop in Figure 4-7, the word "Part" and the current partCounter value are output. Then the following steps execute:

- The loop control variable for the inner loop is initialized by setting questionCounter to 1.

- The loop control variable, questionCounter, is evaluated by comparing it to QUESTIONS. While questionCounter does not exceed QUESTIONS, the loop body executes: the value of questionCounter is output, followed by a period and a fill-in-the-blank line.

- At the end of the loop body, the loop control variable is altered by adding 1 to questionCounter, and the questionCounter comparison is made again.

In other words, when partCounter is 1, the part heading is output and lines are output for questions 1, 2, and 3. Then partCounter becomes 2, the part heading is output, and lines are created for another set of questions 1, 2, and 3. Then partCounter in turn becomes 3, 4, and 5, and lines are created for question sets for each part.

Mixing Constant and Variable Sentinel Values

The number of times a loop executes can depend on a constant or a value that varies. Suppose you own a factory and have decided to place a label on every product you manufacture. The label contains the words "Made for you personally by" followed by the first name of one of your employees. Assume that for one week's production, you need 100 personalized labels for each employee.

Figure 4-8 shows the application that creates 100 labels for each employee entered. The user enters an employee's name, and while the user does not type the QUIT value ("ZZZ"), the program continues. The loopCounter variable is set to 0 and a label that contains the employee's name is output. Then the loop control variable labelCounter is incremented. Its value is tested again, and if it is not equal to the constant value LABELS (100), another label is output. When the value of labelCounter reaches 100, the user is prompted for a new employee name.

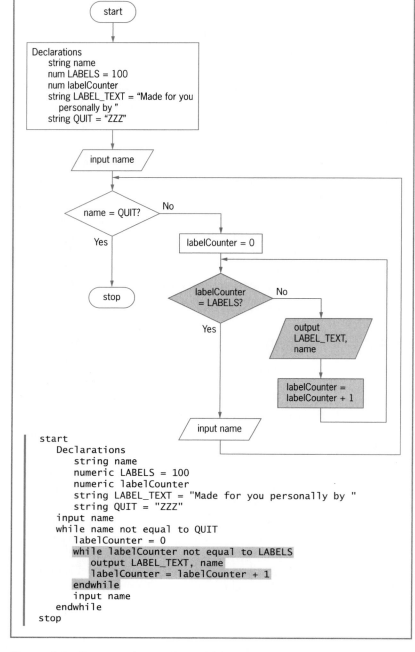

Setting `labelCounter` to 0 within the outer loop is important. After `labelCounter` reaches 100 for the first employee entered, a second employee is entered and you need to start counting from 0 again. If `labelCounter` is never reset after the first employee, no labels will be output for any subsequent employees.

```
start
   Declarations
      string name
      numeric LABELS = 100
      numeric labelCounter
      string LABEL_TEXT = "Made for you personally by "
      string QUIT = "ZZZ"
   input name
   while name not equal to QUIT
      labelCounter = 0
      while labelCounter not equal to LABELS
         output LABEL_TEXT, name
         labelCounter = labelCounter + 1
      endwhile
      input name
   endwhile
stop
```

Figure 4-8 Program that produces 100 labels for every employee

Figure 4-8 contains two loops:

- *An indefinite outer loop* that is controlled by the value of the name that the user enters

- *A definite inner loop* that executes exactly 100 times

In the inner loop (shaded in Figure 4-8), while the counter, named `labelCounter`, continues to be less than 100, a label is printed and `labelCounter` is increased. When 100 labels have printed, control returns to the outer loop, where the next employee `name` is retrieved.

Sometimes you don't want to be forced to repeat every pass through a loop the same number of times. For example, instead of printing 100 labels for each employee, you might want to vary the number of labels based on how many items a worker actually produces. That way, high-achieving workers won't run out of labels, and less productive workers won't have too many. Instead of producing the same, constant number of labels for every employee, a more sophisticated program prints a different number of labels for each employee, depending on that employee's usual production level.

Figure 4-9 shows a slightly modified version of the label-producing program. The changes from Figure 4-8 are shaded. In this version, after the user enters a valid name for an employee, the user is prompted for a production level. The Boolean expression used in the `while` statement in the inner loop compares `labelCounter` to `production`, instead of to a constant, fixed value. Some employees might get 100 labels, but some might get more or fewer.

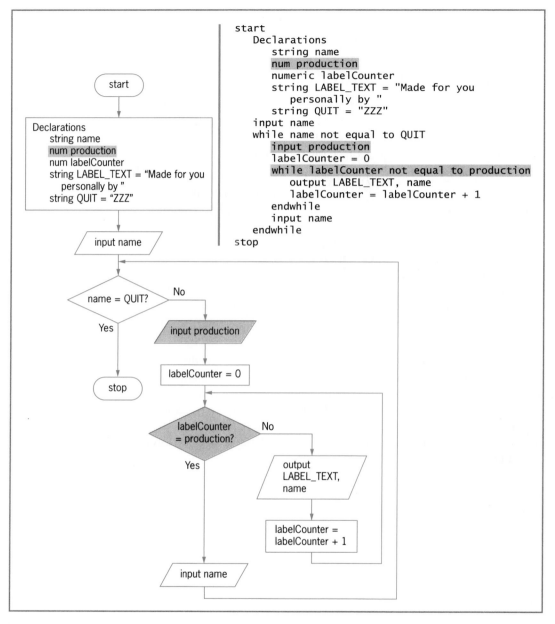

```
start
    Declarations
        string name
        num production
        numeric labelCounter
        string LABEL_TEXT = "Made for you
            personally by "
        string QUIT = "ZZZ"
    input name
    while name not equal to QUIT
        input production
        labelCounter = 0
        while labelCounter not equal to production
            output LABEL_TEXT, name
            labelCounter = labelCounter + 1
        endwhile
        input name
    endwhile
stop
```

Figure 4-9   Program that produces a variable number of labels for every employee

Avoiding Common Loop Mistakes

The mistakes programmers make most often with loops are:

- Neglecting to initialize the loop control variable
- Neglecting to alter the loop control variable
- Using the wrong comparison with the loop control variable
- Including statements inside the loop that belong outside the loop

The following sections explain these common mistakes in more detail.

Mistake: Neglecting to Initialize the Loop Control Variable

It is always a mistake to fail to initialize a loop's control variable. For example, assume you remove either or both of the loop initialization statements that appeared in the label production program in Figure 4-9; Figure 4-10 shows how the incorrect program would look.

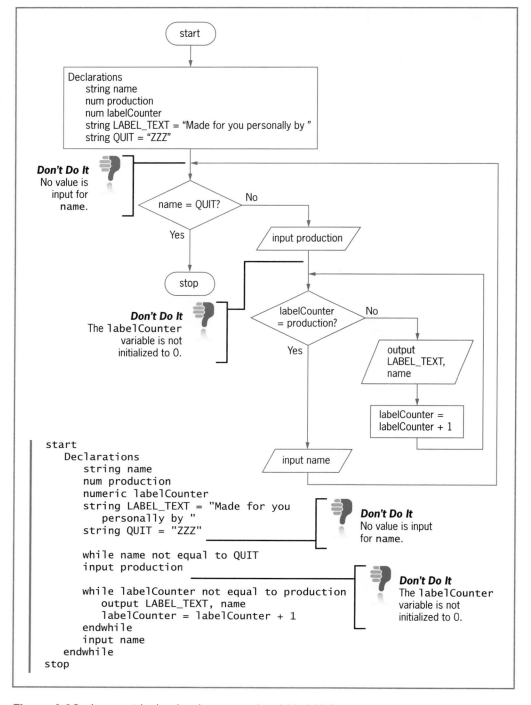

Don't Do It
No value is input for name.

Don't Do It
The labelCounter variable is not initialized to 0.

```
start
    Declarations
        string name
        num production
        numeric labelCounter
        string LABEL_TEXT = "Made for you
            personally by "
        string QUIT = "ZZZ"

    while name not equal to QUIT
    input production

    while labelCounter not equal to production
        output LABEL_TEXT, name
        labelCounter = labelCounter + 1
    endwhile
    input name
    endwhile
stop
```

Don't Do It
No value is input
for name.

Don't Do It
The labelCounter
variable is not
initialized to 0.

Figure 4-10 Incorrect logic when loop control variable initializations are removed from label-making program

If the `input name` statement is removed as shown in Figure 4-10, then when `name` is tested at the start of the outer loop, its value is unknown, or garbage. Is `name` equal to the value of QUIT? Maybe it is, by accident, or, more likely, it is not. If it is, the program ends before any labels can be output. If it is not, the inner loop is entered, and 100 labels are created with an invalid name (the value of QUIT).

If the `labelCounter = 0` assignment statement is removed as shown in the inner loop in Figure 4-10, then in many languages, the value of `labelCounter` is unpredictable. It might or might not be equal to LABELS, and the loop might or might not execute. In a language in which numeric variables are automatically initialized to 0, the first employee's labels will print correctly, but no labels will print for subsequent employees because `labelCounter` will never be altered and will remain equal to LABELS for the rest of the program's execution. Either way, a logical error has occurred.

Mistake: Neglecting to Alter the Loop Control Variable

Different sorts of errors will occur if you fail to alter a loop control variable within the loop. You create such an error if you remove either of the statements that alter the loop control variables from the label-making program in Figure 4-9. Figure 4-11 shows the resulting logic.

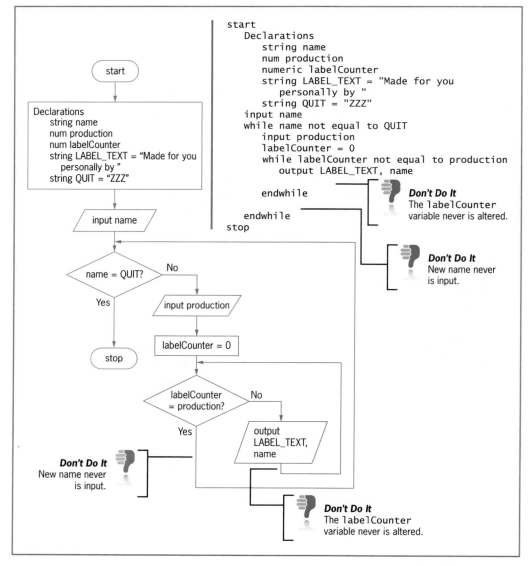

Figure 4-11   Incorrect logic when loop control variable altering statements are removed from label-making program

If you remove the `input name` instruction from the outer loop in the program, the user never has the opportunity to enter a `name` after the first one. For example, assume when the program starts, the user enters "Fred". The name will be compared to the QUIT value, and the inner loop will be entered. After labels print for Fred, no new name is entered, so when the logic returns to the `name = QUIT?` question, the answer will still be No. So, labels containing "Made for you personally by" and the same worker's name will continue to be output infinitely.

Similarly, if you remove the statement that increments labelCounter from the inner loop in the program, then labelCounter never can equal production, and the inner loop executes infinitely. It is always incorrect to create a loop that cannot terminate.

Mistake: Using the Wrong Comparison with the Loop Control Variable

Programmers must be careful to use the correct comparison in the statement that controls a loop. Although there is only a one-keystroke difference between the code segments in Figure 4-12, one performs the loop 10 times and the other performs the loop 11 times.

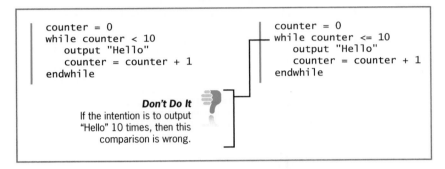

```
counter = 0
while counter < 10
    output "Hello"
    counter = counter + 1
endwhile
```

```
counter = 0
while counter <= 10
    output "Hello"
    counter = counter + 1
endwhile
```

Don't Do It
If the intention is to output "Hello" 10 times, then this comparison is wrong.

Figure 4-12   Two similar but different loops

The seriousness of the error of using <= or >= when only < or > is needed depends on the actions performed within the loop. For example, if such an error occurred in a loan company application, each customer might be charged a month's additional interest; if the error occurred in an airline's application, it might overbook a flight; and if it occurred in a pharmacy's drug-dispensing application, each patient might receive one extra (and possibly harmful and expensive) unit of medication.

Mistake: Including Statements Inside the Loop that Belong Outside the Loop

Consider a program like the one in Figure 4-13. It calculates a user's projected weekly pay raise based on different raise rates from half a percent to 10 percent. The user enters an hourly pay rate and the number of hours he works per week. Then the rate of the raise is set to a starting value of 0.005 (half a percent). While the raise rate is not greater than the maximum the program allows, the user's weekly pay is calculated, and then the raise as a percentage of the weekly amount. The results are displayed, and before the loop ends, the loop control variable, percent, is increased by half a percent. Figure 4-14 shows a typical execution of the program in a command-line environment.

128

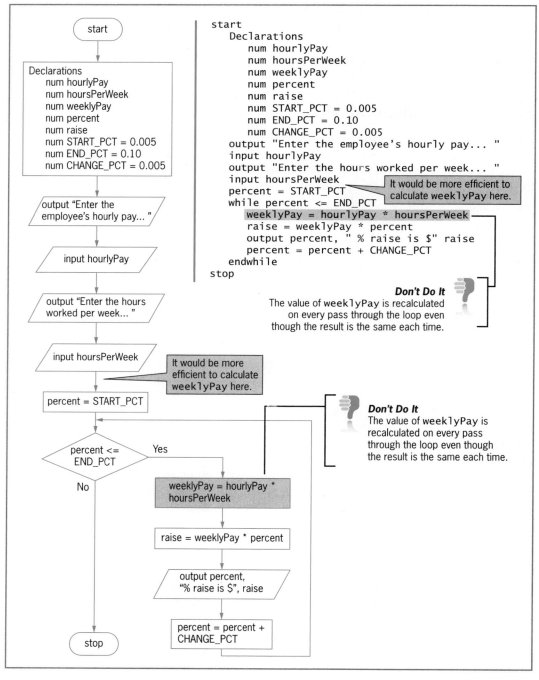

```
start
    Declarations
        num hourlyPay
        num hoursPerWeek
        num weeklyPay
        num percent
        num raise
        num START_PCT = 0.005
        num END_PCT = 0.10
        num CHANGE_PCT = 0.005
    output "Enter the employee's hourly pay... "
    input hourlyPay
    output "Enter the hours worked per week... "
    input hoursPerWeek
    percent = START_PCT
    while percent <= END_PCT
        weeklyPay = hourlyPay * hoursPerWeek
        raise = weeklyPay * percent
        output percent, " % raise is $" raise
        percent = percent + CHANGE_PCT
    endwhile
stop
```

It would be more efficient to calculate weeklyPay here.

Don't Do It
The value of weeklyPay is recalculated on every pass through the loop even though the result is the same each time.

Start / Declarations: num hourlyPay, num hoursPerWeek, num weeklyPay, num percent, num raise, num START_PCT = 0.005, num END_PCT = 0.10, num CHANGE_PCT = 0.005

output "Enter the employee's hourly pay... "

input hourlyPay

output "Enter the hours worked per week... "

input hoursPerWeek

It would be more efficient to calculate weeklyPay here.

percent = START_PCT

percent <= END_PCT — Yes / No

Don't Do It
The value of weeklyPay is recalculated on every pass through the loop even though the result is the same each time.

weeklyPay = hourlyPay * hoursPerWeek

raise = weeklyPay * percent

output percent, "% raise is $", raise

percent = percent + CHANGE_PCT

stop

Figure 4-13   Pay rate projection program

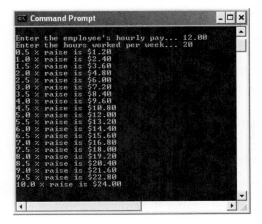

Figure 4-14 Typical execution of pay rate projection program

The program in Figure 4-13 works correctly. However, it is a little inefficient. The user enters his pay rate and hours worked once at the beginning of the program, and at that point, the weekly pay could be calculated. However, the weekly pay calculation does not occur until the loop is entered, so in this program, the same calculation is made 20 times. Of course, it does not take a computer very long to perform 20 multiplication calculations, but if the calculation were more complicated and performed for thousands of employees, the program performance would suffer.

A superior alternative would be to move the weekly pay calculation to just after the `hourlyPay` and `hoursPerWeek` have been entered. As you become more proficient at programming, you will recognize many opportunities to perform the same tasks in alternate, more elegant, and more efficient ways.

When you describe people or events as "elegant," you mean they possess a refined gracefulness. Similarly, programmers use the term "elegant" to describe programs that are well designed and easy to understand and maintain.

Using a `for` Loop

Every high-level computer programming language contains a `while` statement that you can use to code any loop, including both indefinite and definite loops. In addition to the `while` statement, most computer languages also support a `for` statement. You can use the **for statement**, or **for loop**, with definite loops—those that will loop a specific number of times. The `for` statement provides you with three actions in one compact statement. The `for` statement uses a loop control variable that it automatically:

- Initializes
- Evaluates
- Increments

130

The for statement takes the form:

```
for initialValue to finalValue step 1
    do something
endfor
```

For example, to print 100 labels you can write:

```
for count = 0 to 99 step 1
    output LABEL_TEXT, name
endfor
```

This for statement accomplishes several tasks at once in a compact form:

- The for statement initializes count to 0.

- The for statement checks count against the limit value 99 and makes sure that count is less than or equal to that value.

- If the evaluation is true, the for statement body executes, printing the label.

- After the for statement body executes, the value of count increases by the step value, and the comparison to the limit value is made again. A **step value** is a number you use to increase a loop control variable on each pass through a loop. In this case, the step value is 1.

As an alternative to using the loop for count = 0 to 99 step 1, you can use for count = 1 to 100 step 1. To achieve the same results, you can use any combination of values, as long as there are 100 whole number values between (and including) the two limits. However, the superior option would be to avoid the "magic number" and use a constant defined as num LIMIT = 99 and write the following:

```
for count = 0 to LIMIT step 1
    output LABEL_TEXT, name
endfor
```

You never are required to use a for statement; the label loop executes correctly using a while statement. However, when a loop's execution is based on a loop control variable progressing from a known starting value to a known ending value in equal increments, the for loop provides you with a convenient shorthand. It is easy for others to read, and because the loop control variable initialization, testing, and alteration are all performed in one location, you are less likely to leave out one of these crucial elements.

You can provide a for loop with a step value other than 1. For example, you might want to write a program in which you display a country's population projections in 10-year increments. In that case, the for loop might look like the following:

```
for year = 2010 to 2100 step 10
    perform and display population calculations
endfor
```

You first learned about magic numbers in Chapter 1. It is common practice to use 0 and 1 as unnamed constants, but most other constant numeric values in your programs should be named.

The programmer doesn't need to know the starting or the ending value for the loop control variable; only the application must know those values. For example, instead of being a constant, the value compared to count might be entered by the user.

The for loop is particularly useful when processing arrays. You will learn about arrays in Chapter 5.

You might even want to provide a negative step value. For example, a loop that counts from 100 down to 1 might be written as follows:

```
for counter = 100 to 1 step -1
    output counter
endfor
```

In some programming languages, you must always provide a statement that indicates the for loop step value. In others, if you omit the value, the default loop step value is 1.

Common Loop Applications

Although every computer program is different, many techniques are common to a variety of applications. Loops, for example, are frequently used to accumulate totals and to validate data.

Using a Loop to Accumulate Totals

Business reports often include totals. The supervisor requesting a list of employees who participate in the company dental plan is often as interested in the number of participating employees as in who they are. When you receive your telephone bill at the end of the month, you are usually more interested in the total than in the charges for the individual calls.

For example, a real estate broker might want to see a list of all properties sold in the last month, as well as the total value for all the properties. A program might read sales data including the street address of the property sold and its selling price. The data records might be entered by a clerk as each sale is made, and stored in a file until the end of the month; then they can be used in the month-end report. Figure 4-15 shows an example of such a report.

Besides while and for loops, many programming languages support a do-while loop. With a do-while loop, the loop body executes once before the loop-controlling condition is tested. Appendix B describes this loop.

131

Some business reports list no individual detail records, just totals. Such reports are called **summary reports**.

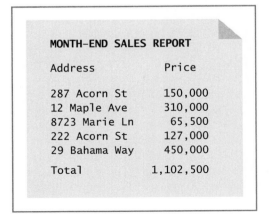

```
MONTH-END SALES REPORT

Address          Price

287 Acorn St     150,000
12 Maple Ave     310,000
8723 Marie Ln     65,500
222 Acorn St     127,000
29 Bahama Way    450,000

Total          1,102,500
```

Figure 4-15 Month-end real estate sales report

Some programming languages assign 0 to a variable you fail to initialize explicitly, but many do not—they either issue an error message or let you incorrectly start with an accumulator that holds garbage. The safest and clearest course of action is to assign the value 0 to accumulators before using them.

To create the sales report, you must input data for each real estate listing, output the address and price, and add the price to an accumulator. An **accumulator** is a variable that you use to gather or accumulate values. An accumulator is very similar to a counter that you use to count loop iterations. The difference lies in the value that you add to the variable; usually you add just 1 to a counter, whereas you add some other, variable value to an accumulator. If the real estate broker wants to know how many listings the company holds, you count them. When the broker wants to know total real estate value, you accumulate it.

To accumulate total real estate prices, you declare a numeric variable at the beginning of the application, as shown in Figure 4-16. You must initialize the accumulator, `accumValue`, to 0. As each real estate transaction is processed, you add its value to the accumulator, as shown in the shaded statement.

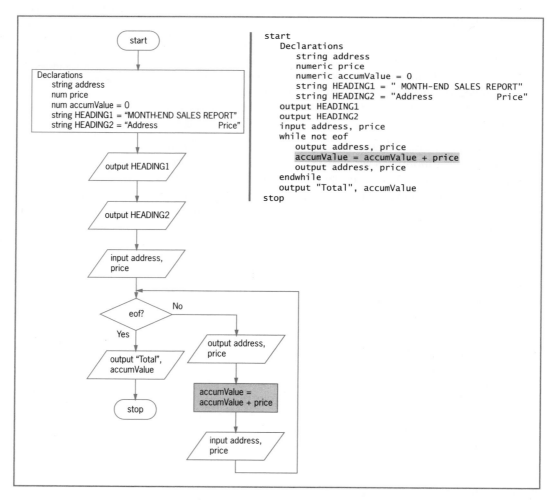

Figure 4-16   Flowchart and pseudocode for real estate sales report program

After the program in Figure 4-16 reads the last record, it reaches the **eof** indicator, and loop execution ends. At that point, the accumulator will hold the grand total of all the real estate values. The program displays the word "Total" and the accumulated value, **accumValue**. Then the program ends.

After outputting the variable **accumValue**, new programmers often want to reset it to 0. Their argument is that they are "cleaning up after themselves." Although you can take this step without harming the execution of the program, it does not serve any useful purpose. You cannot set **accumValue** to 0 in anticipation of having it ready for the next program, or even for the next time you execute this program. Variables exist only for the life of the application, and even if a future application happens to contain a variable named **accumValue**, the variable will not necessarily occupy the same memory location as this one. Even if you run the same application a second time, the variables might occupy physical memory locations different from those they occupied during the first run. At the beginning of any method, it is the programmer's responsibility to initialize all variables that must start with a specific value. There is no benefit to changing a variable's value when it will never be used again during the current execution.

Using a Loop to Validate Data

When you ask a user to enter data into a computer program, you have no assurance that the data the user enters will be accurate. Loops are frequently used to **validate data**; that is, to make sure values fall within an acceptable or reasonable range. For example, suppose part of a program you are writing asks a user to enter a number that represents his or her birth month. If the user types a number lower than 1 or greater than 12, you must take some sort of action. For example:

- You could display an error message and stop the program.

- You could choose to assign a default value for the month, such as 1, before proceeding.

- You could reprompt the user for valid input.

If you choose this last course of action, there are at least two approaches you could take. You could use a selection, and if the month is invalid, you can ask the user to reenter a number as shown in Figure 4-17.

You first learned about using eof to indicate end-of-file in Chapter 1.

You could revise the program in Figure 4-16 to make it a program that creates only a summary report that contains the total of the sale prices (with no individual transaction details). You could accomplish this by removing the first statement in the loop—the one that outputs each address and price.

Most languages provide a built-in way to check whether a value that is entered is numeric or not. When you rely on user input, you frequently accept each piece of input data as a string and then attempt to convert it to a number. The procedure for accomplishing numeric checks is slightly different in different programming languages.

134

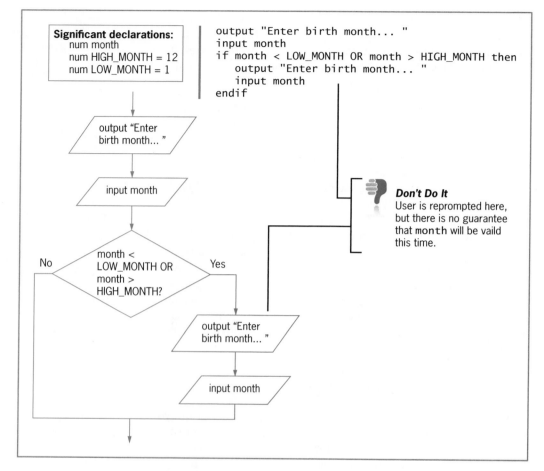

```
output "Enter birth month... "
input month
if month < LOW_MONTH OR month > HIGH_MONTH then
    output "Enter birth month... "
    input month
endif
```

Significant declarations:
num month
num HIGH_MONTH = 12
num LOW_MONTH = 1

output "Enter
birth month... "

input month

month <
LOW_MONTH OR
month >
HIGH_MONTH?

No   Yes

output "Enter
birth month... "

input month

Don't Do It
User is reprompted here,
but there is no guarantee
that month will be vaild
this time.

Figure 4-17   Reprompting a user one time after an invalid month is entered

Just because a data item is valid does not mean that it is correct. For example, a program can determine that 5 is a valid birth month, but not that your birthday actually falls in month 5.

The problem with the logic in Figure 4-17 is that, on the second attempt to enter a month, the user may still not enter valid data. So, you could add a third decision. Of course, you can't control what the user enters that time either.

The superior solution is to use a loop to continuously prompt a user for a month until the user enters it correctly. Figure 4-18 shows this approach.

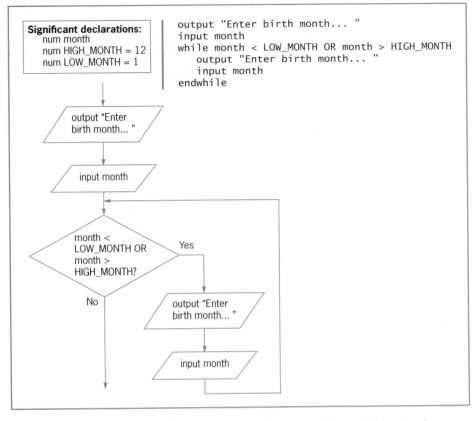

```
Significant declarations:
   num month
   num HIGH_MONTH = 12
   num LOW_MONTH = 1
```

```
output "Enter birth month... "
input month
while month < LOW_MONTH OR month > HIGH_MONTH
    output "Enter birth month... "
    input month
endwhile
```

Figure 4-18 Reprompting a user continuously after an invalid month is entered

Review Questions

1. The structure that allows you to write one set of instructions that operates on multiple, separate sets of data is the _____.

    a. sequence   c. loop

    b. selection   d. case

2. Which of the following is not a step that must occur in every loop?

    a. Initialize a loop control variable.

    b. Set the loop control value equal to a sentinel.

    c. Compare the loop control value to a sentinel.

    d. Alter the loop control variable.

3. The statements executed within a loop are known collectively as the _____.

   a. loop body   c. sequences

   b. loop controls   d. sentinels

4. A counter keeps track of _____.

   a. the number of times an event has occurred

   b. the number of machine cycles required by a segment of a program

   c. the number of loop structures within a program

   d. the number of times software has been revised

5. Adding 1 to a variable is also called _____ it.

   a. digesting   c. decrementing

   b. resetting   d. incrementing

6. When you know the number of times a loop will execute when a program runs, it is a _____ loop.

   a. definite   c. incremented

   b. absolute   d. virtual

7. In the following pseudocode, what is output if a = 1, b = 2, and c = 5?

```
while a < c
    a = a + 1
    b = b + c
endwhile
output a, b, c
```

   a. 1 2 5   c. 5 6 5

   b. 5 22 5   d. 6 22 9

8. In the following pseudocode, what is output if d = 4, e = 6, and f = 7?

```
while d > f
    d = d + 1
    e = e - 1
endwhile
output d, e, f
```

   a. 4 6 7   c. 7 3 7

   b. 8 2 8   d. 5 5 7

9. In the following pseudocode, what is output if g = 4 and h = 6?

```
while g < h
    g = g + 1
endwhile
output g, h
```

    a.   nothing   c.   5 6

    b.   4 6   d.   6 6

10. Most programmers use a `for` loop _____.

    a.   for every loop they write

    b.   when a loop will not repeat

    c.   when they do not know the exact number of times a loop will repeat

    d.   when they know the exact number of times a loop will repeat

11. When two loops are nested, the loop that is contained by the other is the _____ loop.

    a.   captive

    b.   unstructured

    c.   inner

    d.   outer

12. In the following pseudocode, how many times is "Hello" output if j = 2, k = 5, m = 6, and n = 9?

```
while j < k
    while m < n
        output "Hello"
        m = m + 1
    endwhile
    j = j + 1
endwhile
```

    a.   0   c.   6

    b.   3   d.   9

13. In the following pseudocode, how many times is "Goodbye" output if j = 2, k = 5, and n = 9?

```
while j < k
    m = 6
    while m < n
        output "Goodbye"
        m = m + 1
    endwhile
    j = j + 1
endwhile
```

a. 0
c. 6
b. 3
d. 9

14. In the following pseudocode, how many times is "Adios" output if p = 2 and q = 4?

```
while p < q
    output "Adios"
    r = 1
    while r < q
        print "Adios"
        r = r + 1
    endwhile
    p = p + 1
endwhile
```

a. 0
c. 6
b. 4
d. 8

15. If you write a loop, and mistakenly omit the statement that alters to loop control variable, the most likely result is _____.

a. garbage output
c. an infinite loop
b. hardware failure
d. not enough output

Find the Bugs

Your student disk contains files named DEBUG04-01.txt, DEBUG04-02.txt, and DEBUG04-03.txt. Each file contains pseudocode segments with one or more bugs that you must find and correct.

Exercises

1. Design the logic for a program that outputs every number from 1 through 10.

2. Design the logic for a program that outputs every number from 1 through 10 along with its square and cube.

3. Design the logic for a program that outputs every even number from 2 through 30.

4. Design the logic for a program that outputs numbers in reverse order from 10 down to 1.

5. The No Interest Credit Company provides zero-interest loans to customers. (It makes a profit by selling advertising space in its monthly statements and selling its customer lists.) Design an application that gets customer account data that includes an account number, customer name, and balance due. For each customer, display the account number and name; then print the customer's projected balance each month for the next 10 months. Assume that there is no finance charge on this account, that the customer makes no new purchases, and that the customer pays off the balance with equal monthly payments, which are 10 percent of the original bill.

6. The Some Interest Credit Company provides loans to customers at 1.5 percent interest per month. Design an application that gets customer account data that includes an account number, customer name, and balance due. For each customer, display the account number and name; then display the customer's projected balance each month for the next 10 months. Assume that when the balance reaches $10 or less, the customer can pay off the account. At the beginning of every month, 1.5 percent interest is added to the balance, and then the customer makes a payment equal to 5 percent of the current balance. Assume the customer makes no new purchases.

7. The Howell Bank provides savings accounts that compound interest on a yearly basis. In other words, if you deposit $100 for two years at 4 percent interest, at the end of one year you will have $104. At the end of two years, you will have the $104 plus 4 percent of that, or $108.16. Design a program that accepts an account number, the account owner's first and last names, and a balance. Display the projected running total balance for each year for the next 20 years.

8. The Vernon Hills Mail-Order Company often sends multiple packages per order. For each customer order, print enough mailing labels to use on each of the separate boxes that will be mailed. The mailing labels contain the customer's complete name and address, along with a box number in the form "Box 9 of 9". For example, an order that requires three boxes produces three labels: "Box 1 of 3", "Box 2 of 3", and "Box 3 of 3". Design

an application that continuously accepts a customer's title (for example, "Mrs."), a first name, last name, street address, city, state, zip code, and number of boxes in the order until an appropriate sentinel value is entered. Produce enough mailing labels for each order.

9. Secondhand Rose Resale Shop is having a seven-day sale during which the price of any unsold item drops 10 percent each day. The inventory file includes an item number, description, and original price on day one. For example, an item that costs $10.00 on the first day costs 10 percent less, or $9.00, on the second day. On the third day, the same item is 10 percent less than $9.00, or $8.10. Design an application that reads inventory records and produces a report that shows the price of every item on each day, one through seven.

10. The state of Florida maintains a census file in which each record contains the name of a county, the current population, and a number representing the rate at which the population is increasing per year. For example, one record might contain Miami-Dade County, 2,253,000, and 2 percent. The governor wants a report that lists each county and the number of years it will take for the population of the county to double, assuming the present rate of growth remains constant. Design an application that reads records from an input file and displays the county's name and the number of years it will take for the population to double. If a county's record contains a negative growth rate, then instead of displaying the number of years it takes for the population to double, display a message that indicates that the population is never expected to double.

11. The Human Resources Department of Apex Manufacturing Company wants a report that shows its employees the benefits of saving for retirement. Produce a report that shows 12 predicted retirement account values for each employee—the values if the employee saves 5, 10, or 15 percent of his or her annual salary for 10, 20, 30, or 40 years. Design an application that inputs employees' names and salaries and outputs the name followed by the 12 predicted account values for each employee. Assume that savings grow at a rate of 8 percent per year.

12. In Chapter 3, one of the exercises explained that in many programming languages you can generate a random number between 1 and a limiting value named `LIMIT` by using a statement similar to `randomNumber = random(LIMIT)`. You also created the logic for a guessing game in which the application

generates a random number and the player tries to guess it. Now, create a guessing game in which the application generates a random number and the player tries to guess it. After each guess display a message indicating whether the player's guess was correct, too high, or too low. When the player eventually guesses the correct number, display a count of the number of guesses that were required.

13. In Chapter 3, one of the exercises explained that in many programming languages you can generate a random number between 1 and a limiting value named `LIMIT` by using a statement similar to `randomNumber = random(LIMIT)`. Create the logic for a game that simulates rolling two dice by generating two numbers between 1 and 6 inclusive. The player chooses a number between 2 (the lowest total possible from two dice) and 12 (the highest total possible). The player then "rolls" two dice up to three times. If the number chosen by the user comes up, the user wins and the game ends. If the number does not come up within three rolls, the computer wins.

14. In Chapter 3, one of the exercises explained that in many programming languages you can generate a random number between 1 and a limiting value named `LIMIT` by using a statement similar to `randomNumber = random(LIMIT)`. Create the logic for the dice game Pig in which a player can compete with the computer. The object of the game is to be the first to score 100 points. The user and computer take turns rolling a pair of dice, the values of which are determined randomly. The game follows these rules:

- On a turn, each player "rolls" two dice. If no 1 appears, the dice values are added to a running total, and the player can choose whether to roll again or pass the turn to the other player.

- If a 1 appears on one of the dice, nothing more is added to the player's total and it becomes the other player's turn.

- If a 1 appears on both of the dice, not only is the player's turn over, but the player's entire accumulated score is reset to 0.

- In this version of the game, when the computer does not roll a 1 and can choose whether to roll again, generate a new random value of 1 or 2. Use this value to decide whether the computer will continue to play or to pass the turn to the player.

Arrays

After completing this chapter you will be able to:

- ◎ Describe arrays and explain how they occupy computer memory
- ◎ Manipulate an array to replace nested decisions
- ◎ Search an array using a `while` loop
- ◎ Use parallel arrays
- ◎ Avoid violating array bounds
- ◎ Use a `for` loop to process arrays

Understanding Arrays and How They Occupy Computer Memory

An **array** is a series or list of variables in computer memory; all the variables have the same name and data type but are differentiated with special numbers called subscripts. Usually, all the values in an array have something in common. For example, they might represent a list of employee ID numbers or a list of prices for items a store sells. A **subscript**, also called an **index**, is a number that indicates the position of a particular item within an array.

Whenever you require multiple storage locations for objects, you are using a real-life counterpart of a programming array. If you store important papers in a series of file folders and label each folder with a consecutive letter of the alphabet, then you are using the equivalent of an array. When you look down the left side of a tax table to find your income level before looking to the right to find your income tax obligation, you are using an array. Similarly, if you look down the left side of a train schedule to find your station before looking to the right to find the train's arrival time, you also are using an array.

Some programmers refer to an array as a *table* or a *matrix*.

Each of these real-life arrays helps you organize real-life objects. You *could* store all your papers or mementos in one huge cardboard box, or find your tax rate or train's arrival time if both were printed randomly in one large book. However, using an organized storage and display system makes your life easier in each case. Using a programming array will do the same for your data.

How Arrays Occupy Computer Memory

When you declare an array, you declare a structure that contains multiple variables. Each variable within an array has the same name and the same data type; each separate array variable is one **element** of the array. Often, you place values in an array so that you can more easily perform the same tasks with each element. Each array element occupies an area in memory next to, or contiguous to, the others, as shown in Figure 5-1. You can indicate the number of elements an array will hold—the **size of the array**—when you declare the array along with your other variables. For example, you might declare a three-element numeric array named someVals as follows:

```
num someVals[3]
```

143

An error commonly made by beginning programmers is to forget that array subscripts start with 0. If you assume an array's first subscript is 1, you will always be "off by one" in your array manipulation.

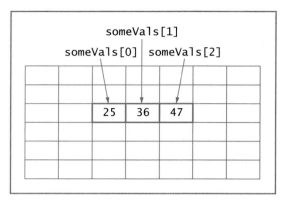

Figure 5-1   Appearance of a three-element array in computer memory

In all languages, subscript values must be nonnegative integers (whole numbers) and sequential.

All array elements have the same group name, but each individual element also has a unique subscript indicating how far away it is from the first element. Therefore, any array's subscripts are always a sequence of integers such as 0 through 3 or 0 through 9.

Depending on the syntax rules of the programming language you use, you place the subscript within parentheses or square brackets following the group name. This text will use square brackets to hold array element subscripts so that you don't mistake array names for method names. Plus, many newer programming languages such as C++, Java, and C# use the bracket notation.

In Figure 5-1, the array named someVals contains three elements, so the elements are someVals[0], someVals[1], and someVals[2]. The value stored in someVals[0] is 25; someVals[1] holds 36, and someVals[2] holds 47. The element someVals[0] is zero positions away from the beginning of the array—in other words, it is located at the same memory address as the array. The element someVals[1] is one position away from the beginning of the array, and someVals[2] is two positions away.

You can picture the memory address of someVals[0] as the address of the someVals array plus zero more positions. Similarly, you can picture the memory address of someVals[1] as the memory address of the someVals array plus one more position.

You can declare an array and then assign a value to each array element individually, for example:

```
num someVals[3]
someVals[0] = 25
someVals[1] = 36
someVals[2] = 47
```

Alternately, you can initialize array elements when you declare the array. Most programming languages use a statement similar to the following to declare a three-element array and assign values to it:

```
num someVals[3] = 25, 36, 47
```

When you use this form of array initialization, the first value you list is assigned to the first array element, and the subsequent values are assigned in order. Most programming languages allow you to initialize an array with fewer values than there are array elements declared, but no language allows you to initialize an array using more values.

Manipulating an Array to Replace Nested Decisions

Consider an application requested by a Human Resources Department to produce statistics on employees' claimed dependents. The department wants a report that lists the number of employees who have claimed 0, 1, 2, 3, 4, or 5 dependents like the one shown in Figure 5-2. (Assume you know that no employees have more than five dependents.)

Dependents	Count
0	43
1	35
2	24
3	11
4	5
5	7

Figure 5-2 Typical Dependents Report

Without using an array, you could write the application that produces counts for the six categories of dependents (for each number of dependents, 0 through 5) by using a series of decisions. Figure 5-3 shows the pseudocode and flowchart for the decision-making part of an application that counts dependents in each of six different categories. Although this logic works, its length and complexity are unnecessary once you understand how to use an array.

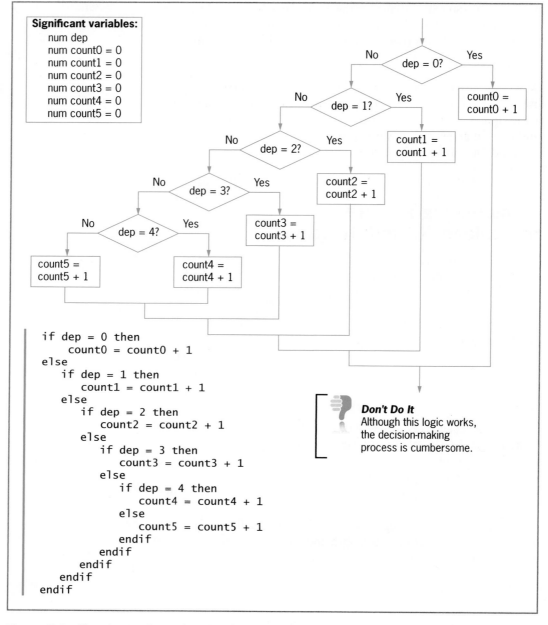

Significant variables:
num dep
num count0 = 0
num count1 = 0
num count2 = 0
num count3 = 0
num count4 = 0
num count5 = 0

```
if dep = 0 then
    count0 = count0 + 1
else
    if dep = 1 then
        count1 = count1 + 1
    else
        if dep = 2 then
            count2 = count2 + 1
        else
            if dep = 3 then
                count3 = count3 + 1
            else
                if dep = 4 then
                    count4 = count4 + 1
                else
                    count5 = count5 + 1
                endif
            endif
        endif
    endif
endif
```

Don't Do It
Although this logic works,
the decision-making
process is cumbersome.

Figure 5-3   Flowchart and pseudocode of counting dependents using a series of decisions—the hard way

In Figure 5-3, the variable dep is compared to 0. If it is 0, 1 is added to count0. If it is not 0, then dep is compared to 1. It is either added to count1, or compared to 2, and so on. Each time the application executes this decision-making process, 1 is added to one of the five variables that acts as a counter for one of the possible numbers of dependents. The dependent-counting application in Figure 5-3 works, but even with only six categories of dependents, the decision-making process is unwieldy. What if the number of dependents might be any value from 0 to 10, or 0 to 20? With either of these scenarios, the basic logic of the program would remain the same; however, you would need to declare many additional accumulator variables and make many additional decisions.

The decision-making process in Figure 5-3 accomplishes its purpose, and nothing is wrong with its logic, though it is cumbersome. Follow its logic here so that you understand how the application works.

147

Using an array provides an alternate approach to this programming problem, greatly reducing the number of statements you need. When you declare an array, you provide a group name for a number of associated variables in memory. For example, the six dependent count accumulators can be redefined as a single array named count. The individual elements become count[0], count[1], count[2], count[3], count[4], and count[5], as shown in the revised decision-making process in Figure 5-4.

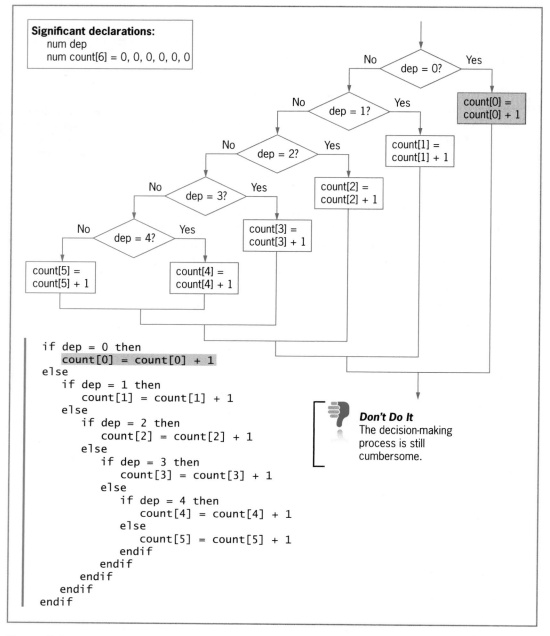

Figure 5-4   Flowchart and pseudocode of counting dependents using an array—but still the hard way

Significant declarations:
  num dep
  num count[6] = 0, 0, 0, 0, 0, 0

dep = 0?   No / Yes

count[0] =
count[0] + 1

dep = 1?   No / Yes

count[1] =
count[1] + 1

dep = 2?   No / Yes

count[2] =
count[2] + 1

dep = 3?   No / Yes

count[3] =
count[3] + 1

dep = 4?   No / Yes

count[5] =
count[5] + 1

count[4] =
count[4] + 1

```
if dep = 0 then
   count[0] = count[0] + 1
else
   if dep = 1 then
      count[1] = count[1] + 1
   else
      if dep = 2 then
         count[2] = count[2] + 1
      else
         if dep = 3 then
            count[3] = count[3] + 1
         else
            if dep = 4 then
               count[4] = count[4] + 1
            else
               count[5] = count[5] + 1
            endif
         endif
      endif
   endif
endif
```

Don't Do It
The decision-making
process is still
cumbersome.

The shaded statement in Figure 5-4 shows that when dep is 0, 1 is added to count[0]. You can see similar statements for the rest of the count elements. When dep is 1, 1 is added to count[1]; when dep is 2, 1 is added to count[2], and so on. When the dep value is 5, it means it was not 1, 2, 3, or 4, so 1 is added to count[5]. In other words, 1 is added to one of the elements of the count array instead of to an individual variable named count0, count1, count2, count3, count4, or count5. Is this version an improvement over the original in Figure 5-3? Of course, it isn't. You still have not taken advantage of the benefits of using the array in this application.

The true benefit of an array lies in your ability to use a variable as a subscript to the array, instead of using a constant such as 0 or 5. Notice in the logic in Figure 5-4 that within each decision, the value you are comparing to dep and the constant you are using as a subscript in the resulting "Yes" process are always identical. That is, when dep is 0, the subscript used to add 1 to the count array is 0; when dep is 1, the subscript used for the count array is 1, and so on. In other words, there is a **direct relationship** between dep and the array position that you want to increment. Therefore, you can just use dep as a subscript to the array. You can rewrite the decision-making process as shown in Figure 5-5.

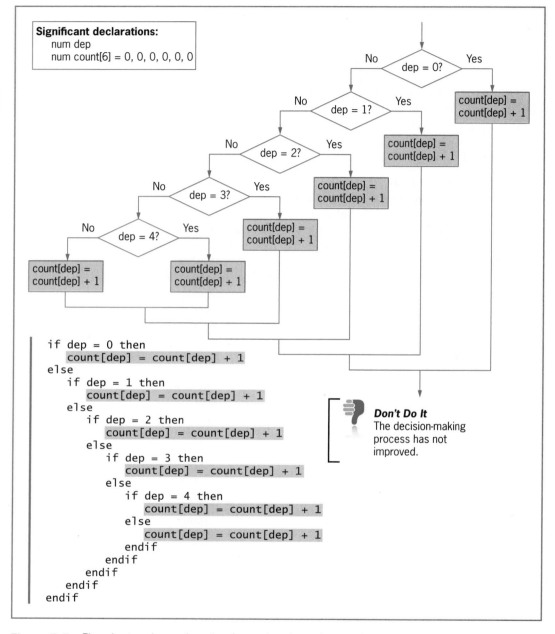

Figure 5-5   Flowchart and pseudocode of counting dependents using an array and a variable subscript—but still a hard way

The code segment in Figure 5-5 looks no more efficient than the one in Figure 5-4. However, notice that in Figure 5-5 the shaded statements that occur after each decision are exactly the same. In each case, no matter what the value of dep is, you always add 1 to count[dep]. If you are always going to take the same action no matter what the answer to a question is, why ask the question? Instead, you can rewrite the decision-making process as shown in Figure 5-6.

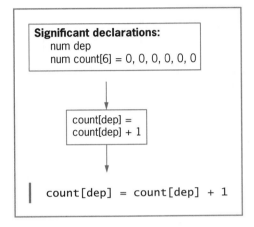

Figure 5-6 Flowchart and pseudocode of efficient counting using an array

The single statement in Figure 5-6 eliminates the *entire* decision-making process that was the original highlighted section in Figure 5-5! When dep is 2, 1 is added to count[2]; when dep is 4, 1 is added to count[4], and so on. *Now* the original process is greatly simplified. What's more, this process does not change significantly whether there are 20, 30, or any other number of possible categories. To use a different number of accumulators, you just declare the array to be the appropriate size.

Figure 5-7 shows an entire program that takes advantage of the array to produce the counts for each dependent category. In the program in Figure 5-7, the first value for dep is read into the program. If it is not the end of the file, then 1 is added to the appropriate element of the count array and the next record is read. When data entry is complete and the end of the file is reached, the final tallies can be output. The heading is output (as shown in Figure 5-2), the variable dep is reset to 0, then count[dep] is displayed. The first output statement displays 0 (as the number of dependents) and the value stored in count[0]. Then, 1 is added to dep, and the same set of instructions is used again to display the counts for each number of dependents. The first loop in Figure 5-7 is an indefinite loop; it continues as long as the user enters more values. The second loop in the program is a definite loop; it executes precisely six times.

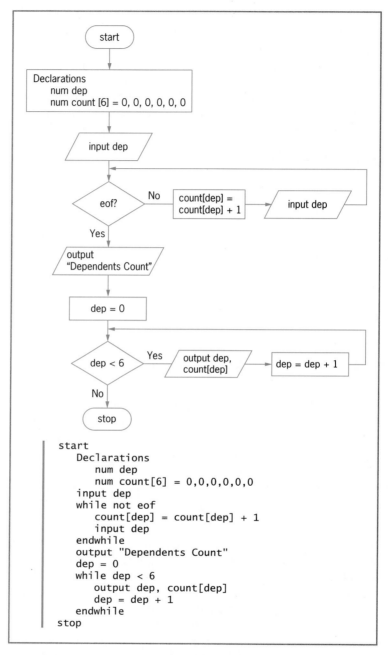

Figure 5-7 Flowchart and pseudocode for Dependents Report program

The dependent-counting program *worked* when it contained a long series of decisions and output statements, but the program is easier to write when you employ arrays. Additionally, the program is more efficient, easier for other programmers to understand, and easier to maintain.

Arrays are never mandatory, but often they can drastically cut down on your programming time and make your logic easier to understand.

Using Constants with Arrays

In Chapter 1 you learned that named constants hold values that do not change during a program's execution. When working with arrays, you can use constants in two ways:

- To hold an array's size

- As the array values

Learning to use arrays correctly can make many programming tasks far more efficient and professional. When you understand how to use arrays, you will be able to provide elegant solutions to problems that otherwise would require tedious programming steps.

153

The logic in Figure 5-7 still contains one minor flaw. Throughout this book you have learned to avoid "magic numbers"; that is, to avoid unnamed constants. As the totals are output in the loop at the end of the program in Figure 5-7, the array subscript is compared to the constant 6. The program can be improved if you use a named constant instead of the unnamed constant. In most programming languages you can take one of two approaches:

- You can declare a named numeric constant such as `ARRAY_SIZE` = 6. Then you can use this constant every time you access the array, always making sure any subscript you use remains less than the constant value.

- In many languages, when you declare an array, a constant that represents the array size is automatically created for you. For example, in Java, after you declare an array named `count`, its size is stored in a field named `count.length`: and in both C# and Visual Basic, the array size is `count.Length`. ('The difference is in the "L" in `Length`.)

Besides making your code easier to modify, using a named constant makes the code easier to understand.

Sometimes the values stored in arrays should be constants. For example, suppose you create an array that holds names for the months of the year. The first month is always "January"—the value should not change. You might create an array as follows:

```
string MONTH[12] = "January", "February", "March", "April",
    "May", "June", "July", "August", "September", "October",
    "November", "December"
```

Recall that the convention in this book is to use all upper-case letters in constant identifiers.

Searching an Array Using a `while` Loop

In the dependent-counting application in this chapter, the fields that the array depended on conveniently held small whole numbers; the number of dependents allowed was 0 through 5, and the `dep` variable directly accessed the array. Unfortunately, real life doesn't always happen in small integers. Sometimes you don't have a variable that conveniently holds an array position; sometimes you have to search through an array to find a value you need.

154

Consider a mail-order business in which orders come in with a customer name, address, item number ordered, and quantity ordered. Assume the item numbers from which a customer can choose are three-digit numbers, but perhaps they are not consecutive 001 through 999. Instead, over the years, items have been deleted and new items have been added to the inventory. There might no longer be an item with number 105 or 129. Sometimes there might be a hundred-number gap or more between items. For example, let's say that this season you are down to offering six items: 106, 108, 307, 405, 457, 688. These are shown in the shaded array declaration VALID_ITEM in Figure 5-8. The array is declared constant because the item numbers will never change.

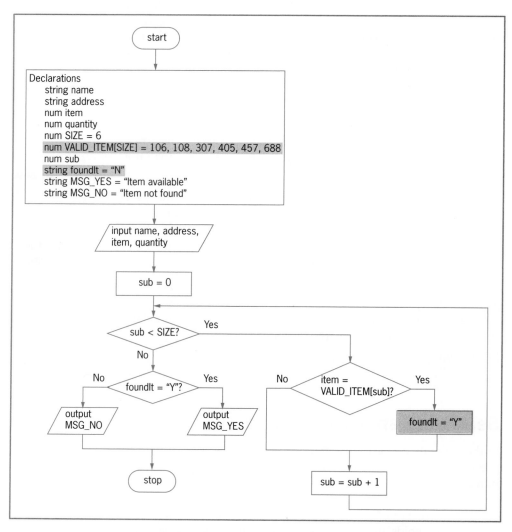

Figure 5-8   Flowchart and pseudocode for program that verifies item availability (*continues*)

(continued)

```
start
   Declarations
      string name
      string address
      num item
      num quantity
      num SIZE = 6
      num VALID_ITEM[SIZE] = 106, 108,307, 405, 457, 688
      num sub
      string foundIt = "N"
      string MSG_YES = "Item available"
      string MSG_NO = "Item not found"
   input name, address, item, quantity
   sub = 0
   while sub < SIZE
      foundIt = "N"
      if item = VALID_ITEM[sub] then
         foundIt = "Y"
      endif
      sub = sub + 1
   endwhile
   if foundIt = "Y" then
      output MSG_YES
   else
      output MSG_NO
   endif
stop
```

Figure 5-8 Flowchart and pseudocode for program that verifies item availability

When a customer orders an item, you want to determine whether the item number is valid. You could use a series of six decisions to determine whether the ordered item is valid by comparing, in turn, each customer order's item number to each of the six allowed values. However, a superior approach is to store the list of valid item numbers in an array and to search through the array for an exact match to the ordered item. If you search through the entire array without finding a match for the item the customer ordered, you can display an error message—for example, "Item not found." When you search through a list from one end to the other, you are performing a **linear search**.

In an office without a computer, if a customer orders item 307, a clerical worker can tell whether it is valid by looking down a list of valid items and verifying that 307 is a member of the list. In a similar fashion, in a computer program, you can use a loop to test each VALID_ITEM against the ordered item number.

The technique for verifying that an item number exists involves setting a subscript to 0 and setting a flag variable to indicate that you have not yet determined whether the customer's order is valid.

Instead of the string `foundIt` variable in the method in Figure 5-8, you might prefer to use a numeric variable that you set to 1 or 0. Most programming languages also support a Boolean data type that you can use for `foundIt`; when you declare a variable to be Boolean, you can set its value to true or false.

A **flag** is a variable that you set to indicate whether some event has occurred; frequently it holds a true or false value. For example, you can set a string variable named `foundIt` to "N", indicating "No". (See the second shaded statement in Figure 5-8.) Then you compare the customer's ordered item number to the first item in the array. If the customer-ordered item matches the first item in the array, you can set the flag variable to "Y", or any other value that is not "N". (See the last shaded statement in Figure 5-8.) If the items do not match, you increase the subscript and continue to look down the list of numbers stored in the array. If you check all six valid item numbers and the customer item matches none of them, then the flag variable `foundIt` still holds the value "N". If the flag variable is "N" after you have looked through the entire list, you can issue an error message indicating that no match was ever found.

Using Parallel Arrays

When you read a customer's order in a mail-order company program, you usually want to accomplish more than simply verifying the item's existence. For example, you might want to determine the price of the ordered item, multiply that price by quantity ordered, and display the amount owed.

Suppose you have a list of item numbers and their associated prices. You could declare two arrays. One contains six elements named `VALID_ITEM`; all six elements are valid item numbers. The other array also has six elements. The array is named `VALID_PRICE`; all six elements are prices. Each price in this `VALID_PRICE` array is conveniently and purposely in the same position as the corresponding item number in the other `VALID_ITEM` array. Two corresponding arrays such as these are **parallel arrays** because each element in one array is associated with the element in the same relative position in the other array. Figure 5-9 shows how the parallel arrays might look in computer memory.

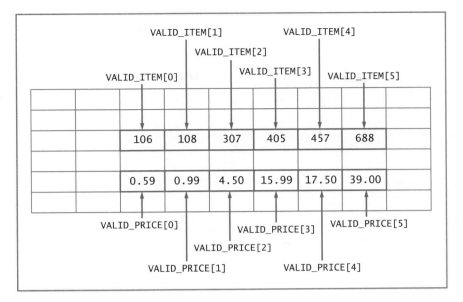

Figure 5-9 How parallel arrays appear in memory

When you use parallel arrays:

- Two or more arrays contain related data.

- A subscript relates the arrays. That is, elements at the same position in each array are logically related.

Figure 5-10 shows a program that declares parallel arrays. The VALID_PRICE array is shaded; each element in it corresponds to a valid item number.

When you create parallel arrays, each array can be a different data type.

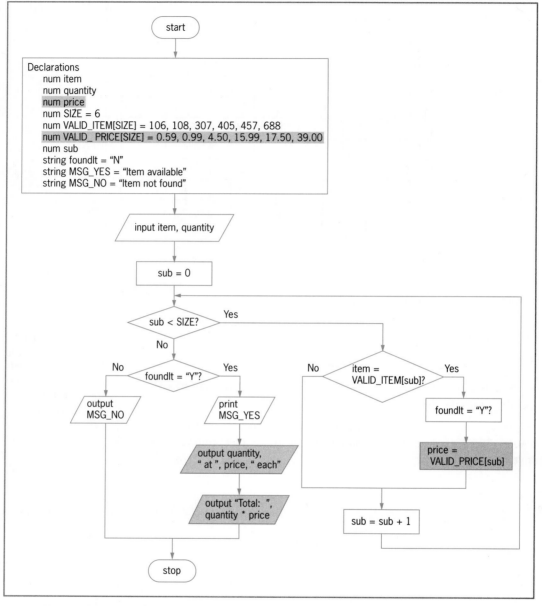

Figure 5-10 Flowchart and pseudocode of program that finds an item's price (*continues*)

(continued)

```
start
   Declarations
      num item
      num quantity
      num price
      num SIZE = 6
      num VALID_ITEM[SIZE] = 106, 108, 307, 405, 457, 688
      num VALID_PRICE[SIZE] = 0.59, 0.99, 4.50, 15.99, 17.50, 39.00
      num sub
      string foundIt = "N"
      string MSG_YES = "Item available"
      string MSG_NO = "Item not found"
   input item, quantity
   sub = 0
   while sub < SIZE
      if item = VALID_ITEM[sub] then
         foundIt = "Y"
         price = VALID_PRICE[sub]
      endif
      sub = sub + 1
   endwhile
   if foundIt = "Y" then
      output MSG_YES
      output quantity, " at ", price, " each"
      output "Total ", quantity * price
   else
      output MSG_NO
   endif
stop
```

Figure 5-10   Flowchart and pseudocode of program that finds an item's price

As the program in Figure 5-10 receives a customer's order data, it looks through each of the VALID_ITEM values separately by varying the subscript sub from 0 to the number of items available. When a match for the item number is found, the program pulls the corresponding parallel price out of the list of VALID_PRICE values and stores it in the price variable. (See shaded statements in Figure 5-10.)

The relationship between an item's number and its price is an **indirect relationship**. That means you don't access a price directly by knowing the item number. Instead, you determine the item number's position and access the price from that. Once you find a match for the ordered item number in the VALID_ITEM array, you know that the price of that item is in the same position in the other array, VALID_PRICE. When VALID_ITEM[sub] is the correct item, VALID_ PRICE[sub] must be the correct price. You can then display the price and multiply it by the quantity ordered to produce a total, as shown in the last shaded statements in Figure 5-10.

Some programmers object to using a cryptic variable name for a subscript, such as sub or x, because such names are not descriptive. These programmers would prefer a name like priceIndex. Others approve of short names when the variable is used only in a limited area of a program, as it is used here, to step through an array. Programmers disagree on many style issues like this one. As a programmer, it is your responsibility to find out what conventions are used among your peers in your organization.

Suppose that a customer orders item 457. Walk through the logic yourself to see if you come up with the correct price per item, $17.50. Then, suppose that a customer orders item 458. Walk through the logic and see whether the appropriate "Item not found" message is displayed.

Improving Search Efficiency

The mail-order program in Figure 5-10 is still a little inefficient. The problem is that if lots of customers order item 106 or 108, their price is found on the first or second pass through the loop. However, the program continues searching through the item array until **sub** reaches the value SIZE. One way to stop the search when the item has been found and **foundIt** is set to "Y" is changing the loop-controlling question. Instead of simply continuing the loop while the number of comparisons does not exceed the array size, you should continue the loop while the searched item is not found *and* the number of comparisons has not exceeded the array size. Leaving a loop as soon as a match is found improves the program's efficiency. The larger the array, the more beneficial it becomes to exit the searching loop as soon as you find what you're looking for. Figure 5-11 shows the improved version of the loop with the altered loop-controlling question shaded.

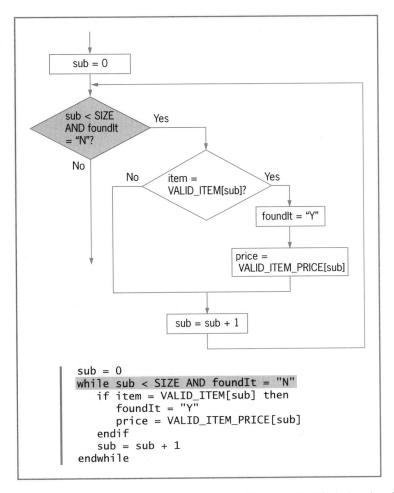

```
sub = 0
while sub < SIZE AND foundIt = "N"
    if item = VALID_ITEM[sub] then
        foundIt = "Y"
        price = VALID_ITEM_PRICE[sub]
    endif
    sub = sub + 1
endwhile
```

Figure 5-11 Flowchart and pseudocode of the loop that finds item's price, exiting the loop as soon as it is found

Notice that the price-finding program is most efficient when the most frequently ordered items are stored at the beginning of the array. Only the seldom-ordered items require many loops before finding a match. Often, you can improve sort efficiency by rearranging array elements.

As you study programming, you will learn search techniques in addition to a linear search. For example, a **binary search** starts looking in the middle of a sorted list, and then determines whether it should continue higher or lower.

Remaining Within Array Bounds

Every array has a finite size. You can think of an array's size in one of two ways—either by the number of elements in the array or by the number of bytes in the array. Arrays are always composed of elements of the same data type, and elements of the same data type always occupy the same number of bytes of memory, so the number of bytes in an array is always a multiple of the number of elements in an array. For example, in Java, integers occupy four bytes of memory, so an array of 10 integers occupies exactly 40 bytes.

In every programming language, when you access data stored in an array, it is important to use a subscript containing a value that accesses memory occupied by the array. For example, examine the program in Figure 5-12. The program accepts a numeric mon and displays the name associated with that month.

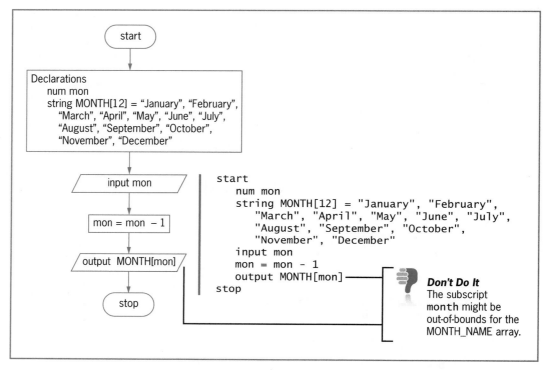

Figure 5-12   Determining the month string from user's numeric entry

In the program in Figure 5-12, notice that 1 is correctly subtracted from mon before it is used as a subscript. That's because although most people think of January as month 1, its name occupies the location in the array with the 0 subscript. However, the logic makes a dangerous assumption: that every number entered by the user is a valid month number. If the user enters a number that is too small or too large, one of two things will happen depending on the programming language you use. When you use a subscript value that is negative or higher than the number of elements in an array:

- Some programming languages will stop execution of the program and issue an error message.

- Other programming languages will not issue an error message but will access a value in a memory location that is outside the area occupied by the array. That area might contain garbage, or worse, it accidentally might contain the name of an incorrect month.

Either way, a logical error occurs. When you use a subscript that is not within the range of acceptable subscripts, your subscript is said to be **out of bounds**. Users enter incorrect data frequently; a good program should be able to handle the mistake and not allow the subscript to be out of bounds.

You can improve the program in Figure 5-12 by adding a test that ensures the subscript used to access the array is within the array bounds. After you test the input value to assure it is between 1 and 12 inclusive, you might prefer to take one of the following approaches if it is not:

- Display an error message and end the program.

- Use a default value for the month. For example, when an entered month is invalid, you might always want to assume it is December.

- Continuously reprompt the user for a new value until it is valid.

Which technique you use depends on the requirements of your program.

Besides entering an invalid number, a user might not enter a number at all. For example, the user might type letters or punctuation. You will handle this type of error when you write programs in a specific language.

163

Using a for Loop to Process Arrays

In Chapter 4, you learned about the for loop—a loop that, in a single statement, initializes a loop control variable, compares it to a limit, and alters it. The for loop is a particularly convenient tool when working with arrays because you frequently need to process every element of an array from beginning to end. As with a while loop, when you use a for loop, you must be careful to stay within array bounds, remembering that the highest usable array subscript is one less than the size of the array. Figure 5-13 shows a for loop that correctly displays all the department names in an array declared as DEPTS. Notice that month is incremented through one less than the number of months because with a five-item array, the subscripts you can use are 0 through 4.

In Java, C++, and C#, the for loop looks like the following:

```
for(dep = 0; dep <
SIZE; dep++)
```

The keyword for is followed by parentheses. The parentheses contain three sections, separated with semicolons. The first section initializes the loop control variable, the middle section makes a comparison, and the last section alters the loop control variable after each execution of the loop body. In Java, C++, and C#, dep++ means "add one to dep".

```
start
   Declarations
      num dep
      num SIZE = 5
      string DEPTS[SIZE] = "Accounting", "Personnel",
         "Technical", "Customer Service", "Marketing"
   for dep 0 to SIZE - 1 step 1
      output DEPTS[dep]
   endfor
stop
```

Figure 5-13 Pseudocode that uses a for loop to display an array of department names

Review Questions

1. A subscript is a(n) _____.

    a.   element in an array

    b.   alternate name for an array

    c.   number that represents the highest value stored within an array

    d.   number that indicates the position of a particular item in an array

2. Each variable in an array must have the same _____ as the others.

    a.   data type   c.   value

    b.   subscript   d.   memory location

3. Each variable in an array is called a(n) _____.

    a.   data type   c.   component

    b.   subscript   d.   element

4. The subscripts of any array are always _____.

    a.   integers   c.   characters

    b.   fractions   d.   strings of characters

5. A subscript used to access an array can be _____.

    a.   a negative integer   c.   a positive integer

    b.   0 (zero)   d.   Two of the above can be used.

6. Suppose you have an array named `number`, and two of its elements are `number[1]` and `number[4]`. You know that _____.

    a.   the two elements hold the same value

    b.   the array holds exactly four elements

    c.   there are exactly two elements between those two elements

    d.   the two elements are at the same memory location

7. Suppose you have an array named number, and two of its elements are number[1] and number[4]. You know that _____.

    a. the array holds at least five elements

    b. the array holds no more than four elements

    c. the value of number[4] is greater than the value of number[2]

    d. the memory address of number[1] is greater than the memory address of number[4]

8. Suppose you want to write a program that reads customer records and displays a summary of the number of customers who owe more than $1,000 each, in each of 12 sales regions. Customer fields include name, zipCode, balanceDue, and regionNumber. At some point during record processing, you would add 1 to an array element whose subscript would be represented by _____.

    a. name   c. balanceDue

    b. zipCode   d. regionNumber

9. Which of the following is true of an array declared as num money[5]?

    a. It can hold strings as well as numeric values.

    b. The assignment money[5] = 0 is valid.

    c. The value of money[0] can never exceed the value of money[1].

    d. It holds exactly five values.

10. You can create an array of _____.

    a. constant numeric values

    b. constant string values

    c. variable string values

    d. any of the above

11. A _____ is a variable that you set to indicate whether some event has occurred.

    a. subscript   c. counter

    b. banner   d. flag

12. What do you call two arrays in which each element in one array is associated with the element in the same relative position in the other array?

    a. cohesive arrays

    b. parallel arrays

    c. hidden arrays

    d. perpendicular arrays

13. In most modern programming languages, the highest subscript you should use with a 10-element array is _____.

    a. 8

    b. 9

    c. 10

    d. 11

14. Each element in a five-element numeric array can hold _____ value(s) at a time.

    a. one

    b. five

    c. at least five

    d. an unlimited number of

15. When you use a subscript value that is negative or higher than the number of elements in an array, _____.

    a. execution of the program stops and an error message is issued

    b. a value in a memory location that is outside the area occupied by the array will be accessed

    c. a value in a memory location that is outside the area occupied by the array will be accessed but only if the value is the correct data type

    d. the resulting action depends on the programming language used

Find the Bugs

Your student disk contains files named DEBUG05-01.txt and DEBUG05-02.txt. Each file contains pseudocode segments with one or more bugs that you must find and correct.

Exercises

1. Design the logic for a program that allows a user to enter 10 numbers, then displays them in the reverse order of their entered order.

2. Design the logic for a program that allows a user to enter 10 numbers, then displays each and its difference from the numeric average of the numbers.

3. a. The city of Cary is holding a special census. The census takers collect one record for each resident. Each record contains a resident's age, gender, marital status, and voting district. The voting district field contains a number from 1 through 22. Design a program that accepts data for each resident until all have been entered and then produces a list of all 22 districts and the number of residents in each.

    b. Design a program that accepts resident data and produces a count of the number of residents in each of the following age groups: under 18, 18 through 30, 31 through 45, 46 through 64, and 65 and older.

4. a. The Midville Park District maintains records containing information about players on its soccer teams. Each record contains a player's first name, last name, and team number. The teams are shown in the accompanying table.

Team Number	Team Name
1	Goal Getters
2	The Force
3	Top Guns
4	Shooting Stars
5	Midfield Monsters

Design a program that accepts player data and creates a report that lists each player along with his or her team number and team name.

    b. Design an application that produces a count of the number of players registered for each team listed in Exercise 4a.

5. a. Watson Elementary School contains 30 classrooms numbered 1 through 30. Each classroom can contain any number of students up to 35. Each student takes an achievement test at the end of the school year and receives a score from 0 through 100. Write a program that accepts data for each student in the school—student ID, classroom number, and score on the achievement test.

    Design a program that lists the total points scored for each of the 30 classrooms.

    b. Modify Exercise 5a so that each classroom's average of the test scores is displayed, rather than each classroom's total.

    c. Watson Elementary School maintains a file containing the teacher's name for each classroom. Each record in this file contains a room numbered 1 through 30, and the last name of the teacher. Modify the program in Exercise 5b so that the correct teacher's name appears on the list with his or her class's average.

6. The Billy Goat Fast-Food restaurant sells the products shown in the accompanying table.

Design the logic for an application that reads in the name of an item ordered by a customer and outputs either the correct price or the message "Sorry, we do not carry that."

Product	Price ($)
Cheeseburger	2.49
Pepsi	1.00
Chips	0.59

7. a. Design the logic for an application for a company that wants a breakdown of payroll by department. Input includes each employee's last name, first name, department number, hourly salary, and number of hours worked. The output is a list of the seven departments in the company (numbered 1 through 7) and the total gross payroll (rate times hours) for each department.

   b. Modify Exercise 7a so that the report lists department names as well as numbers. The department names are shown in the accompanying table.

Department Number	Department Name
1	Personnel
2	Marketing
3	Manufacturing
4	Computer Services
5	Sales
6	Accounting
7	Shipping

8. Create the logic for an application that contains an array of 10 multiple-choice questions related to your favorite hobby. Each question contains three answer choices. Also create a parallel array that holds the correct answer to each question—A, B, or C. Display each question and verify that the user enters only A, B, or C as the answer—if not, keep prompting the user until a valid response is entered. If the user responds to a question correctly, display "Correct!"; otherwise, display "The correct answer is" and the letter of the correct answer. After the user answers all the questions, display the number of correct and incorrect answers.

9. a. Create the logic for a dice game. The application randomly "throws" five dice for the computer and five dice for the player. As each random "throw" is made, store it in an array. The application displays all the values, which can be from 1 to 6 inclusive for each die. Decide the winner based on the following hierarchy of die values. Any higher combination beats a lower one; for example, five of a kind beats four of a kind.

    • Five of a kind

    • Four of a kind

    • Three of a kind

    • A pair

    For this game, the numeric dice values do not count. For example, if both players have three of a kind, it's a tie, no matter what the values of the three dice are. Additionally, the game does not recognize a full house (three of a kind plus two of a kind). Figure 5-14 shows how the game might be played in a command-line environment.

    Figure 5-14 Typical execution of the dice game

    b. Improve the dice game so that when both players have the same combination of dice, the higher value wins. For example, two 6s beats two 5s.

10. Design the logic for the game Hangman, in which the user guesses letters in a hidden word. Store the letters of a word in an array. Display a dash for each missing letter. Allow the user to guess letters continuously until all the letters in the word are correctly guessed. As the user enters each guess, display the word again, filling in the guess if it was correct. For example, if the hidden word is "computer", first display --------. After the user guesses "p", the display becomes ---p----. Make sure that when

a user makes a correct guess, all the matching letters are filled in. For example, if the word is "banana", then when the user guesses "a", all three "a" characters are filled in.

11. A standard deck of 52 playing cards holds cards with the values 1 through 13 representing Ace, 2 through 10, Jack, Queen, and King in each of four suits ("Clubs", "Diamonds", "Hearts", and "Spades"). Create an array so that all 52 card combinations are represented. Create a War card game that randomly selects two cards (one for the player and one for the computer) and declares a winner (or a tie) based on the numeric value of the two cards. The game should play for 26 rounds of War, dealing a full deck with no repeated cards. For this game, assume the cards' values are based on their numbers—that is, the lowest card is the Ace. Display the values of the player's and computer's cards, compare their values, and determine the winner. When all the cards in the deck are exhausted, display a count of the number of times the player wins, the number of times the computer wins, and the number of ties.

Some hints:

- Start by creating an array of all 52 playing cards.

- Select a random number for the deck position of the player's first card and assign the card at that array position to the player.

- Move every higher-positioned card in the deck "down" one to fill in the gap. In other words, if the player's first random number is 49, select the card at position 49 (both the numeric value and the string), move the card that was in position 50 to position 49, and move the card that was in position 51 to position 50. Only 51 cards remain in the deck after the player's first card is dealt, so the available-card array is smaller by one.

- In the same way, randomly select a card for the computer and "remove" the card from the deck.

Using Methods

After completing this chapter you will be able to:

- ◎ Describe modularity
- ◎ Create a method
- ◎ Describe scope
- ◎ Create a method that requires a single parameter
- ◎ Create a method that requires multiple parameters
- ◎ Create a method that returns a value
- ◎ Explain the benefits of implementation hiding
- ◎ Use prewritten, built-in methods

The name that programmers use for their modules usually reflects the programming language they use. For example, Visual Basic programmers use "procedure," C and C++ programmers use "function," C# and Java programmers use "method," and programmers in many older languages are most likely to use "subroutine."

Understanding Modularity

Most programs that you purchase are huge, consisting of thousands or millions of statements. If you've worked with a word-processing program or spreadsheet, think of the number of menu options and keystroke combinations available to the user. Such programs are not the work of one programmer. The modular nature of structured programs means that work can be divided among many programmers; then the modules can be connected, and a large program can be developed much more quickly. Programmers also refer to modules as **subroutines**, **procedures**, **functions**, or **methods**.

To execute a method, you **invoke** it or **call** it from another program or method; the **calling method** invokes the **called method**. Any program can contain an unlimited number of methods, and each method can be called an unlimited number of times.

The process of breaking down a large program into modules is called **modularization**. You are never required to break down a large program into modules in order to make it run on a computer, but there are at least three reasons for doing so:

When a method calls another method, the called method is a **submethod** or **subprocedure**.

- Modularization provides abstraction and eliminates repetition.
- Modularization makes it easier for multiple programmers to work on a problem.
- Modularization makes it easier to reuse your work.

In the following sections, you'll learn more about these three benefits of modularization.

Modularization Provides Abstraction and Eliminates Repetition

One reason modularized programs are easier to understand is that they enable a programmer to see the big picture. **Abstraction** means paying attention to important properties while ignoring nonessential details. Abstraction is selective ignorance. Life would be tedious without abstraction. For example, you can create a list of things to accomplish today:

```
Do laundry
Call Aunt Nan
Start term paper
```

Without abstraction, the list of chores would begin:

```
Pick up laundry basket
Put laundry basket in car
Drive to Laundromat
Get out of car with basket
Walk into Laundromat
Set basket down
Find quarters for washing machine
...and so on.
```

You might list a dozen more steps before you finish the laundry and move on to the second chore on your original list. If you had to consider every small, **low-level detail** of every task in your day, you would probably never make it out of bed in the morning. Using a higher-level, more abstract list makes your day manageable. Abstraction makes complex tasks look simple.

Likewise, some level of abstraction occurs in every computer program. Fifty years ago, a programmer had to understand the low-level circuitry instructions the computer used. But now, newer **high-level programming languages** allow you to use English-like vocabulary in which one broad statement corresponds to dozens of machine instructions. No matter which high-level programming language you use, if you display a message on the monitor, you are never required to understand how a monitor works to create each pixel on the screen. You write an instruction like `output message` and the details of the hardware operations are handled for you.

Modules provide another way to achieve abstraction. For example, a payroll program can call a method named `computeFederalWithholdingTax()`. You can write the mathematical details of the method later, someone else can write them, or you can purchase them from an outside source. When you plan your main payroll program, your only concern is that a federal withholding tax will have to be calculated; you save the details for later.

Additionally, modularization helps eliminate repetition in programs. Let's say a payroll program executes different paycheck-calculating modules based on an employee's status, but each of those modules needs to perform the tasks in the `computeFederalWithholdingTax()` method. Then it is more convenient to call the method from each location where it is needed than to repeat all its individual steps in each location.

Abstract artists create paintings in which they see only the "big picture"—color and form—and ignore the details. Abstraction has a similar meaning among programmers.

Low-level circuitry instructions usually are represented as a long series of 1s and 0s that correspond to the on or off positions of a computer's electronic switches.

Modularization Allows Multiple Programmers to Work on a Problem

When you dissect any large task into modules, you gain the ability to divide the task among various people. Rarely does a single programmer write a commercial program that you buy. Consider any word-processing, spreadsheet, or database program you have used. Each program has so many options, and responds to user selections in so many possible ways, that it would take years for a single programmer to write all the instructions. Professional software developers can write new programs in weeks or months, instead of years, by dividing large programs into modules and assigning each module to an individual programmer or programming team.

Modularization Makes It Easier to Reuse Your Work

If a subroutine or function is well written, you may want to use it more than once within a program or in other programs. For example, a routine that checks the current date to make sure it is valid is useful in many programs written for a business. (A valid date has a month that is not lower than 1 or higher than 12, a day that is not lower than 1 or higher than 31 if the month is 1, and so on.) A program that uses a personnel file containing each employee's birth date, hire date, last promotion date, and termination date can call the date-validation module four times for each employee record. Other programs in an organization can also use the module; these include programs that ship customer orders, plan employees' birthday parties, and calculate when loan payments should be made. If you write the date-checking instructions so they are entangled with other statements in a program, they are difficult to extract and reuse. However, if you place the instructions in their own module, the unit is easy to use and portable to other applications. The feature of modular programs that allows individual modules to be used in a variety of applications is known as **reusability**.

Modularization is sometimes called **functional decomposition**.

You can find many real-world examples of reusability. When you build a house, you don't invent plumbing and heating systems; you incorporate systems with proven designs. This certainly reduces the time and effort it takes to build a house. Assuming the plumbing and electrical systems you choose are in service in other houses, they also improve the reliability of your house's systems—they have been tested under a variety of circumstances and have been proven to function correctly. Similarly, software that is reusable is more reliable. **Reliability** is the feature of programs that assures you a module has been tested and proven to function correctly. Reliable software saves time and money. If you create the functional components of your programs as stand-alone modules and test them in your current programs, much of the work will already be done when you use the modules in future applications.

Although it is not a requirement of any programming language, it frequently makes sense to use a verb as all or part of a method's name, because methods perform some action. Typical method names begin with words such as "get," "calculate," and "display." When you program in visual languages that use screen components such as buttons and text boxes, the method names frequently contain verbs representing user actions, such as "click."

Creating a Method

Most programs consist of a main program that contains the mainline logic; this module then accesses other methods. When you create a method, you give it an identifying name. The rules for naming methods are different in every programming language, but they often are similar to the language's rules for creating identifiers for variables. In this text, method names follow these two rules used for variable names:

- Method names must be one word.
- Method names should have some meaning.

Additionally, in this text, method names are followed by a set of parentheses. This will help you distinguish method names from variable names. This style corresponds to the way methods are named in many programming languages, such as Java, C++, and C#.

When you write a method in a program, it must include the following:

- A header—A **method's header** (also called the **method declaration**) includes the method identifier and possibly other necessary identifying information.
- A body—A **method's body** contains all the statements in the method. The body is also called the **method's implementation**.
- A return statement—A method's **return statement** marks the end of the method and identifies the point at which control returns to the calling program or method.

The flowchart symbol used to call a method is a rectangle with a bar across the top. You place the name of the method you are calling inside the rectangle.

In a flowchart, you draw each method separately with its own sentinel symbols. The symbol that is the equivalent of the `start` symbol in a program contains the header for the method. The name of a method must be identical to the name used in the calling program. In a flowchart of a method, the symbol that is the equivalent of the `stop` symbol in a program does not contain "stop"; after all, the program is not ending. Instead, the method ends with a "gentler," less final term, such as `exit` or `return`. These words correctly indicate that when the method ends, the logical progression of statements will exit the method and return to the calling program. Similarly, in pseudocode, you start each method with its header, and end with a `return` or `exit` statement; the method header and return statements are vertically aligned, and all the method statements are indented between them.

Modularizing Program Logic to Avoid Unnecessary Repetition

Consider the logic in Figure 6-1, which does *not* include a method. Its generic steps might represent any actions, but you should be able to tell the steps are structured. The sequence A is followed by a selection, represented by B. The condition B starts a selection structure with a

In many programming languages, if you do not include a `return` statement at the end of a method, program control will still return to the calling program. This book follows the convention of explicitly including a `return` statement with every method.

Some programmers use a rectangle with stripes down each side to represent a method in a flowchart. This book uses the convention that if a method is prewritten or built into a language, then a rectangle with side stripes is used. If the method is one you write as part of your program, as is the case in all examples in this chapter, then a rectangle with a single stripe across the top is used.

When you call a method, the action is similar to putting a DVD player on pause. You abandon your first action (watching a video) and take care of some other task (for example, making a sandwich). When the secondary task is complete, you return to the main task exactly where you left off.

175

sequence followed by a selection when B is true, and a sequence when B is false. The second selection, represented by G, is nested within the B selection, and it contains a sequence.

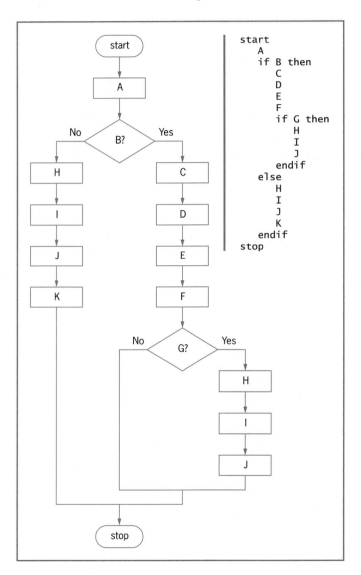

```
start
   A
   if B then
      C
      D
      E
      F
      if G then
         H
         I
         J
      endif
   else
      H
      I
      J
      K
   endif
stop
```

Figure 6-1   Sample logic

If you examine the steps in Figure 6-1, you can see that the sequence represented by H, I, and J occurs in two locations. It is perfectly acceptable to have the same tasks performed in different program locations under different conditions, but when the same tasks are repeated in different places, it can be convenient to create a method that is called at each location where it should execute.

Figure 6-2 shows the same logic as Figure 6-1, but the three statements, H, I, and J, have been contained, or **encapsulated**, into a method named methodHtoJ(). The method has its own terminals (see shading), and it contains a sequence composed of the three actions. When the logic in the original segment is ready to execute the three statements, it calls the method. (See the two shaded calls in the figure.) In the flow-chart, the method calls are represented by process symbols that con-tain a stripe across the top. When you see the stripe you understand that the symbol represents a method that might contain many steps. In the pseudocode, the method call is indicated by using the method's name when you want to call it. (Remember, you can tell it is a method because it is followed by parentheses.) In the program in Figure 6-2, the individual steps H, I, and J need only be written once, and they can be called as a unit from multiple program locations.

A method can call another method, and the called method can call another. The number of chained calls is limited only by the amount of memory available on your computer. The computer keeps track of the correct memory address to which it should return after executing a method by recording the memory address in a loca-tion known as the **stack**.

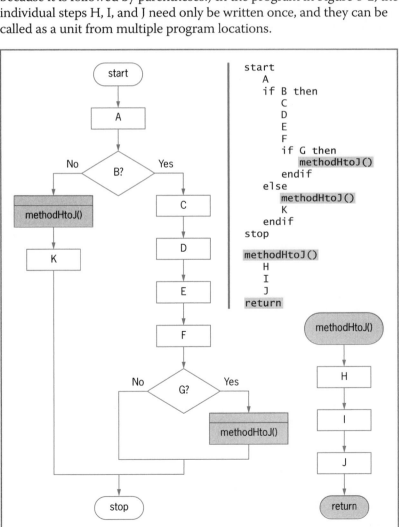

Figure 6-2 Logic from Figure 6-1 using a method

In Figure 6-3, the same logic has been modularized even further. The steps C, D, E, and F have been placed into their own method, not to save repeating them (because they are not repeated anywhere in the program), but just to group them. Just as it is more convenient for you to say "Bake a cake" than it is for you to say "Get out a mixing bowl, get a cup of sugar, get three eggs," and so on, it can be clearer and more convenient to be able to call a method name and have the specific directions listed elsewhere. Creating submethods makes the calling method's logic more concise, easier to read, and somewhat easier to identify as structured. You would not want to place steps C through F into their own method if you didn't have a good reason or if they were unrelated. But you would do so if they represent four closely related steps, and especially if they represent steps to a process that might be needed by another program in the future.

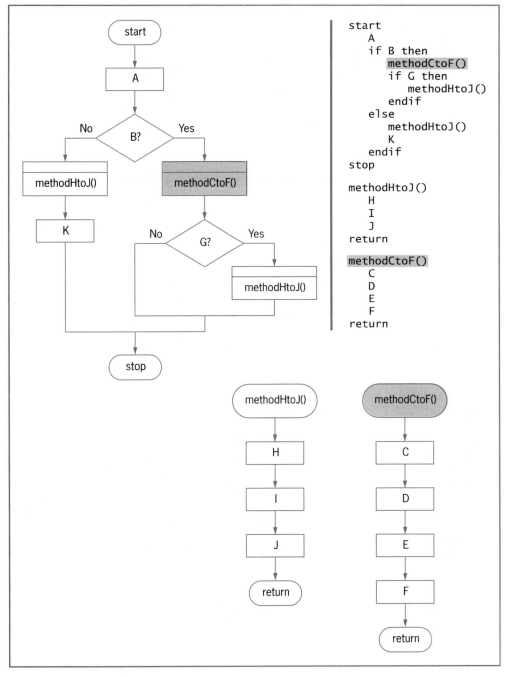

Figure 6-3 Logic from Figure 6-1 using two methods

180

Deciding which steps to place in their own methods requires experience and insight, and two programmers certainly might disagree on which steps to modularize in any given program. However, creating methods makes large programs easier to manage and, in very large programs, allows the work to be split up among multiple programmers more easily. No matter how many methods a program contains, each one must be structured, containing only some combination of sequence, selection, and loop structures, and each must be called as part of a larger program that is also structured.

None of the program segments shown in Figures 6-1, 6-2, and 6-3 is superior to the others logically; in other words, each version performs the same steps in the same order. Determining when to break down any particular method into further submodules does not depend on any fixed set of rules, but you might consider the following:

- A disadvantage to placing program statements in separate methods is that the programs might take slightly longer to execute. That's because it requires time for a program to store the location to which the logic must return when the method is finished.

- Advantages to using separate methods include being able to more easily understand, divide, and reuse the work.

Programmers follow some guidelines when deciding how far to break down subroutines, or how much to put in each of them. Some companies may have arbitrary rules, such as "a method should never have more than 30 statements in it." Rather than use such arbitrary rules, a better policy is to place together statements that contribute to one specific task.

Modularizing a Program for Functional Cohesion and Portability

Sometimes you create modules to avoid repeating instructions, but other times you create modules because the statements seem to belong together, as they constitute parts of a task. The more the statements in a method contribute to the same job, the greater the **functional cohesion** of the method. Functional cohesion is desirable, because the more cohesive the parts of a method are the more reusable and understandable the method is. A routine that checks the validity of a date variable's value, or one that prompts a user and allows the user to type in a value, is considered cohesive. A routine that checks date validity, deducts insurance premiums, and computes federal withholding tax for an employee would be less cohesive.

Consider the simple application in Figure 6-4 that accepts a customer's name and balance due and displays a bill. At the top of the bill, the company's name and address are displayed on three lines. You can simply include three output statements in the mainline logic of a program as shown in Figure 6-4, or you can create both the mainline logic and a `nameAndAddress()` method, as shown in Figure 6-5.

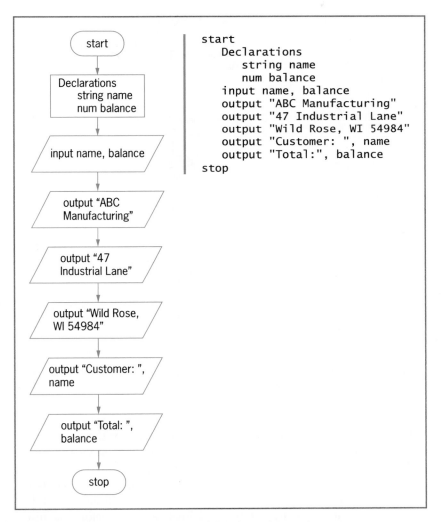

Figure 6-4 Program that outputs a bill using only a main program

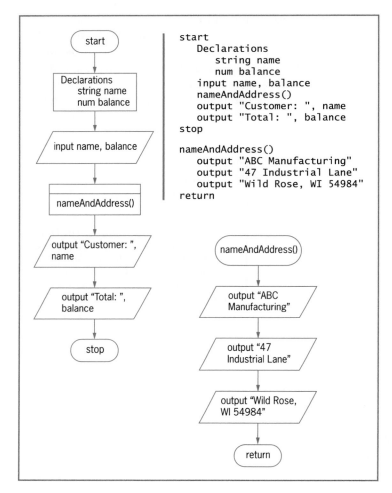

```
start                         start
                                  Declarations
                                      string name
   Declarations                      num balance
   string name                   input name, balance
   num balance                   nameAndAddress()
                                  output "Customer: ", name
                                  output "Total: ", balance
   input name, balance        stop

                              nameAndAddress()
                                  output "ABC Manufacturing"
   nameAndAddress()               output "47 Industrial Lane"
                                  output "Wild Rose, WI 54984"
                              return
   output "Customer: ",
   name                                    nameAndAddress()

   output "Total: ",                       output "ABC
   balance                                 Manufacturing"

   stop                                    output "47
                                           Industrial Lane"

                                           output "Wild Rose,
                                           WI 54984"

                                               return
```

Figure 6-5   Program that outputs a bill using main program that calls the `nameAndAddress()` method

In Figure 6-5, the `nameAndAddress()` method contains three output statements that belong together logically. When the `nameAndAddress()` method is called, logic transfers from the main program to the method. There, each method statement executes in turn, before logical control is transferred back to the main program, where it continues with the statement that follows the method call. There are two major reasons to create a separate method to display the three address lines:

- First, the main program remains short and easy to follow because it contains just one statement to call the method, rather than three separate `output` statements to perform the work of the method.

- Second, the method is easily reusable. After you create the `nameAndAddress()` method, you can use it in any application that needs the company's name and address. In other words, you do the work once, and then you can use the method many times.

Understanding Scope

The program in Figure 6-5 contains several output statements that use literal constants. As you learned in Chapter 1, your programs will be easier to maintain and modify if, in general, you use named constants to hold fixed values. You might decide to modify the program in Figure 6-5 so it looks like the one in Figure 6-6. You would declare named string constants to hold the three company address lines, and then, when you need to display the address, you would use these constants. (See the shaded portions of Figure 6-6.) However, this program will not work.

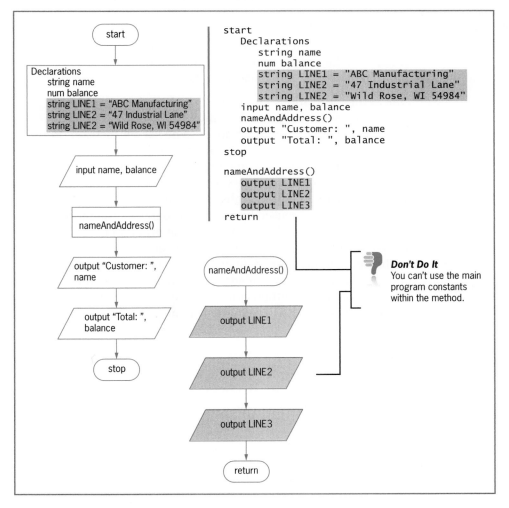

Figure 6-6 Incorrect declarations for customer billing program

In most modern programming languages, the variables and constants declared in the main program are usable only there, and any variables and constants declared within a method are usable only within that method. Programmers say the data items are **visible**, or "can be seen," only within the method or program in which they are declared. They say that variables and constants declared within a method are **in scope** only within that method. They also say that the scope of a variable or constant is **local** to the method or program in which it is declared. Local variables:

When you declare a variable, you cannot choose a physical memory location for it; the location is chosen automatically for you.

- Are created in memory when they are declared within a method or program

- Exist only while the method or program is executing

- Are destroyed when the method or program ends

- Are not known to other methods

This means that, when the strings LINE1, LINE2, and LINE3 are declared in the main program in Figure 6-6, they are not recognized and cannot be used by the nameAndAddress() method.

One of the motivations for creating methods is that you can easily reuse separate methods in multiple programs. If the nameAndAddress() method is going to be used by several programs within the organization, it makes sense that the definitions for the variables and constants it uses must come with it. If you declare variables and constants within the methods that use them, the methods are more **portable**; that is, they can more easily be transported to and reused by multiple programs. Therefore, the superior solution for the customer billing program is to create it as shown in Figure 6-7. In this version, the data items that are needed by the main program are defined in the main program, and the ones needed by the nameAndAddress() method are defined within that method. Each method contains its own data and does not "know about" the data in any other methods.

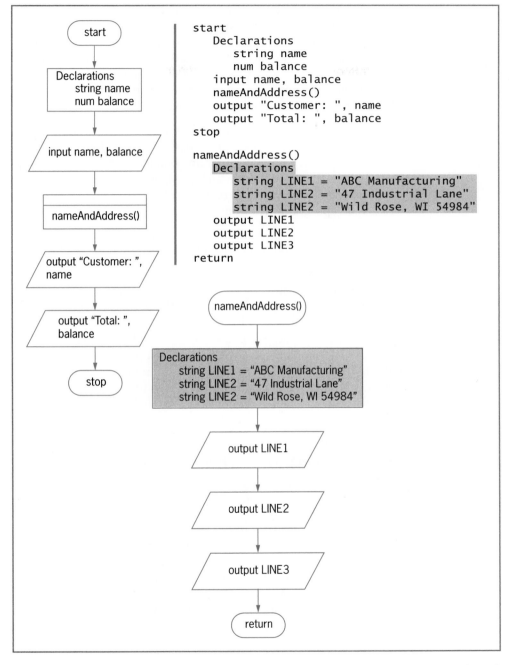

```
start
    Declarations
        string name
        num balance
    input name, balance
    nameAndAddress()
    output "Customer: ", name
    output "Total: ", balance
stop

nameAndAddress()
    Declarations
        string LINE1 = "ABC Manufacturing"
        string LINE2 = "47 Industrial Lane"
        string LINE2 = "Wild Rose, WI 54984"
    output LINE1
    output LINE2
    output LINE3
return
```

Figure 6-7   Bill-displaying program with variables and constants declared locally in each method

Besides local variables and constants, in most languages you can create global variables and constants. **Global** variables and constants are those that are known to the entire program. Variables and constants that are declared outside any method are declared at the **program level**. In general, this is not a recommended practice. However, there are a few occasions in which you might consider declaring variables and constants globally:

- If a data item will be needed in many methods throughout a program, some programmers approve of declaring it globally. For example, if a mathematical program contains many methods that require a constant for a value such as pi, or a business program contains many methods that require a standard tax or discount rate, many programmers would allow these to be declared globally.

- When you learn about object-oriented programming and create a class from which you will derive objects, you can declare the class's data fields at the class level. Chapter 7 will discuss this topic.

In most other circumstances, you should not declare global variables and constants. When you do, you violate the programming principle of **encapsulation**, which states that a task's instructions and its data should be contained in the same method. Using global variables makes it more difficult to find errors in a program, because any method might change the variable's value. Sometimes, however, two or more methods in a program require access to the same data; when this is the case, you usually do not declare global data items. Instead, you **pass the data** from one method to another.

Creating Methods That Require a Single Parameter

Some methods require information to be sent in from the outside. If a method could not receive your communications, called **parameters**, then you would have to write an infinite number of methods to cover every possible situation. As a real-life example, when you make a restaurant reservation, you do not need to employ a different method for every date of the year at every possible time of day. Rather, you can supply the date and time as information to the person who carries out the method. The method, recording the reservation, is then carried out in the same manner, no matter what date and time are involved. In a program, if you design a method to square numeric values, it makes sense to design a `square()` method that you can supply with a parameter that represents the value to be squared, rather than having to develop a `square1()` method (that squares the value 1), a `square2()` method (that squares the value 2), and so on. To call a `square()` method that accepts a parameter, you might write a statement like `square(17)` or `square(86)` and let the method use whatever value you send. When you call a method using a value within its parentheses, the value is an **argument to the method**.

Parameter and *argument* are closely related, but different, terms, similar to *emigrant* and *immigrant*. When you leave a country you are an emigrant; when a value leaves a method to go to another, it is an argument. On the other hand, when you enter a country you are an immigrant; when a value enters a method, it is a parameter. In summary:

- A calling method sends an argument to a called method; an argument appears within the parentheses of a method call.

- A called method accepts the value as its parameter; a parameter appears within the parentheses of a method header.

When you write the method declaration for a method that can receive a parameter, you must include the following items within the method declaration parentheses:

- The type of the parameter

- A local name for the parameter

For example, suppose you decide to write a program that displays the calculated sales tax on an item's price. The program in Figure 6-8 prompts the user for a price. The price is passed to the `computeTax()` method, where it is multiplied by the tax rate and displayed.

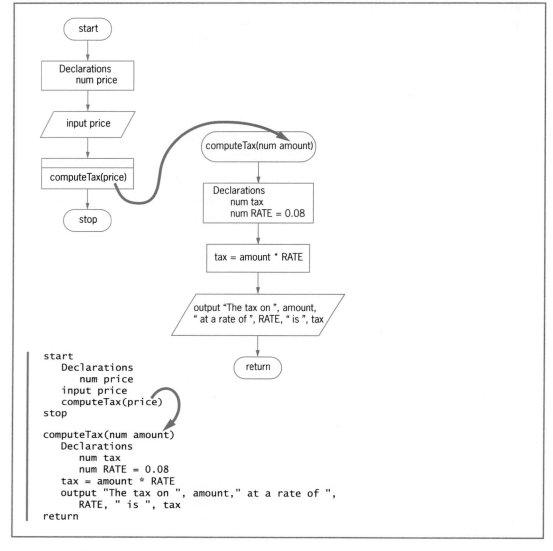

```
start
    Declarations
        num price
    input price
    computeTax(price)
stop

computeTax(num amount)
    Declarations
        num tax
        num RATE = 0.08
    tax = amount * RATE
    output "The tax on ", amount," at a rate of ",
        RATE, " is ", tax
return
```

Figure 6-8   Program that passes a price to a method to compute the sales tax

In the main program in Figure 6-8, a value is retrieved for a numeric variable named price. The value then is passed to the computeTax() method. The method call is computeTax(price), and the method declaration or header is computeTax(num amount). You can think of the parentheses in a method declaration as a funnel into the method—parameters listed there hold values that are "dropped in" to the method.

In the program in Figure 6-8, the numeric variable price is sent as an argument to the method. The parameter defined within the parentheses in the method header (num amount) indicates that the method will receive a value of type num, and that within the method, the passed value representing a price will be known as amount. Within the method, the value is used in a calculation and an output statement.

The computeTax() method could be called from the main program any number of times, if needed. It could be called using any numeric variable or constant as an argument. For example, if you declare a numeric variable named money, you can call computeTax(money). The method also could be called using a literal constant, for example computeTax(42.99). Additionally, it could be called using a numeric element that is part of an array. For example, if you have declared an array as num money[50], then you might call computeTax(money[3]), or you might call computeTax() 50 times, sending it a different array element each time. The only requirement is that each time the computeTax() method is called, it must be called using a numeric argument. Within the computeTax() method, the argument, whether variable or constant, becomes known as amount.

If the value used as an argument in the method call to computeTax() is a variable, it might possess the same identifier as amount, or a different one. Within the computeTax() method, the identifier amount is simply a temporary placeholder; it does not make any difference what name it "goes by" in the calling program.

Each time the computeTax() method in Figure 6-8 executes, an amount variable is redeclared—that is, a new memory location large enough to hold a numeric value is set up and named amount. Within the computeTax() method, amount holds whatever value is passed into the method by the main program. When the computeTax() method ends at the return statement, the local amount variable ceases to exist. A variable passed into a method is **passed by value**; that is, a copy of its value is sent to the method and stored in a new memory location accessible to the method. The memory location that holds amount is released at the end of the method, and if you were to change its value, it would not affect any variable in the calling method. In particular, don't think there would be any change in the variable named price in the main program in Figure 6-8; that variable is a different variable with its own memory address and is totally different from the one that accepts its value in the computeTax() method.

In many languages, besides passing a parameter by value, you can also pass a parameter **by reference**. This means that the method gets access to the original variable's memory address. You will learn about this technique as you study individual programming languages.

Creating Methods That Require Multiple Parameters

A method can require more than one parameter. You indicate that a method requires multiple parameters by listing their data types and local identifiers within the method header's parentheses and separating them by commas. You can pass multiple arguments from a calling method to a called method by listing the arguments within the method call and separating them with commas. For example, suppose you want to create a computeTax() method that accepts two parameters—the amount to be taxed, as well as a percentage figure by which to tax it. Figure 6-9 shows a method that uses two such arguments.

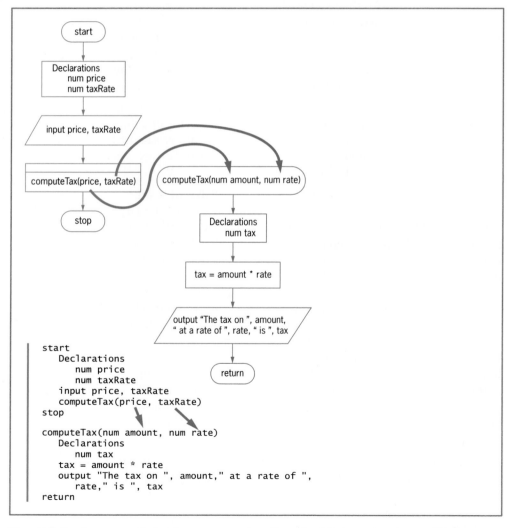

```
start
    Declarations
        num price
        num taxRate
    input price, taxRate
    computeTax(price, taxRate)
stop

computeTax(num amount, num rate)
    Declarations
        num tax
    tax = amount * rate
    output "The tax on ", amount," at a rate of ",
        rate," is ", tax
return
```

Figure 6-9 A program that calls a computeTax() method that requires two parameters

In Figure 6-9, two parameters (num amount and num rate) appear within the parentheses in the method header. A comma separates each parameter, and each requires its own declared type (in this case, both are numeric) as well as its own identifier. When values are passed to the method in a statement such as computeTax(price, taxRate), the first value passed will be referenced as amount within the method, and the second value passed will be referenced as rate. Therefore, arguments passed to the method must be passed in the correct order. A call computeTax(taxRate, price) would result in incorrect values being displayed in the output statement.

You can write a method so that it takes any number of parameters in any order. However, when you call a method, the arguments you send to a method must match in order—both in number and in type—the parameters listed in the method declaration. Thus, a method to compute an automobile salesperson's commission amount might require arguments such as a string for the salesperson's name, a number for the value of a car sold, and a number for the commission rate. The method will execute correctly only when three arguments of the correct types are sent in the correct order.

Creating Methods That Return Values

When a variable is declared within a method, it ceases to exist when the method ends—that is, it goes out of scope. When you want to retain a value that exists in a method, you can **return the value** from the method. In other words, you can send the value back to the calling method. When a method returns a value, the method must have a return type. The **return type** for a method can be any type, including numeric, string, and any other more specific types that exist in the programming language with which you are working. Of course, a method can also return nothing, in which case the return type is usually indicated as void, and the method is a **void method**. (The term *void* means "nothing" or "empty.") A method's return type is known more succinctly as a **method's type**. A method's type is indicated in front of the method name when the method is defined.

For example, a method that returns the number of hours an employee has worked might have the header num getHoursWorked(). This method returns a numeric value, so its type is num.

When a method returns a value, you usually want to use the returned value in the calling method (although using it is not required). Figure 6-10 shows how a program might use the value returned by the getHoursWorked() method. In Figure 6-10, a variable named hours is declared in the main program. The getHoursWorked() method call is part of an assignment statement. When the method

Note that a declaration for a method that receives two or more arguments must list the type for each parameter separately, even if the parameters have the same type.

When multiple parameters appear in a method header, they compose a **parameter list**. If method arguments are the same type—for example, two numeric arguments—passing them to a method in the wrong order results in a logical error; that is, the program will compile and execute, but might produce incorrect results. If a method expects arguments of diverse types, then passing arguments in the wrong order constitutes a syntax error, and the program will not compile.

The arguments sent to a method in a method call are often referred to as **actual parameters**. The variables in the method declaration that accept the values from the actual parameters are the **formal parameters**.

A method's name and parameter list constitute the method's **signature**.

is called, the logic transfers to the `getHoursWorked()` method, which contains a variable named `workHours`. A value is obtained for this variable and is returned to the main program, where it is assigned to `hours`. After the logic returns to the main program from the `getHoursWorked()` method, the method's local variable `workHours` no longer exists. However, its value has been stored in the main program, where, as `hours`, it can be displayed and used in a calculation.

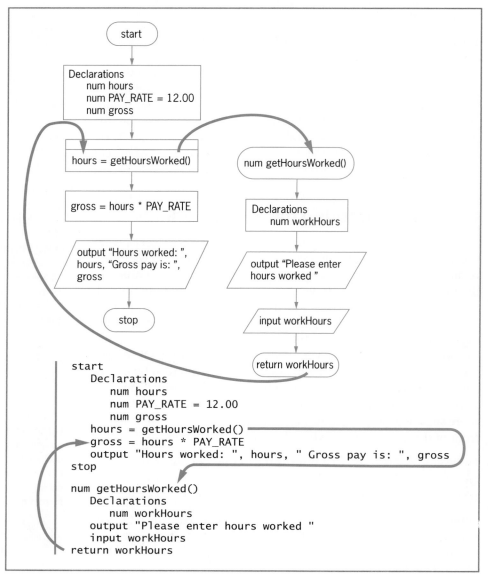

Figure 6-10   A payroll program that calls a method that returns a value

Notice the return type num that precedes the method name in the getHoursWorked() method header. A numeric value is included in the return statement that is the last statement within the getHoursWorked() method. When you place a value in a return statement, the value is sent from the called method back to the calling method. A method's declared return type must match the type of the value used in the return statement; if it does not, the program will not compile.

You are not required to assign a method's return value to a variable in order to use the value. Instead, you can choose to use a method's returned value directly, without storing it. When you use a method's value, you use it the same way you would use any variable of the same type. For example, you can display a return value in a statement such as the following:

```
output "Hours worked is ", getHoursWorked()
```

Because getHoursWorked() returns a numeric value, you can use the method call getHoursWorked() in the same way that you would use any simple numeric value. Figure 6-11 shows an example of a program that uses a method's return value directly without storing it. The shaded workHours returned from the method is used directly in the calculation of gross in the main program.

Along with an identifier and parameter list, a return type is part of a method's declaration. Some programmers claim a method's return type is part of its signature, but this is not the case. Only the method name and parameter list constitute the signature.

Up to this point, this book has not included return types for methods because all the methods have been void methods. From this point forward, a return type is included with every method.

A method's return statement can return, at most, one value. The value can be a simple data type or it can be a more complex type, for example a structure or an object. You will learn about objects in Chapter 7.

The value returned from a method is not required to be a variable. Instead, you might return a constant as in return 0.

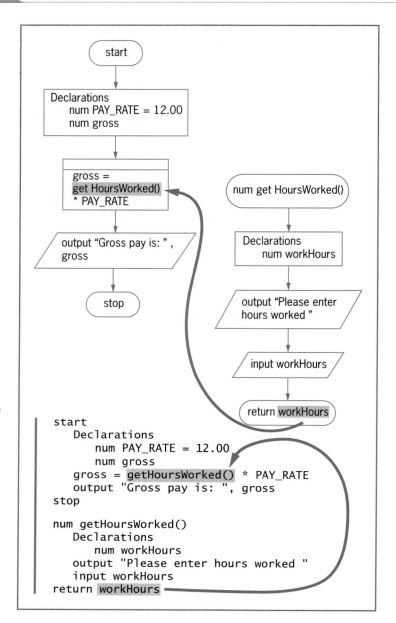

When a program needs to use a method's returned value in more than one place, it makes sense to store the returned value in a variable instead of calling the method multiple times. A program statement that calls a method requires more computer time and resources than a statement that does not call any outside methods. Programmers use the term **overhead** to describe any extra time and resources required by an operation.

Figure 6-11   A program that uses a method's returned value without storing it

In most programming languages, you are allowed to include multiple return statements in a method. For example, consider the findLargest() method in Figure 6-12. The method accepts three arguments and returns the largest of the values. Although this method works correctly (and you might see this technique used in programs written by others), it is not the recommended way to write the method. In Chapter 2, you learned that structured logic requires that each structure contain one entry point and one exit point. The return statements in Figure 6-12 violate this convention by leaving the decision structure before it is complete. Figure 6-13 shows the superior and recommended way to handle the problem. In Figure 6-13 the largest value is stored in a variable. Then, when the decision structure is complete, the stored value is returned.

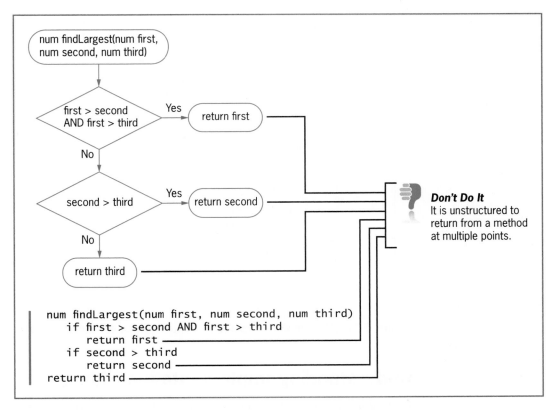

Figure 6-12 Approach not recommended for returning one of several values

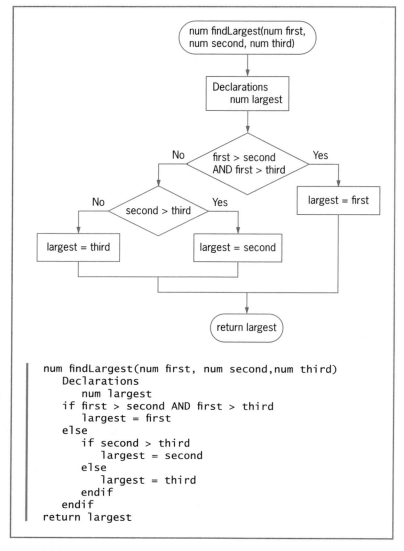

```
num findLargest(num first, num second,num third)
    Declarations
        num largest
    if first > second AND first > third
        largest = first
    else
        if second > third
            largest = second
        else
            largest = third
        endif
    endif
return largest
```

Figure 6-13   Recommended approach to returning one of several values

Understanding Implementation Hiding

An important principle of modularization is the notion of **implementation hiding**, the encapsulation of method details. That is, when you make a request to a method, you don't know the details of how the method is executed. For example, when you make a real-life restaurant reservation, you do not need to know how the reservation is actually recorded at the restaurant—perhaps it is written in a book, marked on a large chalkboard, or entered into a computerized database. The implementation details don't concern you as a patron, and if the restaurant changes its methods from one year to the next, the change does not affect your use of the reservation method. You still call and provide your name, a date, and a time. With well-written methods, using implementation hiding means that a method that calls another must know the name of the called method, what type of information to send it, and what type of return data to expect, but the program does not need to know how the method works internally. The calling method needs to understand only the **interface to the method** that is called. In other words, the interface is the only part of a method with which the method's **client** (or method's caller) interacts. Additionally, if you substitute a new, improved method implementation, as long as the interface to the method does not change, you won't need to make changes in any methods that call the altered method.

When you use methods written by others, you do not need to know how their methods are implemented. When you become a programmer for a business, perhaps many useful methods will already have been created for you by other programmers there. When you start to program in a specific language, you also will be able to take advantage of built-in methods already created for you.

Using Prewritten Built-In Methods

All modern programming languages contain many methods that have already been written for you. Methods are built into a language to save you time and effort. For example, in most languages, printing a message on the screen involves using a built-in method. When you want to display "Hello" on the command prompt screen in C#, you write the following:

```
Console.WriteLine("Hello");
```

In Java, you write:

```
System.out.println("Hello");
```

In these statements, you can recognize `WriteLine()` and `println()` as method names because they are followed by parentheses; the parentheses hold an argument that represents the message that is displayed. If these methods were not written for you, you would have to worry about the low-level details of how to manipulate pixels on a display screen to get the characters to print. Instead, by using the prewritten methods, you can concentrate on the higher-level task of displaying a useful and appropriate message.

Most programming languages also contain a variety of mathematical methods such as those that compute a square root or the absolute value of a number. Other methods perform tasks such as retrieving

Programmers often say that a method's implementation details are hidden in a **black box**. This means that you can examine what goes in and out of the method, but not the details of how it works inside.

In many environments, collections of pre-written methods are called **libraries**.

In C# the convention is to begin method names with an uppercase letter, and in Java the convention is to begin them with a lowercase letter. The `WriteLine()` and `println()` methods follow their respective language's convention.

the current date and time from the operating system or selecting a random number for you to use in a game application. These methods were written as a convenience for you—computing a square root and generating random numbers are complicated tasks, so it is convenient to have methods already written and tested and available to you when you need them. The names of the methods that perform these functions differ among programming languages, so you need to research the language's documentation to use them. Many of a language's methods are described in introductory programming language textbooks, and you can also find language documentation online.

When you want to use a prewritten, built-in method, you should know only four things:

- What the method does in general—for example, compute a square root.

- The method's name—for example, it might be `sqrt()`.

- The method's required parameters—for example, a square root method might require a single numeric parameter.

- The method's return type—for example, a square root method most likely returns a numeric value that is the square root of the argument that was passed to the method.

What you do not need to know is how the method is implemented—that is, how the instruction statements are written within it. Built-in methods are usually black boxes to you. You can use built-in methods without worrying about their low-level implementation details.

Review Questions

1. Which of the following is true?

    a. A program can call, at most, one method.

    b. A program can contain a method that calls another method.

    c. A method can contain one or more other methods.

    d. All of these are true.

2. Which of the following must every method have?

    a. a header   c. a return value

    b. a parameter list   d. all of these

3. Which of the following is most closely related to the concept of "local"?

   a. abstract

   b. object-oriented

   c. in scope

   d. program level

4. Although the terms parameter and arguments are closely related, the difference between them is that "argument" refers to _____.

   a. a passed constant

   b. a value in a method call

   c. a formal parameter

   d. a variable that is local to a method

5. The notion of _____ most closely describes the way a calling method is not aware of the statements within a called method.

   a. abstraction

   b. object-oriented

   c. implementation hiding

   d. encapsulation

6. A method's interface is its _____.

   a. signature

   b. return type

   c. identifier

   d. parameter list

7. When you write the method declaration for a method that can receive a parameter, which of the following must be included in the method declaration?

   a. the name of the argument that will be used to call the method

   b. a local name for the parameter

   c. the return value for the method

   d. all of these

8. When you use a variable name in a method call, it _____ the same name as the variable in the method header.

   a. can have

   b. cannot have

   c. must have

   d. must not have

9. Assume you have written a method with the header `void myMethod(num a, string b)`. Which of the following is a correct method call?

   a. `myMethod(12)`

   b. `myMethod(12, "Hello")`

   c. `myMethod("Goodbye")`

   d. It is impossible to tell.

10. Assume you have written a method with the header `num yourMethod(string name, num code)`. The method's type is _____.

   a. `num`   c. `num and string`

   b. `string`   d. `void`

11. Assume you have written a method with the header `string herMethod(num score, string grade)`. Also assume you have declared a numeric variable named `test`. Which of the following is a correct method call?

   a. `myMethod()`   c. `myMethod(test, test)`

   b. `myMethod(test)`   d. `myMethod(test,"A")`

12. The value used in a method's `return` statement must _____.

   a. be numeric

   b. be a variable

   c. match the data type used before the method name in the header

   d. two of the above

13. When a method receives a copy of the value stored in an argument used in the method call, it means the variable was _____.

   a. unnamed

   b. unassigned

   c. passed by value

   d. assigned its original value when it was declared

14. A `void` method _____.

   a. contains no statements   c. returns nothing

   b. requires no parameters   d. has no name

15. Which of the following is most likely to be a built-in method in a programming language?

   a. a method that computes a number's logarithm

   b. a method that produces a paycheck

   c. a method that accepts a user's name and ID number

   d. All of the above are likely to be built-in methods.

Find the Bugs

Your student disk contains files named DEBUG06-01.txt, DEBUG06-02.txt, and DEBUG06-03.txt. Each file contains pseudocode segments with one or more bugs that you must find and correct.

Exercises

1. Create the logic for a program that calculates and displays the amount of money you would have if you invested $1,000 at 5 percent interest for one year. Create a separate method to do the calculation and return the result to be displayed.

2. a. Create the logic for a program that performs arithmetic functions. Design the program to contain two numeric variables. Prompt the user for values for the variables. Pass both variables to methods named `sum()` and `difference()`. Create the logic for the methods `sum()` and `difference()`; they compute the sum of and difference between the values of two arguments, respectively. Each method should perform the appropriate computation and display the results.

   b. Add a method named `product()` to the program in Exercise 2a. The `product()` method should compute the result when multiplying two numbers, but not display the answer. Instead, it should return the answer to the calling program, which displays the answer.

3. Create the logic for a program that continuously prompts the user for a numeric number of dollars until the user enters 0. Pass each entered amount to a conversion method that displays a breakdown of the passed amount into the fewest bills; in other words, it calculates the number of 20s, 10s, 5s, and 1s needed.

4. Create the logic for a program that continuously prompts a user for a numeric value until the user enters 0. The application passes the value in turn to a method that squares the number and to a method that cubes the number. The program displays the results before prompting the user again. Create the two methods that respectively square and cube a number that is passed to them, returning the calculated value.

5. Create the logic for a program that calls a method that computes the final price for a sales transaction. The program contains variables that hold the price of an item, the salesperson's

commission expressed as a percentage, and the customer discount, expressed as a percentage. Create a `calculatePrice()` method that determines the final price and returns the value to the calling method. The `calculatePrice()` method requires three arguments: product price, salesperson commission rate, and customer discount rate. A product's final price is the original price plus the commission amount minus the discount amount; the customer discount is taken as a percentage of the total price after the salesperson commission has been added to the original price.

6. a. Create the logic for a program that calculates the due date for a bill. The program prompts the user for the month, day, and year a bill is received, then passes the data to a method that calculates the day the bill is due to be paid, which is exactly one month later. If the bill is received, for example, on March 15, 2011, the due date is April 15, 2011. However, if the bill is received on March 31, 2011, then the bill is due on April 30 because April 31 is an invalid date. From the method that calculates the date due, pass the original and calculated date in turn to a display method that displays each date with slashes between the parts of the date—for example 3/15/2011.

   b. Modify the date displaying method so it displays each date using a string for the month—for example, March 15, 2011.

7. a. Plan the logic for an insurance company's premium-determining program. The program calls a method that prompts the user for the type of policy needed—health or auto. Pass the user's response to a second method, where the premium is set—$250 for a health policy or $175 for an auto policy. Pass the premium amount to a third method for display.

   b. Modify Exercise 7a. so that the second method calls one of two additional methods—one that determines the health premium or one that determines the auto premium. The health insurance method asks users whether they smoke; the premium is $250 for smokers and $190 for nonsmokers. The auto insurance method asks users to enter the number of traffic tickets they have received in the last three years. The premium is $175 for those with three or more tickets, $140 for those with one or two tickets, and $95 for those with no tickets. Each of these two methods returns the premium amount to the second method, which sends the premium amount to the display method.

8. Find the current conversion rate for U.S. dollars to any three foreign currencies. Plan the logic for a program that allows the user to enter a dollar amount and choose to which of the three currencies to convert it. Display the answer. Each conversion should take place in its own method.

9. Plan the logic for a program that prompts a user for a customer number, stock number of item being ordered, and quantity ordered. If the customer number is not between 1000 and 7999, inclusive, continue to prompt until a valid customer number is entered. If the stock number of the item is not between 201 and 850, inclusive, continue to prompt for the stock number. Pass the stock number to a method that a colleague at your organization has written; the method's header is `num getPrice(num stockNumber)`. The `getPrice()` method accepts a stock number and returns the price of the item. Multiply the price by the quantity ordered, giving the total due. Pass the customer number and the calculated price to an already written method whose signature is `printBill(num custNum, num price)`. This method determines the customer's name and address by using the customer ID number; and it calculates the final bill, including tax, using the price. Organize your program using as many methods as you feel are appropriate. You do not need to write the `getPrice()` and `printBill()` methods—assume they have already been written.

10. Create the logic for an application that contains an array of five multiple-choice quiz questions related to the topic of your choice. Each question contains four answer choices. Also create a parallel array that holds the correct answer to each question—A, B, C, or D. In turn, pass each question to a method that displays the question and accepts the player's answer. If the player does not enter a valid answer choice, force the player to reenter the answer. Return the valid answer to the main program. After the answer is returned to the main program, pass it and the correct answer to a method that determines whether they are equal and displays an appropriate message. After the user answers all the questions, display the number of correct and incorrect answers.

CHAPTER 7

Object-Oriented Programming

After completing this chapter you will be able to:

- ◎ Explain some basic principles of object-oriented programming
- ◎ Define a class
- ◎ Instantiate an object
- ◎ Distinguish between public and private access
- ◎ Describe inheritance
- ◎ Describe polymorphism
- ◎ Describe encapsulation
- ◎ Describe the advantages of object-oriented programming

An Overview of Some Principles of Object-Oriented Programming

Object-oriented programming (OOP) is a style of programming that focuses on an application's data and the methods you need to manipulate that data. Object-oriented programming uses all of the concepts you are familiar with from modular procedural programming, such as variables, modules, and passing values to modules. Modules in object-oriented programs continue to use sequence, selection, and looping structures and make use of arrays. However, object-oriented programming adds several new concepts to programming and involves a different way of thinking.

In object-oriented terminology, an **object** is one concrete example of a class, and a **class** is a term that describes a group of objects with common properties. A **class definition** describes what attributes its objects will have and what those objects will be able to do. In other words, a class definition describes data and methods. When you define a class you write definitions for its data members in the same way you have defined variables in other programs (using a data type and identifier). You write methods in the same way you have written other methods (using a return type, identifier, optional parameter list, and a method body including a return statement).

For example, `Automobile` is a class of objects. `Automobile` objects contain data or attributes such as a make, model, year, and color. `Automobile` objects also have access to methods such as going forward, going in reverse, and being filled with gasoline. As another example, `Dog` is a class of objects. `Dog` objects contain data such as a breed, name, age, and whether its shots are current. `Dog` objects also have access to methods such as eating and running.

An **instance** of a class is an existing object of a class. For example, my car is one instance of the `Automobile` class and my neighbor's car is another. Every individual `Dog` is an instance of the `Dog` class. Figure 7-1 shows the relationship of some `Dog` objects to the `Dog` class.

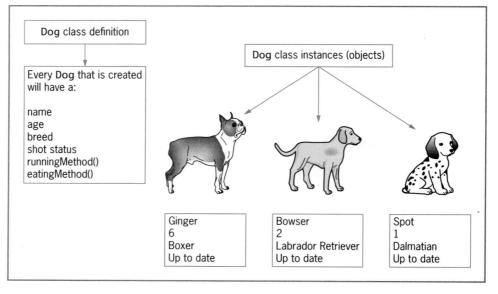

Figure 7-1 A class definition and some objects created from it

For a language to be considered object-oriented, it must include classes and objects. Additionally, it must support three features: polymorphism, inheritance, and encapsulation. Because these three features are so important to object-oriented programming, programmers use the acronym PIE to remember them. You will learn about these features later in this chapter.

When you program in object-oriented languages, you frequently create classes from which objects will be instantiated. Creating an object is called **instantiating** it. (The term comes from the word *instance*; every object is one instance of its class.) You also write applications to use the objects, along with their data and methods. Often, you will write programs that use classes created by others; other times, you might create a class that other programmers will use to instantiate objects within their own programs. A program or class that instantiates objects of another prewritten class is a **class client** or **class user**. For example, your organization might already have written a class named `Customer` that contains attributes such as `name`, `address`, and `phoneNumber`, and you might create clients that include arrays of thousands of `Customer`s. Similarly, in a graphical user interface (GUI) operating environment, you might write applications that include prewritten components that are members of classes with names like `Window` and `Button`. You expect each component on a GUI screen to have specific, consistent attributes, such as a button being clickable or a window being closeable, because each component gains these attributes as a member of its general class.

Defining a Class

A class definition is a set of program statements that tell you the characteristics that each object will have and the methods they can use. In the same way that a blueprint exists before any houses are built from it, and a recipe exists before any cookies are baked from it, so does a class definition exist before any objects are instantiated from it.

A class definition can contain three parts:

- Every class has a name.
- Most classes contain data, although this is not required. Each data variable that exists for every object is called an **instance variable**. Each is also called a **field**.
- Most classes contain methods, although this is not required. Each method that each object can use is an **instance method**.

For example, you can create a class named `Employee`. Each `Employee` object will represent one employee in an organization. Data members, or attributes, of the `Employee` class include the fields `name` and `payRate`. Appropriate methods for an `Employee` class might include `setName()`, `setPayRate()`, `getName()`, and `getPayRate()`. With object-oriented languages, you think of the class name, data, and methods as a single encapsulated unit. Figure 7-2 shows pseudocode for an `Employee` class definition.

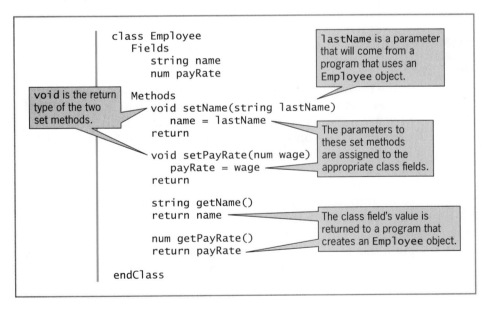

Figure 7-2   The `Employee` class

The syntax used to declare a class differs among programming languages, but for the purposes of the pseudocode, the class in Figure 7-2 begins with the word `class` and ends with `endClass`. The class is divided into two sections—fields and methods. The fields are defined just like other variables you have seen—with a data type and an identifier. Then all the methods are listed.

Set methods are also called **mutator methods**, because they change values within an object.

In the `Employee` class, the `setName()` and `setPayRate()` methods are examples of **set methods**. Their purpose is to assign values to fields of any objects created from the class.

The `setName()` method accepts a string as a parameter. The parameter, locally known as `lastName`, is assigned to the `name` field in the class. Notice, the `setName()` method does not return any values. Because the `setName()` method is a member of the `Employee` class, it has access to the `name` field and can assign a value there.

The `setPayRate()` method accepts a numeric parameter, known locally as `wage`. This value is assigned to the `payRate` field. Like the `setName()` method, the `setPayRate()` method does not need to return any value; it can assign a value to `payRate` by virtue of belonging to the same class.

Both the `setName()` and `setPayRate()` methods are short, and simply assign values. In a more fully developed class, these methods might place restrictions on the values assigned. For example, if the wage passed into the `setPayRate()` method was less than a company minimum or more than a company maximum, a default value might be assigned to `payRate`. The role of some methods in a class is to control the quality of the data that is stored.

Get methods are also called **accessor methods**, because they access an object's values.

In the `Employee` class, the `getName()` and `getPayRate()` methods are **get methods**. Their purpose is to pass the data stored in a field back to a client program. The get methods in this `Employee` class simply return an object's values, but in a more fully developed class, they might do more. For example, the `getName()` method might ensure the first letter in the name is an uppercase letter before returning it, or the `getPayRate()` method might perform some arithmetic with the `payRate` value before returning it. The role of some methods in a class is to control access to data. In fact, if the designers of the `Employee` class deemed that no client program should ever know an `Employee`'s `payRate`, the designers could just omit the `getPayRate()` method.

Instantiating an Object

Declaring a class does not create any actual objects. A class is just an abstract description of what an object will be like if any objects are ever actually instantiated. When you declare a simple variable that is a built-in data type, you write a statement that uses a data type and an identifier. When you write a program that declares an object that is a class data type, you also write a statement that uses a data type and an identifier. Consider these three declarations:

```
num someMoney
string aWord
Employee myAssistant
```

In other words, `Employee` is a data type similar to the way `num` and `string` are data types, and `Employee` defines what operations can be carried out with `myAssistant` in the same way that `num` and `string` define what operations can be carried out with `someMoney` and `aWord` respectively.

When you declare the `myAssistant` object, the object contains all the data fields and has access to all the methods contained within the class. In other words, a larger section of memory is set aside than when you declare a simple variable, because an `Employee` contains several fields. You can use any of an `Employee`'s methods with the `myAssistant` object. The usual syntax is to provide an object name, a dot (period), and a method name. For example, you can write a program that contains statements such as the ones shown in the pseudo-code in Figure 7-3. The output shows how the name and pay rate are accessed for the `myAssistant` object.

```
start
   Declarations
      Employee myAssistant
   myAssistant.setName("Reynolds")
   myAssistant.setPayRate(16.75)
   output "My assistant ", myAssistant.getName(),
      " makes ", myAssistant.getHourlyWage(),
      " per hour"
stop
```

```
Command Prompt                                    _ □ X

My assistant Reynolds makes 16.75 per hour
```

Besides referring to `Employee` as a class, many programmers would refer to it as a **user-defined type**; a more accurate term is **programmer-defined type**. Object-oriented programmers typically refer to a class like `Employee` as an **abstract data type** (ADT); this term implies that the type's data can be accessed only through methods.

Figure 7-3 Application that declares and uses an `Employee` object and program output

When you write a statement such as `myAssistant.setPayRate(16.75)`, you are making a call to a method that is contained within the `Employee` class. Because `myAssistant` is an `Employee` object, it is allowed to use the `setPayRate()` method that is part of its class.

The program segment in Figure 7-3 is very short. In a more useful real-life program, you might read employee data from a data file before assigning it to the object's fields, each Employee might contain dozens of fields, and your application might create hundreds or thousands of objects.

When you write the application in Figure 7-3, you do not need to know what statements are written within the Employee class methods, although you could make an educated guess based on the methods' names. Before you could execute the application in Figure 7-3, someone would have to write appropriate statements within the Employee class methods. If you wrote the methods, of course you would know their contents, but if another programmer has already written the methods, then you could use the application without knowing the details contained in the methods. In the client program segment in Figure 7-3, the focus is on the object—the Employee named myAssistant—and the methods you can use with that object. This is the essence of object-oriented programming.

Understanding Public and Private Access

When you buy a product with a warranty, one of the conditions of the warranty is usually that the manufacturer must perform all repair work. For example, if your computer has a warranty and something goes wrong with its operation, you cannot open the system unit yourself, remove and replace parts, and then expect to get your money back for a device that does not work properly. Instead, when something goes wrong with your computer, you must take the device to a technician approved by the manufacturer. The manufacturer guarantees that your machine will work properly only if the manufacturer can control how the internal mechanisms of the machine are modified.

Similarly, in object-oriented design, usually you do not want any outside programs or methods to alter your class's data fields unless you have control over the process. For example, you might design a class that performs a complicated statistical analysis on some data and stores the result. You would not want others to be able to alter your carefully crafted result. As another example, you might design a class from which others can create an innovative and useful GUI screen object. In this case you would not want others altering the dimensions of your artistic design.

To prevent outsiders from changing your data fields in ways you do not endorse, you force other programs and methods to use a method that is part of the class, such as setName() and setPayRate(), to alter data. Object-oriented programmers usually specify that their data fields will have **private access**—that is, the data cannot be accessed by any method that is not part of the class. The methods themselves, like setPayRate(), support **public access**—which means that other programs and methods may use the methods that control access to the private data. Figure 7-4 shows a complete Employee class to which the access specifier has been added to describe each attribute and method. An **access specifier** (or **access modifier**) is the adjective that defines the type of access that outside classes will have to the attribute or method (`public` or `private`). In the figure, each access specifier is shaded.

```
class Employee
    Fields
        private string name
        private num payRate

    Methods
        public void setName(string lastName)
            name = lastName
        return

        public void setPayRate(num wage)
            payRate = wage
        return

        public string getName()
        return name

        public num getPayRate()
        return payRate

endClass
```

Figure 7-4 `Employee` class including `public` and `private` access specifiers

In many object-oriented programming languages, if you do not declare an access specifier for a data field or method, then it is private by default. This book follows the convention of explicitly specifying access for every class member.

211

In Figure 7-4, each of the data fields is private; that means each field is inaccessible to an object declared in a program. In other words, if a program declares an `Employee` object, such as `Employee myAssistant`, then the following statement is illegal:

`myAssistant.payRate = 15.00` ⎯⎯⎯

Don't Do It
A program cannot alter a private field.

Instead, `payRate` can be assigned only through a public method as follows:

`myAssistant.setPayRate(15.00)`

If you made `payRate` public instead of private, then a direct assignment statement would work, but you would violate an important principle of OOP—that of **data hiding**. According to the principle of data hiding, data fields should usually be private, and a client application should be able to access them only through the public interfaces, that is, through the class's public methods. That way, if you have restrictions on the value of `payRate`, those restrictions will be enforced by the public method that acts as an interface to the

In Chapter 6 you learned that the interface to a method is the only portion an outside client "sees." Similarly, public methods in a class are the only interfaces to the class's data.

private data field. Even when a field has no data value requirements or restrictions, making data private and providing public set and get methods establishes a framework that makes such modifications easier in the future.

Usually, data fields are private and methods are public, but you might choose to make some exceptions. Consider the revised Employee class in Figure 7-5. This class contains a new private field, weeklyPay, and two new methods that use the field.

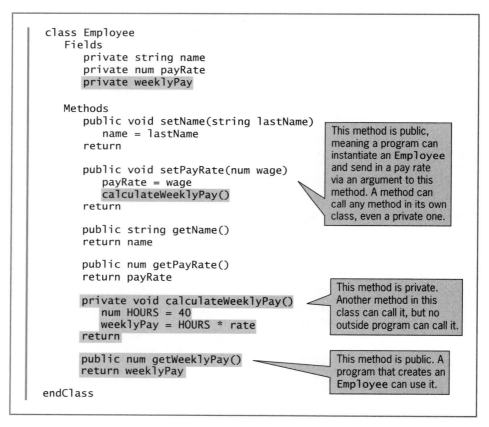

```
class Employee
    Fields
        private string name
        private num payRate
        private weeklyPay

    Methods
        public void setName(string lastName)
            name = lastName
        return

        public void setPayRate(num wage)
            payRate = wage
            calculateWeeklyPay()
        return

        public string getName()
        return name

        public num getPayRate()
        return payRate

        private void calculateWeeklyPay()
            num HOURS = 40
            weeklyPay = HOURS * rate
        return

        public num getWeeklyPay()
        return weeklyPay
endClass
```

This method is public, meaning a program can instantiate an Employee and send in a pay rate via an argument to this method. A method can call any method in its own class, even a private one.

This method is private. Another method in this class can call it, but no outside program can call it.

This method is public. A program that creates an Employee can use it.

Figure 7-5   The Employee class with an added weeklyPay field and associated methods

In the Employee class in Figure 7-5, the calculateWeeklyPay() method is private. That means if you write a program and declare an Employee object such as Employee myAssistant, then the following statement is not permitted:

myAssistant.calculateWeeklyPay()

Don't Do It
The calculateWeeklyPay() method is not accessible outside the class.

Because it is private, the only way to call the `calculateWeeklyPay()` method is from within another method that already belongs to the class. In this example, it is called from the `setPayRate()` method. This prevents any client program from setting `payRate` to one value while setting `weeklyPay` to some incompatible value. By making the `calculateWeeklyPay()` method private, you ensure that the class retains full control over when and how it is used.

Understanding Inheritance

An important feature of object-oriented programs is **inheritance**—the ability to create classes that take on the attributes and methods of existing classes, but with more specific features. When you create a new class using inheritance, you **extend** the existing class. For example, `Automobile` is a class, and all `Automobile` objects share many traits and abilities. `Convertible` is a class that inherits from the `Automobile` class. A `Convertible` is a type of `Automobile` that has and can do everything a "plain" `Automobile` does but with an added mechanism for and an added ability to lower its top. (In turn, `Automobile` inherits from the `Vehicle` class.) `Convertible` is not an object—it is a class. A specific `Convertible` is an object—for example `my1967BlueMustangConvertible`.

Inheritance helps you understand real-world objects. For example, the first time you encounter a `Convertible`, you already understand how the ignition, brakes, door locks, and other `Automobile` systems work. You need to be concerned only with the attributes and methods that are "new" with a `Convertible`. The advantages in programming are the same—you can build new classes based on existing classes and concentrate on the specialized features you are adding.

Suppose your organization decides to hire a team of salespeople who, besides regular pay, make additional pay based on a percentage of the sales they generate for the company. You could design a `Salesperson` class that includes attributes such as `name`, `payRate`, `weeklyPay`, and `commissionRate`, and all the methods associated with those fields, but you would be recreating a lot of work that has already been done for the `Employee` class. Instead of starting from scratch, you might choose to have the `Salesperson` class inherit from the `Employee` class. Figure 7-6 shows a class definition for `Salesperson`.

```
class Salesperson inheritsFrom Employee
    Fields
        private num commissionRate

    Methods
        public void setCommissionRate(num rate)
            commissionRate = rate
        return

        public num getCommissionRate()
        return commissionRate

endClass
```

Figure 7-6   The Salesperson class

Figure 7-6 indicates the Salesperson class inherits from Employee. That means that every Salesperson has all the attributes an Employee has (name, payRate, and weeklyPay) even though you don't see those fields defined in the Salesperson class. Besides those Employee attributes, a Salesperson has one other attribute—commissionRate. Additionally, every Salesperson object can use all Employee methods as well as its own. A class like Employee is called a **base class parent class**, or **superclass**. A class that inherits from a base class, such as Salesperson, is a **derived class, child class**, or **subclass**.

Depending on your needs, you might create a lengthy chain of inheritance. For example, the Employee class might be parent to a Salesperson class, which in turn might be parent to InsideSalesperson (where the customer contacts the salesperson) and OutsideSalesperson (where the salesperson contacts customers) classes. Each class that is used as a base class can have any number of classes derived from it.

Using inheritance saves you time writing and testing code. When you use inheritance you can reuse well-established features of parent classes, and you must only create new features for your derived classes.

Understanding Polymorphism

Another important concept in object-oriented terminology is polymorphism. **Polymorphism**, which means "many forms," describes a language's ability to process objects differently depending on each object's data type. It is the feature of languages that allows the same word or symbol to be interpreted correctly in different situations based on the context. For example, in English the verb "run" means different things if you use it with "a footrace," a "business," or "a computer." You understand the meaning of "run" based on the other words used with it. Object-oriented programs frequently are written so that a method can work appropriately based on the context.

In some languages, a derived class can have more than one parent. For example, suppose you have a Book class and a CD class. If you manufacture books on CD, you might want to inherit the features of both. This capability is called **multiple inheritance**, but not all programming languages support it.

214

As an example, suppose your organization hires employees who are paid for 20 hours of work each week. PartTimeEmployees need the attributes and most of the methods of the Employee class, so it would be convenient to inherit from Employee, but the Employee calculateWeeklyPay() method is not appropriate for a PartTimeEmployee. The solution is to create a PartTimeEmployee class as shown in Figure 7-7. PartTimeEmployee inherits from Employee, and inherits all its fields and methods, except for one. The PartTimeEmployee calculateWeeklyPay() method **overrides** the version in the base class because it has the same name and parameter list. The difference in the method in PartTimeEmployee is in the shaded statement within the method. When you write a program that instantiates Employee objects, the pay will be calculated based on a 40-hour work week, but when you write a program that instantiates PartTimeEmployee objects, the derived class method will be used, and pay will be calculated based on a 20-hour week.

In Chapter 6, you learned that a method's name and parameter list constitute the method's signature.

```
class PartTimeEmployee inheritsFrom Employee
    Methods
        private void calculateWeeklyPay(num rate)
            num HOURS = 20
            weeklyPay = HOURS * rate
        return
endClass
```

Figure 7-7   The PartTimeEmployee class

Because the same method name works appropriately for different object types, your programs are easier to write and clearer for others to read. The advantages of polymorphism will become especially apparent when you begin to create GUI applications containing features such as windows, buttons, and menu bars. In GUI languages, all these objects derive from a common class with a name such as Component. In a GUI application, it is convenient to remember one method name, such as setColor() or setHeight(), and have it work correctly no matter what type of object you are modifying.

When you see a plus sign (+) between two numbers, you understand they are being added. When you see it after an "A" grade on an exam, you are pleased. When you see it carved in a tree between two names, you understand the names are linked romantically. Because the plus symbol has diverse meanings based on context, it is polymorphic.

Understanding Encapsulation

In Chapter 6, you learned that encapsulation is used to describe the act of enclosing data and instructions in a method, making the method portable. Similarly, classes encapsulate data and methods. When you create a class such as Employee, and declare an Employee object, you declare all the data fields and methods that belong to Employee in one declaration statement. Consider an Employee class that contains 30 fields. If you could not encapsulate that data, and you wanted to write a program that passed `Employee` data to a method for display, you would have to pass 30 separate arguments. By encapsulating the data, you pass one argument. Similarly, if you did not encapsulate `Employee` data but maintained separate variables for name, salary, and so on, and you wanted to create arrays that associated each employee's name with the data in all the other variables, you would need 30 parallel arrays. When you create `Employee` objects, you just need one array of `Employee`s.

Figure 7-8 shows a program that declares an `Employee` array and, in turn, passes each object to a method that gets data for the objects. Then, in turn, the program passes each object to a method that displays the data. This program would be more difficult to write and understand if you could not encapsulate the `Employee` data into objects.

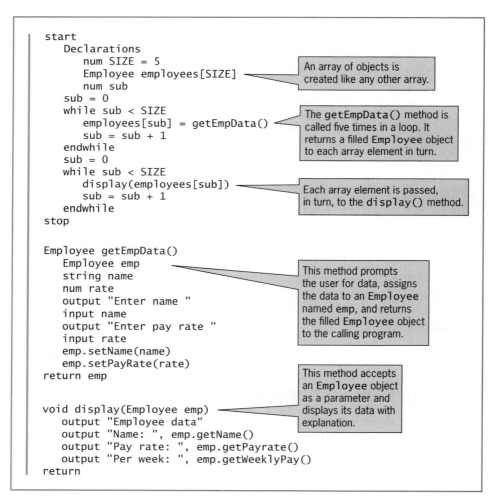

```
start
   Declarations
      num SIZE = 5
      Employee employees[SIZE]          An array of objects is
      num sub                            created like any other array.
   sub = 0
   while sub < SIZE
      employees[sub] = getEmpData()     The getEmpData() method is
      sub = sub + 1                      called five times in a loop. It
   endwhile                              returns a filled Employee object
   sub = 0                               to each array element in turn.
   while sub < SIZE
      display(employees[sub])           Each array element is passed,
      sub = sub + 1                      in turn, to the display() method.
   endwhile
stop

Employee getEmpData()
   Employee emp
   string name                          This method prompts
   num rate                              the user for data, assigns
   output "Enter name "                  the data to an Employee
   input name                            named emp, and returns
   output "Enter pay rate "              the filled Employee object
   input rate                            to the calling program.
   emp.setName(name)
   emp.setPayRate(rate)
return emp                              This method accepts
                                         an Employee object
                                         as a parameter and
void display(Employee emp)              displays its data with
   output "Employee data"               explanation.
   output "Name: ", emp.getName()
   output "Pay rate: ", emp.getPayrate()
   output "Per week: ", emp.getWeeklyPay()
return
```

Figure 7-8   Program that passes `Employee` data to and from methods

216

In the main program in Figure 7-8 an array of five `Employee` objects is declared. Then, in a loop, the `getEmpData()` method is called. Within the method, a temporary `Employee` object is created. The user is prompted for a name and pay rate, and these are assigned to the temporary object using the `Employee` class `setName()` and `setPayRate()` methods. The filled `Employee` object is then returned to the main program, where it is assigned into the array. Remember that a method can return only one item of a data type that matches the return type listed in the method's header. By returning an encapsulated `Employee`, you get to return several pieces of data in one package.

After the first loop in the program in Figure 7-8 ends, a second loop sends each array element to a `display()` method. If `Employee` data was not encapsulated, the parameter list for the method would have to include each field, but because an `Employee` is an encapsulated object, the values are passed in one package.

Advantages of Object-Oriented Programming

At some point, you might have taken a few days to organize your garage or kitchen. It is a lot of work up front, but after the organization is complete, working in those environments becomes easier. Object-oriented programming is similar. Although at first, OOP seems to add a layer of complexity to programming logic, after you master it, understanding program logic and working with programs become easier.

When you design programs using object-oriented principles:

- Objects are separate, like objects in the real world, so each object's features are separate (encapsulated) from all others. Objects are easier to modify, reuse, and manipulate than all their separate data fields and methods would be.

- Objects are easy to understand, like objects in the real word. When you learn how to drive your first car, you automatically know how to drive other cars. A few minor features of a new car might differ from the car in which you learned to drive, but the principles are the same. Because of polymorphism, when you learn how to manipulate an object in a program, you automatically know how to manipulate similar objects. Even though their methods might execute differently, the methods with the same interface that belong to different objects execute appropriately.

- Objects are extensible, meaning one object can inherit characteristics from another, like objects in the real world. When automobile manufacturers create an improved windshield wiper or gas cap, they do not start from scratch, but instead base the new design on existing templates. Similarly, your work as a programmer is reduced when you can employ inheritance by extending existing class features as you construct new classes.

Object-oriented programming is a complicated subject, and you have many more details to learn before you are an expert. However, with what you have learned in this chapter, you have a solid foundation in understanding how to use a major model of programming logic and design.

Review Questions

1. Which of the following means the same as *object*?

    a. class   c. instance

    b. field   d. category

2. Which of the following means the same as *instance variable*?

    a. field   c. category

    b. instance   d. class

3. A program that instantiates objects of another prewritten class is a(n) _____.

    a. object   c. instance

    b. client   d. GUI

4. A(n) _____ is like a blueprint that describes the attributes and methods of a class.

    a. object   c. class definition

    b. instance   d. object characterization

5. Every class definition must contain _____.

    a. a name   c. methods

    b. data   d. all of the above

6. Assume a working program contains the following statement:

   `myDog.setName("Bowser")`

   Which of the following do you know?

   a. `setName()` is a public method

   b. `setName()` accepts a string parameter

   c. both of these

   d. none of these

7. Which of the following is the most likely scenario for a specific class?

   a. Its data fields are private and its methods are public.

   b. Its data fields are public and its methods are private.

   c. Its data fields and methods are both public.

   d. Its data fields and methods are both private.

8. Assume you have created a class named Dog that contains a data field named `weight` and an instance method named `setWeight()`. Further assume the `setWeight()` method is public and accepts a numeric parameter named `pounds`. Which of the following statements correctly sets a Dog's weight within the `setWeight()` method?

   a. `weight = pounds`   c. either of these

   b. `pounds = weight`   d. none of these

9. An object can be _____.

   a. stored in an array   c. returned from a method

   b. passed to a method   d. all of the above

10. The process of acquiring the traits of one's predecessors is _____.

    a. inheritance   c. polymorphism

    b. encapsulation   d. orientation

11. Advantages of creating a class that inherits from another include all of the following except _____.

    a. You save time because subclasses are created automatically from those that come built-in as part of a programming language.

b. You save time because you need not recreate the fields and methods in the original class.

c. You reduce the chance of errors because the original class's methods have already been used and tested.

d. You make it easier for anyone who has used the original class to understand the new class.

12. Employing inheritance reduces errors because _____.

a. the new classes have access to fewer data fields

b. the new classes have access to fewer methods

c. you can copy and paste methods that you already created

d. many of the methods you need have already been used and tested

13. A class that is used as a basis for inheritance is called a _____ class.

a. derived class   c. child class

b. subclass   d. base class

14. A class that has inherited from another is a _____ class.

a. derived class   c. base class

b. superclass   d. parent class

15. The feature that describes how a method named `register()` works appropriately and correctly for both a `WashingtonSchoolStudent` and a `LincolnSchoolStudent` is known as _____.

a. inheritance   c. polymorphism

b. encapsulation   d. orientation

Find the Bugs

Your student disk contains files named DEBUG07-01.txt and DEBUG07-02.txt. Each file contains pseudocode segments with one or more bugs that you must find and correct.

Exercises

1. Identify three objects that might belong to each of the following classes:

   a. `Automobile`

   c. `CollegeCourse`

   b. `NovelAuthor`

   d. `BankTransaction`

2. Identify three different classes that might contain each of these objects:

   a. Wolfgang Amadeus Mozart

   b. my pet cat named Socks

   c. apartment 14 at 101 Main Street

   d. the final exam for this course

3. Name three classes that might derive from each of these classes:

   a. `Student`

   c. `School`

   b. `Tree`

   d. `Country`

4. Name a base class from which each of these classes might have been derived:

   a. `Student`   b. `Tree`   c. `School`

5. Design a class named `CustomerRecord` that holds a customer number, name, and address. Include methods to get and set the values for each data field.

6. Design a class named `House` that holds the street address, price, number of bedrooms, and number of baths in a `House`. Include methods to get and set the values for each data field.

7. Design a class named `Loan` that holds an account number, name of account holder, amount borrowed, term, and interest rate. Include methods to get and set values for each data field.

8. Complete the following tasks:

   a. Design a class named `Book` that holds a stock number, author, title, price, and number of pages for a book. Include methods to set and get the values for each data field.

   b. Design an application that declares two `Book` objects and sets and displays their values.

c. Design an application that declares an array of 10 Books. Prompt the user for data for each of the Books, and then display all the values.

d. Design a class named TextBook that is a child class of Book. Include a new data field for the grade level of the book. Override the Book class display method so that you accommodate the new grade-level field.

e. Design an application that instantiates a Book and a TextBook and demonstrates all the methods of each class.

9. Complete the following tasks:

a. Design a class named Player that holds a player number and name for a sports team participant. Include methods to set the values for each data field and print the values for each data field.

b. Design two classes named BaseballPlayer and BasketballPlayer that are child classes of Player. Include a new data field in each class for the player's position. Include an additional field in the BaseballPlayer class for batting average. Include a new field in the BasketballPlayer class for free-throw percentage.

c. Design an application that instantiates an object of each type and demonstrates all the methods.

10. a. Playing cards are used in many computer games, including versions of such classics as Solitaire, Hearts, and Poker. Design a Card class that contains a string data field to hold a suit (spades, hearts, diamonds, or clubs) and an integer data field for a value from 1 to 13. Include get and set methods for each field. Write an application that randomly selects two playing cards and displays their values.

b. Using two Card objects, design an application that plays a very simple version of the card game War. Deal two Cards—one for the computer and one for the player—and determine the higher card, then display a message indicating whether the cards are equal, the computer won, or the player won. (In this game, playing cards are considered equal when they have the same value, no matter what their suit is.) For this game, assume the ace (value 1) is low. Make sure that the two Cards dealt are not the same Card. For example, a deck cannot contain more than one Card representing the 2 of spades.

11. a. Computer games often contain different characters or creatures. For example, you might design a game in which alien beings possess specific characteristics such as color, number of eyes, or number of lives. Create an `Alien` class. Include at least three data members of your choice. Get and set methods for each field.

   b. Create two classes—`Martian` and `Jupiterian`—that descend from `Alien`. Supply each with methods that override the `Alien` set methods to force `Martian` and `Jupiterian` object data fields with default values of your choice. For example, you can decide that a `Martian` has four eyes but a `Jupiterian` has only two.

   c. Create an application that instantiates one `Martian` and one `Jupiterian` and set and display their data.

Understanding Numbering Systems and Computer Codes

The numbering system with which you are most familiar is the decimal system—the system based on 10 digits, 0 through 9. When you use the decimal system, there are no other symbols available; if you want to express a value larger than 9, you must resort to using multiple digits from the same pool of 10, placing them in columns.

When you use the decimal system, you analyze a multicolumn number by mentally assigning place values to each column. The value of the rightmost column is 1, the value of the next column to the left is 10, the next column is 100, and so on, multiplying the column value by 10 as you move to the left. There is no limit to the number of columns you can use; you simply keep adding columns to the left as you need to express higher values. For example, Figure A-1 shows how the value 305 is represented in the decimal system. You simply sum the value of the digit in each column after it has been multiplied by the value of its column.

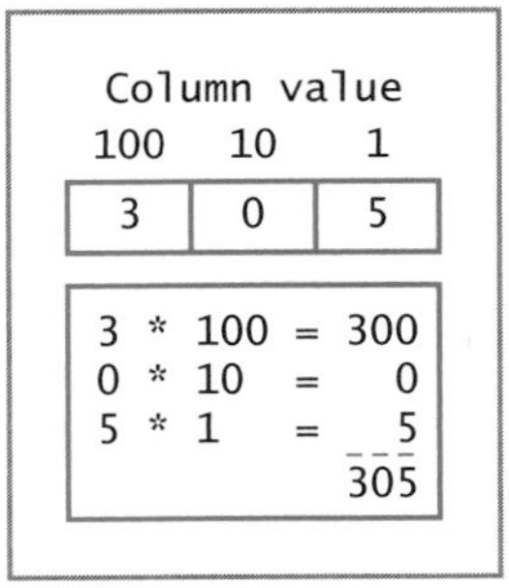

```
       Column value
    100    10     1
  +-----+-----+-----+
  |  3  |  0  |  5  |
  +-----+-----+-----+

    3 * 100 = 300
    0 *  10 =   0
    5 *  1  =   5
             -----
              305
```

Figure A-1 Representing 305 in the decimal system

The binary numbering system works in the same way as the decimal numbering system, except that it uses only two digits, 0 and 1. When you use the binary system, if you want to express a value greater than 1, you must resort to using multiple columns, because no single symbol is available that represents any value other than 0 or 1. However, instead of each new column to the left being 10 times greater than the previous column, when you use the binary system, each new column is only two times the value of the previous column. For example, Figure A-2 shows how the numbers 9 and 305 are represented in the binary system. Notice that in both binary numbers, as well as in the decimal system, it is perfectly acceptable—and often necessary—to write a number that contains 0 as some of the digits. As with the decimal system, when you use the binary system, there is no limit to the number of columns you can use—you use as many as it takes to express a value.

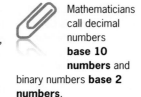

Mathematicians call decimal numbers **base 10 numbers** and binary numbers **base 2 numbers**.

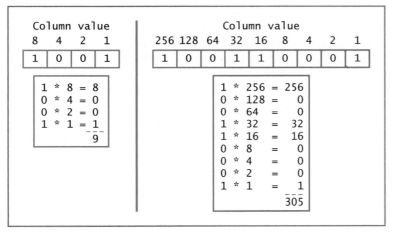

Figure A-2 Representing decimal values 9 and 305 in the binary system

Every computer stores every piece of data it ever uses as a set of 0s and 1s. Each 0 or 1 is known as a **bit**, which is short for binary digit. Every computer uses 0s and 1s because all values in a computer are stored as electronic signals that are either on or off. This two-state system is most easily represented using just two digits.

Every computer uses a set of binary digits to represent every character it can store. If computers used only one binary digit to represent characters, then only two different characters could be represented, because the single bit could be only 0 or 1. If they used only two digits, then only four characters could be represented—one that used each of the four codes 00, 01, 10, and 11, which in decimal values are 0, 1, 2, and 3, respectively. Many computers use sets of eight binary digits to represent each character they store, because using eight binary digits provides 256 different combinations. One combination can represent an "A", another a "B", still others "a" and "b", and so on.

A set of eight bits is called a **byte**. Half a byte, or four bits, is a **nibble**.

Most of the values not included in Table A-1 have a purpose. For example, the decimal value 7 represents a bell—a dinging sound your computer can make, often used to notify you of an error or some other unusual condition.

Each binary number in Table A-1 is shown containing two sets of four digits; this convention makes the long eight-digit numbers easier to read.

Two hundred fifty-six combinations are enough so that each capital letter, small letter, digit, and punctuation mark used in English has its own code; even a space has a code. For example, in some computers 01000001 represents the character "A". The binary number 01000001 has a decimal value of 65, but this numeric value is not important to ordinary computer users; it is simply a code that stands for "A". The code that uses 01000001 to mean "A" is the **American Standard Code for Information Interchange**, or **ASCII**.

The ASCII code is not the only computer code; it is typical, and is the one used in most personal computers. The **Extended Binary Coded Decimal Interchange Code**, or **EBCDIC**, is an eight-bit code that is used in IBM mainframe computers. In these computers, the principle is the same—every character is stored as a series of binary digits. However, the actual values used are different. For example, in EBCDIC, an "A" is 11000001, or 193. Another code used by languages such as Java and C# is **Unicode**; with this code, 16 bits are used to represent each character. The character "A" in Unicode has the same decimal value as the ASCII "A", 65, but it is stored as 0000000001000001. Using 16 bits provides many more possible combinations than using only eight—65,536 to be exact. With Unicode, not only are there enough available codes for all English letters and digits, but also for characters from many international alphabets.

Ordinary computer users seldom think about the numeric codes behind the letters, numbers, and punctuation marks they enter from their keyboards or see displayed on a monitor. However, they see the consequence of the values behind letters when they see data sorted in alphabetical order. When you sort a list of names, "Andrea" comes before "Brian," and "Caroline" comes after "Brian" because the numeric code for "A" is lower than the code for "B", and the numeric code for "C" is higher than the code for "B" no matter whether you are using ASCII, EBCDIC, or Unicode.

Table A-1 shows the decimal and binary values behind the most commonly used characters in the ASCII character set—the letters, numbers, and punctuation marks you can enter from your keyboard using a single key press.

Decimal Number	Binary Number	ASCII Character
32	0010 0000	Space
33	0010 0001	! Exclamation point
34	0010 0010	" Quotation mark, or double quote
35	0010 0011	# Number sign, also called an octothorpe or a pound sign
36	0010 0100	$ Dollar sign
37	0010 0101	% Percent
38	0010 0110	& Ampersand
39	0010 0111	' Apostrophe, single quote
40	0010 1000	(Left parenthesis
41	0010 1001	) Right parenthesis
42	0010 1010	* Asterisk
43	0010 1011	+ Plus sign
44	0010 1100	, Comma
45	0010 1101	– Hyphen or minus sign
46	0010 1110	. Period or decimal point
47	0010 1111	/ Slash or front slash
48	0011 0000	0
49	0011 0001	1
50	0011 0010	2
51	0011 0011	3
52	0011 0100	4
53	0011 0101	5
54	0011 0110	6
55	0011 0111	7
56	0011 1000	8
57	0011 1001	9
58	0011 1010	: Colon
59	0011 1011	; Semicolon
60	0011 1100	< Less-than sign
61	0011 1101	= Equal sign
62	0011 1110	> Greater-than sign
63	0011 1111	? Question mark
64	0100 0000	@ At sign
65	0100 0001	A
66	0100 0010	B
67	0100 0011	C
68	0100 0100	D
69	0100 0101	E
70	0100 0110	F
71	0100 0111	G
72	0100 1000	H
73	0100 1001	I
74	0100 1010	J
75	0100 1011	K
76	0100 1100	L
77	0100 1101	M
78	0100 1110	N
79	0100 1111	O
80	0101 0000	P
81	0101 0001	Q
82	0101 0010	R
83	0101 0011	S
84	0101 0100	T
85	0101 0101	U
86	0101 0110	V
87	0101 0111	W
88	0101 1000	X
89	0101 1001	Y
90	0101 1010	Z
91	0101 1011	[Opening or left bracket

Table A-1   Decimal and Binary Values for Common ASCII Characters (*continues*)

(continued)

Decimal Number	Binary Number	ASCII Character
92	0101 1100	\ Backslash
93	0101 1101	] Closing or right bracket
94	0101 1110	^ Caret
95	0101 1111	_ Underline or underscore
96	0110 0000	` Grave accent
97	0110 0001	a
98	0110 0010	b
99	0110 0011	c
100	0110 0100	d
101	0110 0101	e
102	0110 0110	f
103	0110 0111	g
104	0110 1000	h
105	0110 1001	i
106	0110 1010	j
107	0110 1011	k
108	0110 1100	l
109	0110 1101	m
110	0110 1110	n

Decimal Number	Binary Number	ASCII Character
111	0110 1111	o
112	0111 0000	p
113	0111 0001	q
114	0111 0010	r
115	0111 0011	s
116	0111 0100	t
117	0111 0101	u
118	0111 0110	v
119	0111 0111	w
120	0111 1000	x
121	0111 1001	y
122	0111 1010	z
123	0111 1011	{ Opening or left brace
124	0111 1100	| Vertical line or pipe
125	0111 1101	} Closing or right brace
126	0111 1110	~ Tilde

Table A-1   Decimal and Binary Values for Common ASCII Characters

Two Special Structures—case and do-while

Convenient, Additional Structures

You can solve any logic problem you might encounter using only three structures: sequence, selection, and loop. However, many programming languages allow two more structures: the `case` structure and the `do-while` loop. These structures are never *needed* to solve any problem—you can always use a series of selections instead of the `case` structure, and you can always use a sequence plus a `while` loop in place of the `do-while` loop. However, sometimes these additional structures are convenient. Programmers consider them all to be acceptable, legal structures.

The case Structure

You can use the **case structure** when there are several distinct possible values for a single variable you are testing, and each value requires a different course of action. Suppose you administer a school at which tuition varies per credit hour, depending on whether a student is a freshman, sophomore, junior, or senior. The structured flowchart and pseudocode in Figure B-1 show a series of decisions that assigns different `tuition` values depending on the value of `year`.

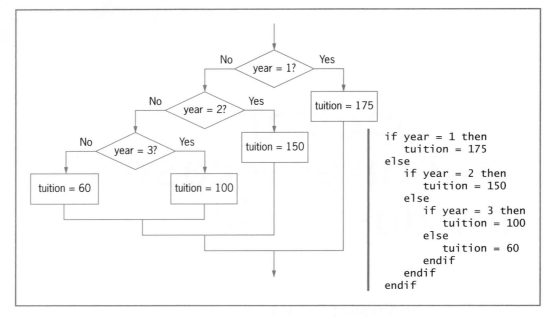

```
if year = 1 then
    tuition = 175
else
    if year = 2 then
        tuition = 150
    else
        if year = 3 then
            tuition = 100
        else
            tuition = 60
        endif
    endif
endif
```

Figure B-1 Flowchart and pseudocode of tuition decisions

The logic shown in Figure B-1 is absolutely correct and completely structured. The **year** = 3? selection structure is contained within the **year** = 2? structure, which is contained within the **year** = 1? structure. (In this example, if **year** is not 1, 2, or 3, it is assumed the student receives the senior tuition rate.)

Even though the program segments in Figure B-1 are correct and structured, many programming languages permit using a **case** structure, as shown in Figure B-2. When using the **case** structure, you test a variable against a series of values, taking appropriate action based on the variable's value. Many people feel such programs are easier to read, and the **case** structure is allowed because the same results *could* be achieved with a series of structured selections (thus making the program structured). That is, if the first program is structured and the second one reflects the first one point by point, then the second one must be structured also.

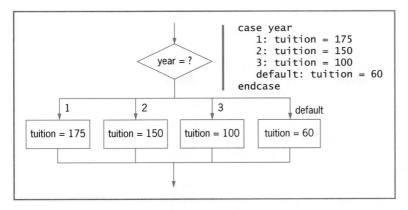

```
case year
    1: tuition = 175
    2: tuition = 150
    3: tuition = 100
    default: tuition = 60
endcase
```

Figure B-2   Flowchart and pseudocode of `case` structure that determines tuition

Even though a programming language permits you to use the `case` structure, you should understand that the `case` structure is just a convenience that might make a flowchart, pseudocode, or actual program code easier to understand at first glance. When you write a series of decisions using the `case` structure, the computer still makes a series of individual decisions, just as though you had used many `if-then-else` combinations. In other words, you might prefer looking at the diagram in Figure B-2 to understand the tuition fees charged by a school, but a computer actually makes the decisions as shown in Figure B-1—one at a time. When you write your own programs, it is always acceptable to express a complicated decision-making process as a series of individual selections.

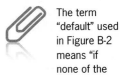 The term "default" used in Figure B-2 means "if none of the other cases is true." Each programming language you learn may use a different syntax for the default case.

 You use the `case` structure only when a series of decisions is based on different values stored in a single variable. If multiple variables are tested, then you must use a series of decisions.

The do-while Loop

Recall that a structured loop (often called a `while` loop) looks like Figure B-3. A special-case loop called a `do-while` loop looks like Figure B-4.

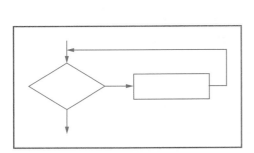

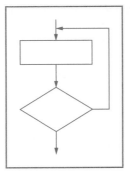

Figure B-3   The `while` loop, which is a pretest loop

Figure B-4   Structure of a `do-while` loop, which is a posttest loop

Notice that the word "do" begins the name of the do-while loop. This should remind you that the action you "do" precedes testing the condition.

An important difference exists between these two structures. In a `while` loop, you ask a question and, depending on the answer, you might or might not enter the loop to execute the loop's procedure. Conversely, in a **do-while loop**, you ensure that the procedure executes at least once; then, depending on the answer to the controlling question, the loop may or may not execute additional times.

In a `while` loop, the question that controls a loop comes at the beginning, or "top," of the loop body. A `while` loop is a **pretest loop** because a condition is tested before entering the loop even once. In a `do-while` loop, the question that controls the loop comes at the end, or "bottom," of the loop body. A `do-while` loop is a **posttest loop** because a condition is tested after the loop body has executed.

You encounter examples of `do-while` looping every day. For example:

```
do
    pay a bill
while more bills remain to be paid
```

As another example:

```
do
    wash a dish
while more dishes remain to be washed
```

In these examples, the activity (paying bills or washing dishes) must occur at least one time. With a `do-while` loop, you ask the question that determines whether you continue only after the activity has been executed at least once.

You never are required to use a posttest loop. You can duplicate the same series of actions generated by any posttest loop by creating a sequence followed by a standard, pretest `while` loop. Consider the flowcharts and pseudocode in Figure B-5.

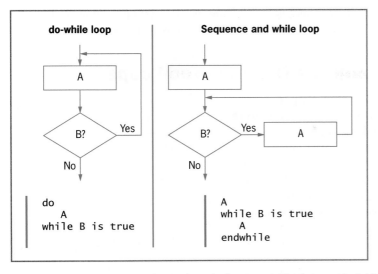

```
do-while loop                    Sequence and while loop


        A                                A


       B?        Yes                     B?        Yes        A


      No                                No


   do                               A
      A                             while B is true
   while B is true                     A
                                     endwhile
```

Figure B-5 Flowchart and pseudocode for do-while loop and while loop that do the same thing

On the left side of Figure B-5, A executes, and then B is asked. If B is yes, then A executes and B is asked again. On the right side of the figure, A executes, and then B is asked. If B is yes, then A executes and B is asked again. In other words, both sets of flowchart and pseudocode segments do exactly the same thing.

Because programmers understand that any posttest loop (do-while) can be expressed with a sequence followed by a while loop, most languages allow at least one of the versions of the posttest loop for convenience. Again, you are never required to use a posttest loop; you can always accomplish the same tasks with a sequence followed by a pretest while loop.

Recognizing the Characteristics Shared by All Structured Loops

As you examine Figures B-3 and B-4, notice that with the while loop, the loop-controlling question is placed at the beginning of the steps that repeat. With the do-while loop, the loop-controlling question is placed at the end of the sequence of the steps that repeat.

All structured loops, both pretest and posttest, share these two characteristics:

- The loop-controlling question must provide either entry to or exit from the repeating structure.

- The loop-controlling question provides the *only* entry to or exit from the repeating structure.

In other words, there is exactly one loop-controlling value, and it provides either the only entrance to or the only exit from the loop.

Recognizing Unstructured Loops

Figure B-6 shows an unstructured loop. It is neither a `while` loop (which begins with a decision and, after an action, returns to the decision) nor a `do-while` loop (which begins with an action and ends with a decision that might repeat the action). Instead, it begins like a posttest loop (a `do-while` loop), with a process followed by a decision, but one branch of the decision does not repeat the initial process. Instead, it performs an additional new action before repeating the initial process.

 Especially when you are first mastering structured logic, you might prefer to use only the three basic structures—sequence, selection, and `while` loop. Every logical problem can be solved using only these three structures, and you can understand all of the examples in this book using only these three.

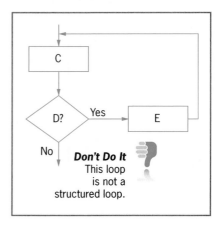

Figure B-6 Unstructured loop

If you need to use the logic shown in Figure B-6—performing a task, asking a question, and perhaps performing an additional task before looping back to the first process—then the way to make the logic structured is to repeat the initial process within the loop, at the end of the loop. Figure B-7 shows the same logic as Figure B-6, but now it is structured logic, with a sequence of two actions occurring within the loop.

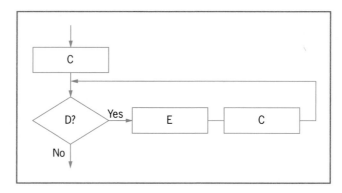

Figure B-7 Sequence and structured loop that accomplish the same tasks as Figure B-6

Index